Gold EXPERIENCE

B1+

Pre-first
for Schools

Teacher's
Book

Genevieve White

1

Contents

Gold Experience
Introduction

Welcome to *Gold Experience*, a five-level exam preparation and general English course for teenagers. The five levels, which correspond to the Common European Framework of Reference levels A1, A2, B1, B1+ and B2, provide thorough preparation for Cambridge English Key for Schools, Preliminary for Schools and First for Schools examinations and comprehensive language development.

Gold Experience is a fast-paced course written to engage and motivate teenage students with varied, age-appropriate topics and activities which will make English lessons enjoyable and productive for both you and your class.

The topics are from contemporary contexts such as the Internet, social media, television and magazines, as well as content-rich CLIL topics from which your students will learn about the world.

Gold Experience offers a complete package of print and digital materials which provide maximum flexibility for your teaching situation.

Blended package	Print package	Digital package
Print and digital *Gold Experience* package offers maximum flexibility with both print and online components.	Print *Gold Experience* is a complete teaching package with a print Workbook.	Digital *Gold Experience* is the ideal package for schools working in a fully digital environment.
For the student:  Students' Book MyEnglishLab	**For the student:**  Students' Book & Multi-ROM with audio and video Grammar and Vocabulary Workbook	**For the student:**  Students' eText MyEnglishLab
For the teacher:  eText IWB software MyEnglishLab Teacher's Online Resource Materials	**For the teacher:**  Students' Book & Multi-ROM with audio and video Grammar and Vocabulary Workbook Teacher's Online Resource Materials	**For the teacher:**  eText IWB software MyEnglishLab Teacher's Online Resource Materials

Gold Experience B1+ Components

Gold Experience B1+ is ideal for teenagers at intermediate level in general English classes and those who are starting to work towards the Cambridge First (FCE) for Schools examination.

Students' Book

The twelve topic-based units offer thorough input and practice of reading, writing, listening and speaking skills, with topic vocabulary and grammar presented in situations which exemplify the meaning and use.

There are many opportunities for students to share their ideas, opinions and knowledge of the world. Lessons start with a **Power Up** activity which is designed to activate students' existing knowledge and stimulate their interest in the topic.

Learner training is an important aspect of *Gold Experience*. **Skill** and **Exam** tips give clear, simple advice on how students can develop their language and exam skills. **Word XP** boxes highlight aspects of lexis, for example, collocation and forming nouns from verbs, so students develop good vocabulary-learning strategies.

Each unit in *Gold Experience* has a **Video** clip either from TV or filmed especially for the course. The TV clips are fully integrated with the main reading text, while the other clips show teenagers involved in topic-based tasks and activities that students use as a basis for project work.

After every unit there is a **Revision** page which reinforces the vocabulary and grammar students have learnt.

eText for students

eText is the students' online or tablet component which contains the Students' Book pages with integrated links to audio, video and games.

Workbook

The Workbook offers practice of all the vocabulary and grammar areas taught in the Students' Book and is suitable for both classroom self-study and homework.

MyEnglishLab

Gold Experience MyEnglishLab includes all the Workbook exercises in interactive format along with additional reading, writing, listening and speaking skills, as well as practice and review tests. With instantly graded activities plus tips and feedback, students are supported and guided to successfully complete the exercises.

Also on *Gold Experience* MyEnglishLab are the Students' Book video and audio.

Teacher's Online Resource Materials

All the support a busy teacher needs is available online on the Pearson Portal or through your local Pearson rep.

- Teaching notes with a wealth of additional classroom ideas, integrated answer keys and audio scripts
- Photocopiable worksheets
- Unit, mid- and end-of-year tests

eText for teachers

eText for teachers is a digital component for classroom use on an interactive whiteboard. Available online or on disk, it contains the Students' Book in digital format with audio, video, games and teacher's resources.

MyEnglishLab for teachers

The teacher view of MyEnglishLab gives you a full learning management system with a range of practical, problem-solving teaching tools.

- You can assign tasks to the whole class, groups or individual students depending on their needs.
- The communication tools allow you to send messages to your students and, if you wish, keep in contact outside of class.
- The gradebook lets you see how individual students and the whole class are progressing.
- The common error report enables you to see which problems are the most common and which of your students are making these mistakes. With this information, you can focus classroom time on the areas that need the most work.
- The review tests can be assigned at the time that suits your teaching programme.

Students' Book Organisation

Spread 1, pp 8–9

1 Discussion-based task to raise interest in the topic

2 Gist activities to familiarise students with the reading text

3 Main reading task in the style of the Cambridge First for Schools exam

4 A tip to help develop exam skills

5 A task to help students identify, summarise and rephrase main ideas in the text

6 An activity that allows the students to use English in a personalised context

7 Topics are brought to life in the classroom through motivating video clips

Spread 2, pp 10–11

1 New vocabulary presented in context through a variety of tasks

2 A useful vocabulary learning tip

3 A fun activity that encourages use of the key words

4 Clearly presented grammar with example sentences from the main reading text and usage notes

5 Students practise the grammar though a series of tasks moving towards freer practice

6 An activity that allows the students to use the grammar in a personalised context

Students' Book Organisation

Spread 3, pp 12–13

1 New presented vocabulary in context

2 Carefully-staged activities lead into an exam-style task

3 Clear explanation of the language point with sample sentences and usage notes

4 Carefully-staged activities give practice of the language palette

5 Final task allows the students to use the vocabulary and grammar in a personalised context

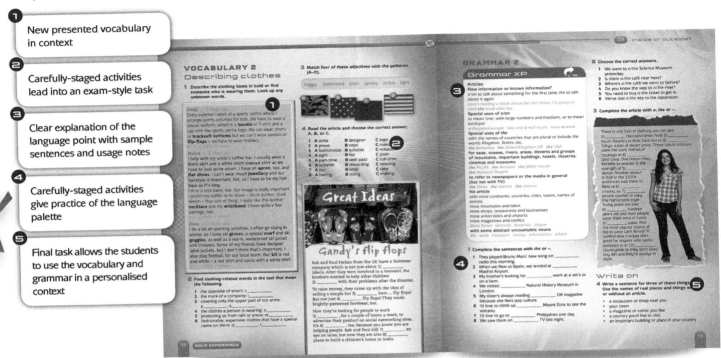

Spread 4, pp 14–15

1 Lead-in discussion to introduce vocabulary and get students thinking about the topic

2 Carefully-staged activities that develop listening skills

3 Carefully-staged activities that develop speaking skills and confidence

4 Useful functional language that students need to express themselves

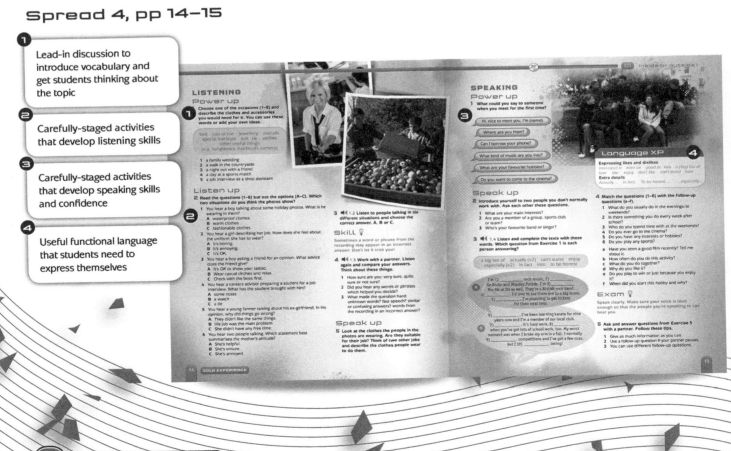

Students' Book Organisation

Spread 5, pp 16–17

1. A task which includes an example of the text type for students to use as a model

2. Carefully-staged activities that develop writing skills

3. Activities to work on useful language for the task type

4. Teen-appropriate writing tasks that also prepare students for the Cambridge First for Schools exam

5. Preparation tasks help students to plan their writing

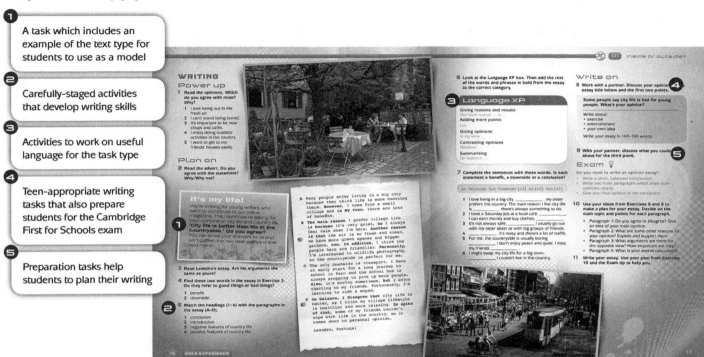

Spread 6, pp 18–19

1. An engaging video clip which allows students to see and hear English in use

2. Pre-, while and post-view activities so students get the most from watching the video

3. An open activity so students present their ideas to their classmates

4. Unit word list to help students revise vocabulary

5. Revision tasks after every unit

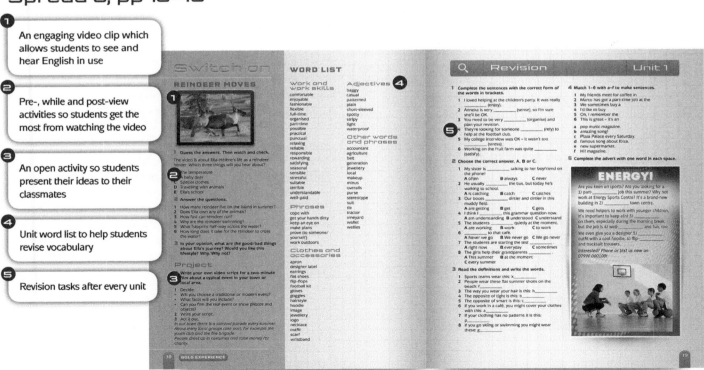

Starter

READING (SB page 6)

To start

Draw a five-pointed star on the board. On each point write one thing which is important and meaningful to you, e.g. your best friend's name, a number of significance to you, an important date and the name of a place. On the fifth point draw a symbol, e.g. *If you love nature, draw a flower; if you love surfing draw a wave.*

Show your students the star you have drawn and ask them to guess what the symbol, numbers and words represent. Then ask them to draw their own star, including names, numbers and symbols of significance to them.

Organise students into pairs to share their stars and guess the significance of the words on their partners' stars. Nominate a few students to report back on what they have learned about their partners.

1 Focus students' attention on the words and pictures. Ask them to match four of the words with the pictures. Check answers around the class, drilling the pronunciation of any tricky words, e.g. *certificate* /səˈtɪfɪkət/. Ask students about the words which they didn't use: *Who would you write a note to?* (e.g. your mum, a friend) *What do you have to write on an information form?* (e.g. phone number, email address, etc.) *How many text messages do you send every day?*

Then refer students to the questions and challenge them to see who can be the first to find the answers. Conduct class feedback.

A ticket   **B** poster   **C** advert   **D** certificate

1 £25 pounds, 14–18-year-old teenagers
2 12–14 July, Mayday Park
3 national (from New York to Los Angeles – within the USA), 8.50 a.m.
4 three hours, one person

2 Ask students to work with a partner to complete the task. Check answers around the class. Give students a few moments to think of four words related to each topic, e.g.
hobby: free time, surfing, enjoy, relaxing
music: band, concert, instrument, singer
sport: fitness, football, team, coach
travel: foreign country, flight, destination, far
Ask them to compare their answers with a partner. Collect answers around the class. Ask students to tell you which topic interests them the most.

A travel   **B** music   **C** sport   **D** hobby

Students' own answers.

LISTENING (SB page 6)

3 Focus students' attention on the prepositions in the box and the photos of the teenagers. Ask them to read what the teenagers say and complete the gaps.

1 In   2 to   3 at   4 on   5 out   6 at   7 from

4 Play the recording, twice if necessary, while students check their answers to Exercise 3.

➤ Track S.1

Interviewer: So what did you do this summer, everyone?
Sophie: In August, we went to the beach a lot. It was good fun and I learnt how to surf!
Interviewer: How about you, Alex?
Alex: We spent a day at an amazing amusement park when we were on holiday. It was the best day out!
Interviewer: And you, Julie?
Julie: We stayed at home this year, but we had visitors from Australia. We took them to see all the sights!

5 Focus students' attention on the photos. Ask them to describe what they see (Photo A: a beach with people on surfboards; Photo B: a group of people taking photos of something). Tell students that they are going to listen to a teacher. Each time they hear an instruction they must match it with Photo A or Photo B. Play the recording, twice if necessary, while students complete the task. Allow them to check their answers with a partner before conducting class feedback.

➤ Track S.2

1 Teacher: OK, everybody. You must be ready for tomorrow's lessons at 9 a.m. And remember your camera! You can't do the lesson without it!

2 Teacher: It's easy to get burnt without realising it when you're in the water, so put some sun cream on before you start.

3 Teacher: OK, guys. When you're ready, try to stand up. That's good. Don't fall off!

4 Teacher: So, tomorrow we'll be climbing some really big hills. Please bring your walking boots.

5 Teacher: Tomorrow's lesson starts at 10 a.m., the same as today. Don't forget your towels this time!

6 Teacher: So, we'll go to the park after lunch. Can you all bring your painting things with you?

7 Teacher: Right, I'm going to take a group photo. Get ready ... and smile, please! Excellent!

1 B 2 A 3 A 4 neither 5 A 6 neither 7 both

SPEAKING (SB page 7)

6 Focus students' attention on the two photos (A and B). Organise students into pairs and ask them to discuss the questions about the activities in the photos. Circulate, offering support as necessary. Conduct class feedback.

Students' own answers.

7 Give students a few moments to look at the list and the questions in the speech bubbles. Nominate a confident student to demonstrate the interview with you. Ask one or two questions and encourage them to ask you questions about the topics on the list. Then ask students to interview their partner. Monitor and make a note of any issues for class feedback. Nominate a few students to report back on what they have learned about their partner.

Students' own answers.

WRITING (SB page 7)

8 Ask students: *What plans do you have for this school year? Will you take up any new activities?* Tell them they are going to write a message to their friends. Focus their attention on the list of questions. As a class, brainstorm some possible ideas for each. Students write their messages and share them with a partner. Ask a few students to read their messages aloud to the rest of the class.

Students' own answers.

Model answer

Hi, I'm Sasha! At the moment I'm really into football. I go to football training once a week. It's great because all of my friends go, too. I haven't learned so much this year because the term's only just begun, but I've started to learn French and can say a few things already. This year I hope to learn to play the saxophone. I'm starting lessons after school next week.

To finish

Play a game to test how much students can remember about each other. Throw a soft ball to one of your students. The student who catches the ball has to say one thing they have learned about you this lesson, e.g. *your name, where you come from*. This student then throws the ball to someone else, who has to say something about the student who threw it to them. Continue until everyone has had a turn.

01 Inside or outside?

Unit objectives

Reading:	multiple matching; questions
Vocabulary:	work and work skills; describing clothes
Grammar:	present tenses; articles
Listening:	multiple-choice questions
Speaking:	exchanging personal information about likes and dislikes
Writing:	writing an opinion essay

READING (SB pages 8–9)

To start

Draw a Venn diagram on the board. In one circle, write something we do indoors, e.g. *baking*. In the other circle, write something we do outdoors, e.g. *gardening*. In the overlapping circles write an activity which can be done both indoors and outdoors, e.g. *swimming*.

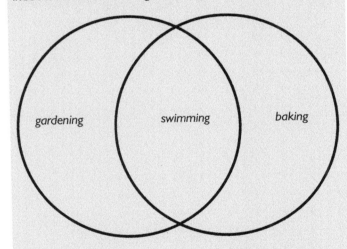

gardening   swimming   baking

Organise students into small groups and ask them to draw a similar diagram. Tell them they have one minute to fill their diagram with 'indoor', 'outdoor' and 'both indoor and outdoor' activities. After one minute, nominate a student from each group to read out their lists. Encourage students from other groups to challenge the ideas, e.g. If a group writes *cooking* in the 'indoor' box, this could be challenged as people often barbecue their food outdoors. The group who has collected the greatest number of unchallenged points at the end of the game is the winner.

Power up

1 Focus students' attention on the different outdoor activities. Write the headings *Summer* and *Winter* on the board. Organise students into pairs and tell them they have one minute to create a list of outdoor activities for each season. After one minute, elicit how many activities they had for each season. Nominate students to tell you their activities and write them on the board. Ask which activities they enjoy the most and why. Generate as much vocabulary as possible.

Students' own answers.

2 Nominate a confident student to read out the phrases. Tell students which of the situations you dislike most and why, e.g. *I dislike being cold the most. I hate it when my fingers are frozen and my nose is red!* Organise students into small groups and ask them to tell each other which of the phrases they dislike most and why. Monitor as they complete the task, encouraging them to give specific examples from their own experience whenever possible, e.g. *I don't like being muddy or dirty because it's not good for my clothes.*

Students' own answers.

Read on

3 Focus students' attention on the photos and ask them to describe what they see. Encourage them to guess where in the world these photos might have been taken. Read the title of the article aloud and ask students to predict what the text is about. Write their ideas on the board. If necessary, pre-teach the following words and phrases: *boarding school, sensible, overalls, keeping an eye on something* and *rewarding*. Use concept questions to check students' understanding, e.g. *If I go to boarding school, do I come home every evening?* (No) *Do I only come home in the holidays?* (Yes) *If I'm a sensible person, would I go out on a very cold day without a jacket?* (No) *Are overalls the same as trousers?* (No) *Why not?* (They go on your legs and over your shoulders.). *Why might you need to keep an eye on a very small child?* (To make sure they don't do anything dangerous.). *What would be a rewarding job for you?*

Students' own answers.

4 Point to the board and remind students of their predictions on what the text might be about. Ask them to read the article quickly and find out if they were right.

5 Before they try to complete the task, refer students to the Skill advice. Focus students' attention on the questions and ask them to underline the keywords in each question as this will help them to focus on the information they need. Check understanding of the following: *works full-time* (works around forty hours per week) and *to move around* (to move house often). Explain that they are going to read the article again more slowly and match each question to the people (A–D). Allow students to check their answers with a partner before class feedback.

1 B **2** C **3** D **4** A **5** C **6** B **7** A **8** D **9** B **10** A

6 Draw students' attention to the list of definitions. Explain that they need to match the definitions to words from the text. Point out that the first letter of each word has been given to help them, as well as the text (e.g. text A). Students check their answers in pairs. During feedback for each question elicit the text first and then the answer so students can follow along.

1 generations **2** minus **3** stereotypes
4 agriculture **5** tractor **6** local
7 vineyard **8** accountant

Sum up

7 Organise students into pairs and ask them to think about the things in 1–5 and make sentences about the people they read about. Nominate a confident student to provide an example in front of the whole class. As students complete the activity, remind them to use *both, either, only, all, three/four of them*. Monitor and pay special attention to word order and where they position *both, neither, only*, etc. Note down any common errors for class feedback.

1 Neither Bunny nor Will was born on a farm.
2 Both Bunny and Will can drive a tractor.
3 Three of them work with animals (Katya, Bunny and Will).
4 Only Will works long hours.
5 Possible answers
  Three of them come from farming families: Katya, Bunny and Pablo.
  Three of them go to school or college: Katya, Bunny and Pablo.
  Neither Katya nor Pablo live in the UK.
  All of them are quite young.
  Only Bunny wants to live in a different country.

Speak up

8 Share one thing you would like to do from the article and one thing you wouldn't like to do, e.g. *I'd like to work in a vineyard because I love grapes and I'd like to eat some as I work! I wouldn't like to deliver a new-born lamb as I think it would be really stressful.* Students talk about their answers in pairs. Monitor and encourage students to make their answers as full as possible. Nominate one or two students to share their choices and reasons.

To finish

Organise students into small groups. Ask them to brainstorm five or six questions they would like to ask the young farmers they read about (the answers must not be included in the text). When students have had two minutes to do this, conduct feedback. Write any particularly interesting questions on the board.

Nominate one student from each group to be a talk show host. Tell them they are hosting a talk show and have invited the young farmers from the article to appear on it. The other students in the group must choose which of the young farmers they would like to be. Give them a few minutes to practise their questions and answers. Circulate, providing support where necessary. Ask one or two of the strongest groups to perform their talk show to the rest of the class.

Homework
MyEnglishLab

VOCABULARY 1 (SB page 10)
Work and work skills
To start

Organise students into pairs and ask them to write down the names of two jobs they would like to do. When they have done this, ask them to think of adjectives to describe the jobs they have chosen, e.g.

Firefighter – I'd like to be a firefighter because it's an exciting job.

Lawyer – I want to be a lawyer because it's a well-respected job.

Encourage students to tell you what qualities you would need to be good at these jobs, e.g. *To be a firefighter, you need to be brave and quite fit. To be a lawyer, you need to be intelligent and hard-working.*

Note down any useful adjectives on the board, e.g. *exciting, well-respected, brave, fit.* Tell students they are going to learn all about ways of describing jobs and skills in this lesson and that you will come back to the jobs they have chosen at the end of the lesson to see if they can say more with the new language they will have learned.

1 Read the adjectives in the box aloud. Focus in particular on correct word stress, writing the words and marking the stress patterns on the board (all of the words are stressed on the first syllable, apart from *relaxing* and *rewarding* which are stressed on the second syllable). Drill the words chorally and individually. Ask students to match the adjectives with the statements and allow them to check their answers with a partner before conducting whole class feedback.

1 relaxing 2 part-time 3 well-paid

4 stressful 5 full-time 6 seasonal

7 rewarding/satisfying (*rewarding* and *satisfying* have a similar meaning)

2 Refer students to the example and complete it on the board, e.g. *Looking after animals is relaxing.* Elicit which is the adjective (*relaxing*) and which is the verb *be* (*is*). Students rewrite the statements in Exercise 1. During feedback, collect answers around the class, focusing on accurate word stress of the adjectives.

1 Looking after animals is relaxing.

2 My job at the hairdresser's is part-time.

3 My newspaper round is well-paid.

4 Rushing around in the restaurant is often stressful.

5 My mum's job is full-time.

6 I usually help with the olive-picking, which is seasonal.

7 Seeing a car that I've cleaned is rewarding/satisfying.

3 Tell students they are going to listen to people from the article in the previous lesson. Play the recording, twice if necessary. Allow students to check their answers with a partner and then check answers orally.

Draw students' attention to the phrases in bold. Check understanding by asking personalised concept questions, e.g. *Do you think you're good at coping with problems, Nergis? Why/Why not? Can you think of a time you wanted to prove something to yourself? Do you sometimes have to keep an eye on your little sister, Attila?*

➤ Track 1.1

1

Man: Hey, Will? Can you keep an eye on the new-born lambs for me? They need warm blankets and milk.

2

Will: Looking after the cows is hard work, but I'm happy to get my hands dirty helping on the farm.

3

Woman: Katya is giving medicine to her reindeer. She wants to prove to herself that she can do a difficult job.

4

Katya: My sister and I love living in tents. We like being able to work outdoors in any weather.

5

Pablo: We have to do this work on a sunny day. Farmers can't make plans until they know the weather forecast.

6

Bunny: My brother's very practical and can cope with many problems, but he can't drive a tractor and I can!

1 keep 2 get 3 prove 4 work 5 make 6 cope

4 Tell students they are going to learn more useful adjectives for describing people and the way they do their jobs. Students work with a partner to make the sentences. Read them around the class, focusing on the pronunciation of potentially tricky words, e.g. *punctual* /pʌŋktʃuəl/. Then ask students to work individually to translate the words in bold into their own language.

1 c 2 b 3 a 4 e 5 f 6 d

Word XP

Read the adjectives in the box aloud. Drill the pronunciation chorally and individually. Focus on the unstressed pronunciation of the last two syllables in each case: /əbəl/ or /ɪbəl/. Ask students if they can think of other adjectives which end in -*able* or -*ible*. Write the new adjectives on the board.

5 Students choose the correct word to complete each sentence. Fast finishers can make sentences which use the incorrect option. Conduct class feedback, eliciting reasons for students' choices.

1 terrible 2 comfortable 3 reliable

4 possible 5 sensible 6 enjoyable

Game on

Read the instructions with students and focus their attention on the example. Distribute bits of paper for students to write their sentences on. Circulate and help with accuracy. Collect the papers and shuffle them. Place them on your desk and nominate a student to pick one and read it aloud. Encourage the rest of the class to guess who wrote it and why. Keep the pace fast and energetic, so that you can get through the entire class.

To finish

Ask students to remember the two jobs they chose at the beginning of the lesson. Give them a minute or two to think about words and phrases they have learned in this lesson which could be used to describe the jobs. Elicit ideas around the class.

Homework

Workbook page 4

MyEnglishLab

GRAMMAR 1 (SB page 11)

Present tenses

To start

Organise students into small groups. Ask each group to choose three of the adjectives ending in -ible and -able they learned in the previous lesson and write sentences with them. Refer them to the Word XP box on page 10 if necessary. Monitor as they write their sentences, checking that they are using the new language correctly. Students from each group then take turns reading out their sentences, leaving the adjective blank, e.g. *Skinny jeans are very _____ at the moment.* (fashionable).

The other groups have to listen carefully and decide on the correct -ible or -able adjective, writing their answers on the board. The group with the most correctly spelled adjectives at the end of the game is the winner.

Grammar XP

Refer students to the Grammar XP box. Write a few sentences about yourself using present tenses, e.g.

I'm a teacher and I live in Istanbul. I'm standing in front of my desk at the moment. I often cycle to work. In winter I take the bus because it's cold.

Ask students: *Which sentences are about my habits? Which sentence talks about what I'm doing now?*

Elicit how we form the present continuous (am/is/are + verb + -ing) and what we need to remember when we are using the third person present simple form (we add -s to the end of the verb). Generate examples of present tense sentences which are true for your students and write them on the board.

Tell students that for one day only they can ask you any question they like. However you will only answer questions which use present tense forms correctly. Give students a minute to think of their questions and then invite them to ask you questions. Answer correct questions and write them on the board, focusing on the form of both present simple and present continuous questions. Address any incorrectly formed questions and ask your students to work together to correct them.

1 Focus students' attention on the conversation and ask them to complete the gaps with the correct form of the verbs in brackets. Organise students into pairs and ask them to read out the conversation with a partner: this will give them the opportunity to check and discuss their answers. Nominate one pair to read the conversation to the rest of the class.

1 sometimes want

2 usually have

3 don't often wear

4 don't usually stay

5 are always getting/always get

6 often stays up

7 is always worrying

8 are getting

9 don't often see

10 usually like

2 Students complete the sentences using the correct form of the verbs in the box. During feedback, encourage students to give reasons for their choice in each case.

1 is always talking

2 meets

3 don't understand

4 are swapping

5 is learning

6 Do you usually wake up

7 writes

8 gets/is getting

3 Ask students to write the sentences using either the present simple or present continuous. Refer students back to the information in the Grammar XP box and elicit where adverbs of frequency and adverbial phrases are usually positioned in sentences. Encourage students to refer to this information as they complete this task.

1 My family spends a week at the seaside in summer./In summer, my family spends a week at the seaside.

2 My brother is always borrowing my favourite T-shirt – it's annoying!

3 My mum usually gets home at 6 p.m.

4 I play football for a local team most weekends./Most weekends, I play football for a local team.

5 We never have chewing gum in the classroom – it's not allowed.

6 Francesca is waiting for me at the bus stop right now./Right now, Francesca is waiting for me at the bus stop.

7 Tom is running faster and faster to catch the bus at the moment./At the moment, Tom is running faster and faster to catch the bus.

8 After all his adventures, Harry goes home to his parents' house in the end./In the end, after all his adventures, Harry goes home to his parents' house.

Write on

4 Tell your students about two things which people do which annoy you, e.g. *My flatmate is always leaving her clothes on the floor so I have to pick them up and she's always borrowing my clothes without asking me.* Elicit which present tense you have used here (present continuous). Remind students that we often use this tense when we are describing people's annoying habits. Ask students to write down two annoying habits using the present continuous. Organise them into groups and ask them to share their sentences with each other. Bring the class back together and ask each group to report back on some of the most annoying things which were discussed. Conduct a class vote, where your students vote for the most annoying habit they have heard about.

Students' own answers.

To finish

Prepare a few present tense sentences with adverbial phrases, but with the words in jumbled order, e.g.

it's warm sunny usually and summer in

(It's usually warm and sunny in summer.)

school he wears trainers always to

(He always wears trainers to school.)

my asking always without borrowing my sister clothes is

(My sister is always borrowing my clothes without asking.)

Organise students into small groups. Write the first sentence on the board. Challenge students to see which group can be the first to put the words into the correct order. Give the fastest group one point each time they unjumble a sentence successfully. Then ask groups to write some jumbled sentences of their own. The groups should take it in turns to come up to the board and write their sentences while the rest of the class puts the words in the correct order.

Homework

Workbook page 6

MyEnglishLab

VOCABULARY 2 (SB page 12)

Describing clothes

To start

Describe to the class what one of the students is wearing (do not look at the student as you describe his/her clothes). Say something like:

This student is wearing dark blue jeans with a pair of brightly patterned trainers. This student has a hoodie with a logo on the front.

Ask the class to name the student you are talking about. Then nominate a student to choose someone else's clothes to describe. The other students listen and guess who is being spoken about.

1 Focus students' attention on the words in bold and ask them to read the text quickly. Elicit descriptions of each of the clothing items and examples of the items in the class. Generate as much discussion as you can about the items by asking questions, e.g. *Why do you need to wear goggles when you go skiing?* (to protect your eyes from the snow) *Why do you think Eloise needs to wear flat shoes when she's working for her uncle?* (so she doesn't slip when she's carrying hot food).

Students' own answers.

2 Ask students to read the text again and match the clothing-related words with the definitions. Check answers quickly around the class.

1 casual

2 logo

3 short-sleeved

4 outfit(s)

5 waterproof

6 designer label

3 Focus students' attention on the patterns and ask them to match them to four of the adjectives. Ask students to identify people in the class who are wearing the patterns, e.g. *Omar is wearing a stripy T-shirt today.*

A patterned **B** spotty **C** plain **D** stripy

4 Give students a few minutes to read the article. Ask questions to check their understanding, e.g. *Why did Rob and Paul decide to set up their footwear company?* (Because they were involved in a tsunami and wanted to help other children.). *Were the flip-flops plain?* (No, they were brightly coloured.). *How do they advertise their flip-flops?* (On social networking sites.). Ask students to complete the text by choosing the correct answers.

1 B 2 B 3 A 4 C 5 A 6 B 7 B 8 C

To finish

Ask one student to start saying the alphabet in their head. Nominate another student to call 'Stop!' The first student should tell the class the letter of the alphabet which she or he has reached. Organise students into small groups. They have thirty seconds to find and write down as many things to wear as they can which begin with the letter called out. So for example, if the letter is *j*, answers could include *jeans, jogging bottoms, jumper, jewellery*, etc. Award one point to each group per item of clothing.

Continue until students have worked through a few letters of the alphabet. The group with the most points at the end of the game is the winner.

Homework

Workbook page 5

MyEnglishLab

GRAMMAR 2 (SB page 13)
Articles

To start

Bring in some photos from a fashion magazine (or use photos of people in the SB if you prefer). Ask a confident student to come up to the front of the class. Give another student a picture of a person (preferably choose one wearing brightly coloured and interesting clothes) and ask this student to describe the clothes to the first student, who must listen and draw the person and clothes described.

When the student has finished their description, the picture on the board and the picture in the magazine/book can be compared. Repeat the process a couple of times. Make a note of any problems or inaccuracies you noticed with use of the new language.

Grammar XP

Read the information in the Grammar XP box aloud to your students. For each example which is given, encourage the students to give you more examples. Ask them to give examples of rivers, important buildings, restaurants, names of streets in their own town or city, and write them on the board.

1 Remind students to refer to the Grammar XP box to help them decide whether the nouns in this task take a definite or zero article. Allow students to check their answers with a partner before conducting feedback around the class.

1 the   2 –   3 –   4 the   5 –   6 –   7 the   8 –

2 Ask students to choose the correct answer to complete each sentence. Check answers around the class, encouraging students to give reasons for their choices.

1 the   2 a   3 the   4 the   5 a   6 the

3 Before students read the article, ask them to put their hands up if they are wearing something made of denim. Ask them if they can tell you anything about denim. Ask: *What is it made of? When/Where was it invented? Why is it so popular?* Ask students to read the article quickly and tell you what they found out. Students complete the task. Read the article around the class, pausing occasionally and asking students to give reasons for their choices.

1 a   2 –   3 –   4 the   5 –   6 the   7 –   8 a   9 a   10 the

Write on

4 Write sentences about yourself on the board, using some of the prompts given.

The 'Taj Mahal' Indian restaurant in my home town is the best place I've ever eaten.

I'd love to visit Cuba.

Ben Nevis is an important place in my country – it's the highest mountain.

Elicit why you have or haven't used an article in each case. Ask students to write their own sentences using the prompts. Organise students into groups to share their sentences, and monitor as they read their sentences, checking for accurate use of articles. Ask students to find things their sentences have in common. Nominate a student from each group to report back. Encourage students to use the language they learned in the reading lesson where possible, e.g. *none of us, only one of us.*

Students' own answers.

To finish

Ask students to read the sentences they wrote in Exercise 4 to their partner, missing out the articles. Students have to listen to their partner and write down the article they think is missing.

After students have worked with their partner for a few minutes, open this up into a whole class game. Divide the class into two groups. Students should take it in turns to read their sentences to students in the other group, who should decide whether the sentences they hear need an article or not. The group with most correct sentences at the end of the game is the winner.

Homework

Workbook page 7

MyEnglishLab

To start

Do a dictogloss activity with your students to practise article use. Choose a very short passage. It could be from the SB, or if you prefer, you could use the following:

The White House is one of the most famous buildings in the world. It's famous because the president of the United States and his family live there. American presidents have lived there since the beginning of the nineteenth century.

Read the passage two or three times at normal speed, but do not allow students to write anything down. Then organise your students into groups and ask them to write down what they remember, paying particular attention to their use of articles.

When students have had time to discuss their ideas write down the passage you read and ask students to check their use of articles.

Power up

1 Read the situations (1–5) aloud. Ask students to choose one of the situations and give them a minute to write down what kind of clothes/accessories are needed. After one minute, ask them to find a partner who chose the same situation, to share their ideas and add any new ones to their list. Write the headings on the board. Ask one student from each pair to go to the board and write down their ideas. Conduct class feedback. Encourage students to disagree with the ideas. Ask questions to elicit specific responses, e.g. If students have written *shoes* under the heading 'a night out with a friend', ask: *What kind of shoes?* Elicit as much vocabulary as possible, e.g. *high-heeled shoes, designer trainers*.

Students' own answers.

Listen up

2 Focus students' attention on the photographs and ask them to describe what they see. Give students a moment to look at the questions. Elicit why it is important not to look at the options first (because students might focus on listening for these words rather than answering the question). Students should decide which photos are being discussed. Conduct class feedback.

2 (the photo shows a girl in a uniform) and 5 (the photo shows a young farmer)

3 Read the Skill advice aloud to your students before they begin the task. Give them a minute to read through the answer options and encourage them to ask you about anything they are not sure of. Play the recording while students answer the questions. Allow students to check their answers with a partner before conducting whole class feedback.

➤ **Tracks 1.2 and 1.3**

1

Olga: What did you think of England, then?

Will: It was great! We stayed with my cousins in the Lake District. We went sailing and climbing and hill walking. I'm definitely a bit fitter now. Look, here are some photos.

Olga: Are you the one wearing the, erm, *stylish* green waterproof jacket?

Will: Hey! That's my cousin, Louise!

Olga: Well, it's hard to tell – everyone's got hats on.

Will: I'm the one in the big woolly jumper and scarf. There – next to my dad in the big green wellies!

2

Uncle: So, are you enjoying your new job at the café? Or is it hard work?

Francesca: A bit of both, really. I like meeting people and I'm learning some new skills, like working the till and making coffee, so it's not dull. We have to wear a kind of uniform – a smart shirt and tie with a black skirt. The outfit's not too bad, really, but I'm always getting coffee on my shirt – it's so annoying! But the hardest part is that it's an early start because the coffee shop opens at eight a.m.

3

Luke: I start my Saturday job tomorrow and my dad reckons I should wear a long-sleeved shirt to cover the tattoo on my arm, but I think people shouldn't judge me!

Annie: Yeah, but you should listen to your dad. And remember: you need the money! What's the job, anyway?

Luke: It's at that new pizza restaurant. But it's not a waiter's job – I'll be washing up.

Annie: Well, maybe your tattoo's not important if you're in the kitchen, but wear the long-sleeved shirt tomorrow, then ask your manager if it's OK to wear a T-shirt next time.

4

Advisor: So, Jamie, when's your job interview? Is it next week?

Jamie: Yes. It's on Monday, at nine a.m.

Advisor: OK, good. So, what's the most important thing to do on Monday?

Jamie: Um … look smart?

Advisor: Yes, but what's even more important than wearing a shirt and tie?

Jamie: Er … be on time!

Advisor: Exactly. So set your alarm clock. Now, have you got the list of questions to ask them?

Jamie: Yes, I wrote it last night. It's here.

Advisor: Right, let's have a look. OK. And whatever happens, remember to smile!

5

Jake: I know. We got on really well, too.

Sara: You both looked really happy when I saw you.

Jake: Yeah. We have so many things in common. She's a real animal-lover, she likes being outdoors. She loves helping with the fruit-picking, too. She's just really normal and fun.

Sara: So what went wrong?

Jake: I wish I knew! In the end maybe I was too busy helping Dad on the farm. She wanted to spend more time together, but that's just not possible.

6

Jen: Mum, I've got a basketball match tomorrow. Is my kit ready?

Mum: I don't know. I haven't seen it. Did you put it in the wash?

Jen: No. Oh, hang on. It might still be in my sports bag. Aha!

Mum: Ew! Jen, it's really smelly and disgusting! How long has it been here?

Jen: Um ... maybe a week.

Mum: Right, let's put it in the wash right now, but you can take those trainers outside. I think they need some fresh air!

Jen: You might be right.

---

1 B   2 C   3 C   4 A   5 B   6 A

4   Explain to students that they are going to check their answers in Exercise 3 and they are also going to identify how they found their answers. Read the questions aloud. Play the recording again and give students a couple of minutes to discuss their answers with a partner before class feedback.

Students' own answers.

Speak up

5   Organise students into groups and ask them to discuss the question. Monitor as they complete this task, offering support as necessary. Collect ideas around the class.

Students' own answers.

To finish

Organise students into small groups. They need to choose one of the situations from Exercise 1 and design the worst outfit for each case, e.g. *a night out with a friend* (pyjamas), *a family wedding* (a hoodie and trainers). Nominate students from each group to report back on their answers and explain in each case why their choice is inappropriate. Talk about how dress codes differ in different countries. Ask your students to tell you what they know about how people in different countries and cultures might dress on these occasions.

Homework

MyEnglishLab

SPEAKING (SB page 15)

To start

Tell students about the first time you met your best friend, e.g. *I met my best friend many years ago when we both had the same part-time job. I asked her what kind of music she liked and it turned out we both had the same favourite band! After that we found we had lots more in common.*

Ask students to remember the first time they met their best friend and tell their partner what they spoke about. Nominate a few students to report back.

Power up

1   Nominate students to read the sentences in the speech bubbles. Encourage them to use natural sounding pronunciation and intonation, e.g. falling intonation for *wh-* questions; rising and falling intonation for *Can I borrow your phone?* and *Do you want to come to the cinema?* Ask students to tell you which of these would be fine to say on a first meeting. There may be some debate, e.g. usually we wouldn't ask to borrow someone's phone on a first meeting, but in an emergency this would be OK.

Students' own answers.

Speak up

2   Read the questions aloud, focusing on friendly intonation. Drill the questions chorally. Ask students to get up, move around and find someone they don't usually work with. If your students are very shy, you can read out pre-prepared pairs which you have decided on in advance. Students should introduce themselves to each other and ask each other the questions. Nominate a student from each pair to report back on what they learned about their partner.

Students' own answers.

3   Refer students to the texts in the speech bubbles and the phrases in the box. Play the recording, twice if necessary, while students complete the texts. Allow students to compare their answers with a partner before eliciting the answers around the class. Elicit which question from Exercise 1 each person is answering.

➤ Track 1.4

A: I'm a big fan of rock music, especially *Go Radio* and *Mayday Parade*. I'm into *You Me at Six* as well. They're a British rock band. Actually, I'd love to see them live in a big arena. In fact, I'm planning to get tickets for their next tour.

B: Actually, I've been learning karate for nine years now and I'm a member of our local club. To be honest, it's hard work, especially when you've got lots of school work, too. My worst moment was when I broke my arm in a fall. I normally enjoy competitions and I've got a few cups, but I can't stand losing!

1 a big fan of
2 especially
3 into   **4** Actually
5 In fact
6 Actually
7 To be honest
8 especially
9 enjoy
10 can't stand

A is answering the question: *What kind of music are you into?*
B is answering the question: *What are your favourite hobbies?*

4 Ask a student the question: *Do you ever go the cinema?* When your student has answered, say *Oh, right ...* and look away. Ask another student the same question. This time, ask a follow-up question after your student's response, e.g. *Oh, really? How often do you go?* or *Why not?* Ask learners to tell you which example sounded more friendly and interested and elicit why (because you asked a follow-up question). Ask students to match the questions with the follow-up questions. Allow students time to check their answers with a partner before whole class feedback.

1 b **2** d **3** c **4** a **5** f **6** e

5 Focus students' attention on the phrases in the Language XP box. Read the words and phrases and ask students to give you examples of how to use them in sentences. Focus students' attention on the Exam advice and read it aloud to them. Organise students into pairs and ask them to read the tips and then take it in turns to ask and answer the questions in Exercise 4. Monitor as students complete the activity, ensuring that they are speaking loudly and clearly enough, and that they are using the new vocabulary accurately.

Students' own answers.

To finish

Organise students into two teams. Tell the class that you are going to ask individual students questions about their free time and hobbies. After the students have answered the question, the teams must compete to see who can be first to ask a follow-up question. They are not allowed to call out but must raise their hand once they have thought of their question. Award points for sensible and accurately formed follow-up questions. The team with the most points is the winner.

Homework
MyEnglishLab

WRITING (SB pages 16–17)

To start

Write an opinion sentence on the board, e.g. *Unhealthy food should be made illegal.*
Organise students into two teams: 'for' and 'against'. Give students a minute to prepare reasons for or against the statement you have written. Conduct a speed debate where students take it in turns to stand up and give their opinion one at a time. The other team should reply for or against the sentence by stating their opinion. Award points for ideas which are sensible and well expressed. The team with the most points at the end of the game is the winner.

Power up

1 Give an example of which opinion you agree with most, e.g. *I love being out in the fresh air because I think it's healthy and makes me feel calm and relaxed.* Organise students into pairs and ask them to tell their partner which opinion they agree with the most and why. Monitor as students do this, encouraging them to give reasons for their answers. Conduct class feedback and find out which statement most of your students agreed with.

Students' own answers.

Plan on

2 Focus students' attention on the photos and ask them to describe what they see. Ask: *Where would you like to be right now, if you had the choice. Why?* Ask students to follow along as you read the advert. Ask: *Do you agree with the statement?* Ask for a show of hands to see if they agree/disagree with the statement. Organise students so they are working with a partner who has the same idea as they do. Give them a minute to discuss their reasons for thinking that life is better in the city (or not). Conduct class feedback and write students' ideas on the board.

Students' own answers.

3 Give students two minutes to silently read Leandro's essay. When they have finished, ask them to tell their partner if they found ideas which were different to their own.

Students' own answers.

4 Ask students to tell you whether they think the two words refer to good or bad things. Ask them to find the words in the text and draw their attention to the surrounding words in both cases, e.g. (benefit) ... *there are lots of benefits.* (downside) *The only downside is* ... . Personalise the language by asking students questions about their own area, e.g. *What are the benefits of living in* ... (students' town)? *Are there any downsides to living here?*

1 good things
2 bad things

5 Explain that it is very important to organise essay writing so that it has a clear beginning, middle and end. Elicit why it is important to do this (so that readers can follow your argument easily). Students match the headings with the correct paragraphs. Check answers around the class.

1 D **2** A **3** C **4** B

6 Refer students to the Language XP box and read the categories aloud. Ask students to look at the words and phrases in bold in the essay. Ask them to copy the categories into their notebooks and give them a two-minute time limit to write the words in bold under the correct category. Conduct class feedback and ask your students if they can think of any more examples to add to the different categories.

Giving reasons and results: The main reason ... is, because, so, Another reason is (that)

Adding more points: too, In addition, Also

Giving opinions: in my view, Personally, I disagree that

Contrasting opinions: However, In spite of that, but

Summarising: On balance, ...

7 Focus students' attention on the linking words in the box. Ask them to complete the gaps using the words. As you check answers around the class, elicit whether the statements are talking about benefits, downsides or conclusions.

1 However, because (benefit)
2 so, too (benefit)
3 so (downside)
4 However (downside)
5 as, too (downside)
6 but (conclusion)

Write on

8 Direct students' attention to the essay prompt and read it aloud to them. Organise students into pairs and ask them to discuss the title and the first two points ('exercise' and 'entertainment'). After a couple of minutes bring the class together. Conduct feedback, generating as much useful and relevant language as possible and write it on the board.

Students' own answers.

9 Ask students to think about other points which they could discuss. Refer them back to the discussion they had in Exercise 2 if they are having difficulty thinking of ideas.

Students' own answers.

10 Read through the essay plan together. Ask students to write a brief plan for their essay using their ideas from Exercises 8 and 9. Encourage them to compare their plan with a partner. Circulate as students plan their essay, checking that they are following a clear and organised structure.

Students' own answers.

11 Read the Exam advice together. Students should use their plan from Exercise 10 to write their essay. Offer support where necessary. When students have finished writing their essays, ask them to ensure that they have included all of the information from their plans. Ask students to swap their essays with a partner. They should check each other's work for spelling and grammar mistakes. Read a selection of the best essays out to the class and/or display them on your classroom wall.

Students' own answers.

Model answer

Some people say that city life is bad for young people because they think that it is unhealthy and dangerous for them. However, I come from a big city and in my opinion, there are a lot of benefits for young people who live in cities.

The main benefit of city life is the educational opportunities. Young people living in cities can visit museums and go to the theatre and cinema much more often than people who live in the countryside. In addition, they have a greater choice of friends to go to these places with.

Some people think that young people living in cities have an unhealthier lifestyle than people who live in the country, but I disagree. There are many parks and sports centres where young people can go to get exercise.

Finally, I think that young people living in cities are more independent because they do not need their parents to drive them everywhere they need to go. This is because public transport is usually very good in big cities.

On balance, I disagree that city life is bad for young people, as I think it is exciting and educational. In spite of that, I have friends who couldn't cope with life in the city. I think it depends on what you're used to.

To finish

Dictate the following words and ask students to write them down:

comfortable, seasonal, accountant, agriculture, flip-flops, terrible, well-paid, tight, waterproof, get your hands dirty, prove (to someone) and stereotype.

Nominate students to come to the board to write the words from the dictation. Check that they have used the correct spelling. Then organise students into groups. Challenge them to think of a story which uses all of the words from the dictation.

After five minutes, nominate a student from each group to tell the rest of the class their story. Award points for the story which manages to accurately use the most words.

Homework

MyEnglishLab

SWITCH ON (SB page 18)

Reindeer moves

1 Read the question aloud to your students. Organise students into pairs and ask them to guess which three things they will hear about. Play the video and ask students to check their predictions.

Students' own answers.
The narrator doesn't mention C (special clothes) or E (Ella's school).

2 Give students a moment to look at the questions. Play the video again so that students can answer the questions. Check answers around the class.

1 3,000
2 yes (She was given some the day she was born.)
3 (up to) 80 kilometres an hour
4 They must get from the island to the mainland (for winter food).
5 a baby deer turns round
6 one hour

3 Ask students to discuss their opinions. Monitor during the task, offering support as necessary. Elicit students' ideas during class feedback.

Students' own answers.

Project

4 Tell students that they are going to write their own video script for an event in their local town or area. Organise them into groups and focus their attention on the three questions. Nominate a confident student to read the example aloud to the rest of the class. Allow students time to come to a decision on the event they have chosen and bring the class back together again to discuss ideas. Students then write their script and rehearse it. Monitor, modelling pronunciation and intonation where necessary. Students film the scripts in the classroom or on location if possible. Bring the class together to watch the films and give constructive feedback.

Students' own answers.

REVISION (SB page 19)

I

1 enjoyable
2 sensible
3 organised
4 reliable
5 stressful
6 satisfying

2

1 B **2** C **3** A **4** C **5** A **6** B **7** A **8** C

3

1 kit
2 flip-flops
3 hairstyle
4 baggy
5 casual
6 apron
7 plain
8 goggles

4

1 c **2** e **3** a **4** f **5** d **6** b

5

1 time
2 the
3 eye
4 paid
5 label
6 flops

Homework
Workbook pages 8–9

Making it happen

Unit objectives

Reading:	multiple-choice questions
Vocabulary:	technology; inventors and inventions
Grammar:	past simple, past continuous, used to, would; pronouns
Listening:	sentence completion
Speaking:	collaborative task
Writing:	writing an article

READING (SB pages 20–21)

To start

Bring a large ball or soft toy in the class. Ask students to stand or sit in a circle. Tell students that the theme of this unit is *technology* and that they will learn lots of really useful vocabulary on this subject.

Say that you want to find out how much your students already know. Explain that you are going to throw the ball around the class to different students. The students need to catch the ball and say a word to do with technology: it can be a verb, a noun or an adjective. If students repeat a word which has already been said, they are out of the game. Continue until there is only one student (the winner) left. Write new vocabulary on the board.

Power up

1 Focus students' attention on the list of items. Tell them which one you find most useful and why, e.g. *I find social networking sites the most useful because I can use them to keep in touch with all my friends and find out what's happening in the world.* Organise students into pairs. Give them a few minutes to talk about what they find most useful. Circulate as students complete the activity, encouraging them to give reasons for their answers. Open this up into a class discussion, generating as much vocabulary as possible and writing useful vocabulary on the board. Conduct a class vote to see which of the items discussed are most (and least) popular.

Students' own answers.

Read on

2 Elicit the meaning of the word *entrepreneur* (a person who sets up a business) and drill its pronunciation: /ˌɒntrəprəˈnɜː/. Check understanding by asking students if they can think of any famous entrepreneurs in their own country.

Read the title of the article aloud and elicit the meaning of the word *triumph* (a great success). If necessary, pre-teach the following words: *summarise* (to shorten a text to give the main points of something), *out of the blue* (when something happens which you weren't expecting), *inspired* (made someone feel that it is possible to achieve something great) and *set your mind on something* (to decide what you want to do and stick with it). Check students understanding by asking questions, e.g. *If you summarise something do you make it longer or shorter?* (shorter) *Is it easier to understand or more difficult?* (easier) *If something happens out of the blue, is it a surprise?* (yes) *Do your English tests usually come out of the blue?* (no) *Who inspires you? Why? If you set your mind on something, are you very sure you want to do it?* (yes) *Who can tell me about a time they set their minds on something?* Focus students' on the question: *What did Nick and Nina create?* and ask them to read the text quickly to find the answer.

Nick created an app that summarises news stories.
Nina created an app that gives users prompts/tips to help them remember their passwords more easily.

3 Read the Skill advice aloud to your students and then focus their attention on the questions. Students then read the article again more slowly and choose the correct answer for each question. Allow students to check their answers with a partner before conducting whole class feedback.

1 C   2 D   3 D   4 B   5 A   6 C

4 Students read the definitions and then find words in the article which have the same meaning. Check answers around the class, focusing on the pronunciation of difficult words, e.g. *achievable* /əˈtʃiːvəbəl/. Write words with more than one syllable on the board and elicit where the stressed syllable lies in each one.

1 d   2 c   3 f   4 g   5 b   6 e   7 a

Sum up

5 Ask students to choose either Nick or Nina. Tell them that they are going to summarise the story of their chosen entrepreneur. Read the questions aloud to your students and give them a few minutes to prepare what they are going to say. Use a show of hands to find out which entrepreneurs your students have chosen. Ask those who have chosen Nick to find a partner who has chosen Nina. Students then tell their partner about their chosen entrepreneur. Monitor and support students as necessary. Note down inaccuracies and good use of the new language for the feedback session.

Students' own answers.

Speak up

6 Tell students about your favourite phone app, e.g. *I have a phone app which helps me to manage my money. It reminds me when I have bills to pay and lets me know how much money I have to spend every month. I love it because I'm not very good with money and it really helps me.* Give students a minute to tell their partner about their favourite phone app before opening this up into a whole class discussion. Generate as much vocabulary as possible and encourage students to give reasons for their choices. Organise students into small groups to talk about the phone app they would create and what it would do. When time is up, ask one student from each group to report back on their app. (If you have plenty of confident students in your class they can come up to the front of the class to talk about their idea and write the name of their app on the board.) Encourage students to give feedback to their peers and conduct a class vote to see which idea is the most popular.

Students' own answers.

To finish

Ask students if they have ever watched *Dragon's Den* or an equivalent TV programme in their country. Elicit what happens on this programme (an entrepreneur pitches their business idea to some investors in the hope that they will get some money to fund their project). Organise students into pairs. Tell them to choose one of the apps they invented in Exercise 6 to present to *Dragons' Den* to get some money to help grow their business. Give them a few minutes to think about the following:

Why is their app so unique?

Why will it sell well?

Why should Dragon's Den invest their money in it?

Divide the class into two groups: dragons and entrepreneurs. The entrepreneurs have one minute to pitch their idea to the dragons. The dragons are only allowed to invest their money in one idea. Once all the entrepreneurs have had a minute to pitch their ideas they should swap sides, so that the dragons get a chance to pitch their ideas. Conduct class feedback and elicit which ideas got the most money. Was this because the ideas were good or because they were well-presented?

Homework

MyEnglishLab

VOCABULARY 1 (SB page 22)
Technology

To start

Ask your students to remind you who Nick and Nina are (they are the entrepreneurs students read about in the reading lesson). Organise the class into two groups: one side for Nick and one side for Nina. Within the large groups students should work in pairs. They have one minute to remember and write down as many facts as they can about their entrepreneur. Stop the class after one minute and count up the facts from each pair. Award extra points for good use of new language. The pair with the most points is the winner.

1 Read the words in the box aloud to your students. Drill pronunciation chorally and individually, focusing on potentially tricky words, e.g. virus /ˈvaɪrəs/. Write the words on the board. Elicit and mark the stressed syllables. Students complete the sentences using the words in the box. Allow students to check their answers with a partner before conducting class feedback. Try to personalise the new language where possible by asking students questions about themselves, e.g. *Are you on Twitter, Akeel? How often do you tweet?*

1 code   2 virus   3 website   4 battery   5 connection   6 tweet

2 Students choose the correct verb to complete the conversations. When they are ready, ask them to practise the conversations in pairs. Circulate, focusing on accurate pronunciation of the new language and natural sounding intonation. Conduct class feedback. Ask students to suggest alternative sentences for the verbs which weren't needed, e.g. *hacked, charge, access, programmed* and *program*.

1 deleted   2 update   3 scroll   4 downloaded   5 charge

Word XP

Read the information in the Word XP aloud to your students. Elicit some examples of phrasal verbs from your students. Remind them that it can be difficult to guess the meaning of phrasal verbs even if you know the meaning of their separate parts.

3 Ask students to complete the sentences with the words and phrases in the box. When they are finished they compare their answers with a partner. Play the recording so that students can check their answers.

Student A: I had great fun doing my technology project last night – not!

Student B: Oh! What happened?

Student A: Well, I wanted to follow up an interesting idea my teacher mentioned to me about looking at the inside of a computer. I belong to an online technology forum, but when I tried to log on to the website, I found that I couldn't remember my password! So then I had to email them for a new one! After a bit, they sent me a new password, so I keyed that in and I could finally start working. I found some good diagrams, but they were really detailed – I needed ones that were much simpler. Finally, I worked out a solution to that problem as well – I zoomed in on different bits of the diagram and printed them off. Then I put the bits together to make a nice big diagram to go in my project. In the end, I was happy with what I'd done, but by the time I turned off the computer, it was after midnight.

---

1 f (an interesting idea)

2 e (website)

3 a (password)

4 d (solution)

5 c (diagram)

6 b (computer)

---

4 Ask students to find and circle the phrasal verb in each sentence in Exercise 3. Check answers around the class, ensuring that students understand the meaning of the phrasal verbs by using concept questions, e.g. *If you zoom in on something, does it become bigger or smaller?* (bigger).

---

1 followed up

2 log on

3 key in

4 work out

5 zoom in

6 turn off

---

5 Give students a minute to silently skim read the article. Ask questions to check their understanding, e.g. *Why did Cameron's father get such a large bill?* (because Cameron had bought a lot of extras when he was playing computer games). *Did Cameron mean to spend all the money?* (no, he didn't realise he was spending real money). *What cost £77.98?* (a chest of gold coins). Focus students' attention on the words in the box and tell them to complete the article with the words (there are two which aren't needed). Allow students to check their answers with a partner before reading the article around the class.

---

1 online   **2** click   **3** virtual   **4** software

Game on

Organise the class into two teams (ideally facing each other in two lines). Move along the lines, asking students from alternate teams to say a new technology word they have learned this lesson. Award extra points for accurate pronunciation and bonus points if students can make a sentence using their word. The team with the most points at the end of the game is the winner.

To finish

Ask: *What technology can you find in this school?* Elicit as much vocabulary as possible. Ask students to make a leaflet for new students arriving at the school. It should contain the following information: how to access the school computer, how to navigate the school website, how to find the school on Facebook. Display the posters on the wall and photocopy the best example to give to new students.

Homework

Workbook pages 10–11

MyEnglishLab

GRAMMAR 1 (SB page 23)

Past tenses

To start

Ask students to think about what they did yesterday. Give them one minute to write down all the technology they remember using. When time is up, ask them to write sentences about all the technology they used. Keep the pace brisk, by giving another time limit of one minute. Students read out their sentences. Check for correct usage of past tenses. Ask students to decide who used the most technology yesterday.

Grammar XP

Read the information and examples in the Grammar XP box with the students. Write some sentences about yourself on the board using the target language, e.g.

I really liked learning languages at school. I went to university and studied French and Italian.

When I was studying languages at university, I decided to be a teacher.

I used to like playing basketball.

When I was at university, I would go swimming every day.

Focus on the past simple and past continuous sentences. Point to the past simple sentence and ask: *What happened first?* (liking languages at school) *What happened next?* (going to university) Write the numbers '1' and '2' over the sentence to show the past simple is used to describe a sequence of events. Draw students' attention to the verb forms (regular *liked* and irregular *went*).

Then focus on the past continuous example. Ask: *Which happened first?* (studying languages) Draw a wavy line on the board and write *studying languages* underneath it. Then draw an arrow to show the past simple verb *decided* interrupting the continuing (unfinished) process of studying. Focus students' attention on the past continuous form (*was/were + verb + -ing*).

Finally, look at the two examples of *would* and *used to*. Elicit why *would* could not substitute *used to* in the sentence *I used to like playing basketball* (because liking is a situation rather than a habit). Ask students to write their own *used to* and *would* sentences. Conduct class feedback.

1 Ask students if they have ever been to a technology exhibition and elicit what you might expect to find at one, e.g. *exciting new gadgets, robots, computers*. Students complete the text messages with the past simple or continuous forms of the verbs in brackets. Allow students to check their answers with a partner before conducting class feedback.

1 tried on
2 was walking
3 lit up
4 told
5 were talking
6 checked out
7 informed

2 Students read the sentences and choose *used to*, *would* or both. Check answers around the class, asking students to explain their choices.

1 Did he use to
2 used to/would (both answers are correct)
3 didn't use to
4 used to
5 used to/would (both answers are correct)

3 Give students a minute to quickly read the blog. Ask questions to check understanding, e.g. *What was the advertisement for?* (a table tennis robot); *Why couldn't Tom get one for his birthday?* (it was too expensive); *Why didn't Tom want to play table tennis with Cheng?* (because he's too good). Students complete the blog with the correct form of the verbs in brackets, using *used to* wherever possible. Read the blog post around the class during feedback.

1 was reading 2 saw 3 thought 4 was/used to be
5 was dreaming 6 came 7 asked 8 took
9 shook 10 used to go

Write on

4 Tell students about a gadget you enjoyed using when you were younger, e.g. *When I was younger I had a little electronic tennis game which I really enjoyed playing because it played music.* Alternatively, you could amuse your students by telling them that there were no gadgets when you were younger, giving some examples of all the old-fashioned things you used to do. Ask students to write about a gadget they used to like. Circulate as students write, offering support where necessary and checking they are using the past simple, past continuous, *used to* and *would* accurately. Nominate a few students to read their work aloud to the rest of the class.

Students' own answers.

To finish

Play *Two truths and a lie* with your students to practise the use of *would* and *used to*. Write three sentences on the board (two true and one lie), e.g.

I used to have blonde hair.

I used to be a long distance runner.

When I was a child, I would sleepwalk almost every night.

Ask students to see if they can spot which of the three sentences is a lie. Now ask students to write two truths and a lie of their own. Encourage them to use both *used to* and *would*. Students then play the game in small groups. Circulate, checking they are using the new language correctly.

Homework
Workbook pages 12–13
MyEnglishLab

VOCABULARY 2 (SB page 24)

Inventors and inventions

To start

Write the headings *food*, *clothes* and *games* on the board. Write one sentence about what you used to do as a child for each, using *used to*, e.g.

I used to hate spinach, but I don't mind it now.

I used to wear terrible clothes because my mum dressed me.

I used to love skipping with a rope.

Ask students to write down sentences about themselves for each heading and share them with a partner. Ask students to report back and share something funny or surprising they learned about their partner.

1 Focus students' attention on the four nouns. Write them on the board and drill the pronunciation of each. Elicit and mark the stressed syllables. Ask students to tell you what each item does, e.g. *What does a calculator do?* (It does your sums for you). Students write down the verb that each noun comes from. Conduct feedback orally.

1 calculate   2 invent   3 program   4 transmit

Word XP

Read the information in the Word XP box with the students. Ask if they can think of any more nouns which have -er/-or endings, and write ideas on the board.

2 Students complete the sentences by forming nouns from the verbs in brackets. Allow students to check their answers with a partner before reading the sentences around the class. Focus on natural sounding pronunciation and word stress.

1 amplifier(s)   2 receiver   3 generators   4 scanner, photocopier

Word XP

Write the word *play* on the board. Add the prefix *re-* to the beginning of play. Ask students what they think *replay* means (to play again) and elicit the meaning of the prefix *re-* (to do something again). Now write the word *agree* on the board. Add the prefix *dis-* and elicit how you have just changed the word's meaning (you have made it mean the opposite). Elicit that adding *dis-* to some verbs can make them have the opposite meaning.

Read the information in the Word XP box with the students. Encourage them to think of other examples of verbs which can have their meanings changed by these two prefixes.

3 Students complete the sentences with the correct form of the verbs, adding the prefixes *re-* and *dis-*. Check answers orally.

1 replay   2 disappear, reappear   3 disconnect   4 rerecord

4 Focus students' attention on the title of the article, and ask them to predict which inventions might be mentioned. Write students' ideas on the board. Give students one minute to read the article in silence. Check understanding by asking students: *Which four inventions does the article mention?* (the printing press, canned food, computers and transmitters). Students complete the article with the correct form of the words in capitals. Allow students to check their answers quickly with a partner before reading the article around the class. Ask students to close their books and remember one fact about each of the inventions.

1 printer   2 explorer   3 creator   4 inventor   5 distrusted
6 refrigerator   7 programmer   8 transmitter

Speak up

5 Look at the board and direct students' attention to their predictions about inventions in Exercise 4. Organise students into pairs and ask them to discuss what they think the great inventions in history are, encouraging them to add to the examples already collected on the board. Circulate as students discuss their ideas, encouraging them to give reasons for their suggestions. Conduct class feedback, nominating a student from each pair to report back on their ideas.

Students' own answers.

To finish

Write vocabulary words from the lesson on a piece of paper and cut them up into strips. Organise the class into two teams. Give one member of each team a word. They must describe the word to the rest of their team (without saying the actual word). Give them a strict time limit of one minute to do this. As soon as the team has guessed their word, give them a new word (and choose a new student to describe the word). The team which manages to guess the most words correctly is the winner.

Homework
Workbook page 11
MyEnglishLab

GRAMMAR 2 (SB page 25)

Pronouns

To start

Remind your class that the last lesson focused on great inventions. Tell students that there have also been some very bad inventions. Give an example of an invention you think is bad, e.g.

I think that mobile phones are a bad invention because it's really hard to be alone now.

Ask students to work with a partner and decide what their bad invention is and why they think it is bad. Elicit ideas from a few pairs.

Grammar XP

Read the information and examples in the Grammar XP box with the students. Then write personal examples of each type of pronoun use on the board. Make sure that you muddle the order, so that the examples you use do not correspond to those given, e.g.

a) *I emailed my project to* **myself** *so that I didn't lose it.*

b) *You're so clever! You've done this grammar exercise all* **by yourself!**

c) *My mum taught* **herself** *how to read when she was three years old.*

Ask students to identify which kind of reflexive pronoun is used in each case (a = with a preposition, b = for emphasis, c = when the subject and object are the same). Draw students' attention to the word stress (in reflexive pronouns the stress is on the second syllable, and the first syllable is often pronounced very weakly, e.g. *yourself* /jɔːˈself/.)

1 Students complete the sentences with reflexive pronouns. Check answers around the class, asking students to justify their answers.

1 (all by) yourself
2 herself, itself
3 myself
4 themselves
5 ourselves

2 Give students a minute to quickly read the text. Check students' understanding by asking: *What were the friends playing?* (Sports Connection on Wii U); *What kind of sports did they play?* (tennis and go-kart racing); *Did they play anything else?* (no). Ask students if they like playing sports on Wii and ask them to tell you about sports they like. Students find the possessive pronouns in the text. Read the text around the class, asking students to say 'Beep!' (or something similar) when they find a possessive pronoun.

Last night, two friends of <u>ours</u>, Stella and Ricky, came round to our house to play *Sports Connection* on Wii U. They brought a couple of other games of <u>theirs</u> for us to play as well, but we didn't have time in the end. Since the game was <u>his</u>, Ricky started off with the game pad, but he also let us have a turn with it later. It was really good fun! My best game was tennis and Stella was happy too, because <u>hers</u> was go-kart racing.

3 Students complete the sentences with possessive pronouns. Check answers orally.

1 mine **2** ours **3** yours **4** his **5** hers **6** theirs

4 Focus students' attention on the title of the blog. Ask them to tell you what they think the different uses of robots are, and write ideas on the board. Give students one minute to quickly read the text and ask them questions to check their understanding, e.g. *What uses for robots does the writer speak about?* (exploring space, performing operations) *What did the writer used to think about robots?* (that robots were only in science fiction films). Students complete the blog with one word in each space. Conduct class feedback, making sure you don't accept the first answer you hear; go around the class and listen to a range of student responses.

1 mine **2** myself **3** used **4** would **5** own **6** themselves
7 himself **8** each

To finish

Remind students of the Japanese inventor who invented a robot just like himself. Ask students: *If you invented a robot what would it look like? What would it be able to do? Would it be useful or would it be entertaining?*

Ask students to work with a partner and design a robot. They should also draw a picture of their robot. At the end of the lesson, students can present their robot to the rest of the class and describe what it can do.

Homework
Workbook page 13
MyEnglishLab

LISTENING (SB page 26)

To start

Write a short conversation with errors on the board, e.g.

A: *What a lovely dress? Did you make it by you?*

B: *Yes, I did! I made it yourself. I'm going to wear it to a party tomorrow.*

A: *Really! Well, enjoy you!*

Organise students into pairs and challenge them to correct the errors in the conversation as quickly as they can. The first pair to find and correct all the errors can read the conversation out to the class.

Power up

1 Organise students into different pairs. Give them a one minute time limit to list the equipment in their home which depends on electricity and batteries, e.g. microwave, fridge, television, alarm clock, mobile phone, laptop, cooker, torch, freezer.

When the minute is up, find out which pair collected the largest number of items. Ask students to read out their lists, writing down new vocabulary on the board.

Students' own answers.

2 Focus students' attention on the words in the box and explain that they are going to listen to a radio programme which contains these words. Read the words aloud to your students, drilling pronunciation chorally and individually. Students match the words in the box with their meanings. Check answers quickly around the class.

1 broadcast **2** engineering **3** research **4** electronic part **5** supply

Listen up

3 Focus students' attention on the photograph of Kelvin Doe and explain that he is a young inventor from Africa. Tell students that they are going to listen to the recording and write down all the different things he has made. If necessary, pre-teach the following: *dustbin* (where you throw your rubbish), *advisor* (a person who can help you and give you advice), *went viral* (instantly became very popular online). Check students' understanding by asking questions, e.g. *If I really like something, do I put it in the dustbin?* (no) *What does an advisor give me?* (advice) *If something goes viral, do very few people watch it?* (no) *Do lots of people watch it?* (yes). Play the recording. Allow students to check their ideas with a partner before conducting class feedback.

> ➤ **Tracks 2.2 and 2.3**

Kelvin Doe is a young inventor from Freetown in Sierra Leone, a small West African country that is bordered on one side by the Atlantic Ocean. He loves his country and he wants to do all he can to help it move forward into the technological age.

When Kelvin was only eleven years old, he started picking up electronic parts and bits of metal from the dustbins in his area, and making things from them. He even discovered how to make batteries by himself!

Kelvin was the youngest of five children. He used to go to bed early, at around 7 p.m., then wake up again at midnight. He would then spread all the bits he'd found over the living room floor and use the space as his workshop! He did what he could until his mother came downstairs and made him go back to bed again!

Kelvin's house often had only one or two hours of electricity a day, so Kelvin made a generator for their own supply. He also made a sound amplifier and a microphone receiver. By the time he was fourteen, he was able to use all that equipment to start up his own radio station!

So Kelvin became a DJ – DJ Focus as he calls himself – and broadcast to the residents of his local neighbourhood. Radio is a very popular form of entertainment in Sierra Leone, with about eighty-five percent of the population having a radio and about seventy-two percent listening to it on a daily basis.

Meanwhile, in 2012, Kelvin's radio transmitter was one of the winning entries in a competition organised by David Sengeh from the Massachusetts Institute of Technology – or MIT as it is known – and Kelvin was invited to travel to America. For a boy of fifteen who had never travelled further than ten miles from his home, this was a life-changing event. Fortunately, he had David as his advisor and he could rely on him for any help and guidance.

Kelvin gave talks to the students at MIT on the subject of his inventions and he took part in research projects in the area of engineering. A YouTube video that David made about Kelvin's US trip went viral within a few weeks, with over 3.5 million views!

A year later, Kelvin was back in the States, this time as a speaker at TEDxTeen, a programme of events that highlight the work of teens around the globe. He admitted that he was a bit nervous about speaking to such a large audience, but, in fact, he wowed them with his inspiring presentation. Kelvin was voted number forty-five of the one hundred most creative people in business in 2013.

batteries, a generator, an amplifier,
a microphone receiver, a radio transmitter,
a radio station

4 Read the Skill advice with the students. Give them one minute to read the gapped sentences and encourage them to think about what the missing words might be. Play the recording again. Check answers around the class.

1 country
2 dustbins
3 living room
4 electricity
5 radio
6 72/seventy-two
7 competition
8 advisor
9 inventions
10 nervous

Speak up

5 Ask students if the radio is important in Sierra Leone. (yes). Ask if they remember any more information about radio-listening habits in Kelvin's country (about 85 percent of people have a radio, and about 72 percent of people listen to radio on a daily basis). Ask students to discuss radio in their country with a partner.

Students' own answers.

To finish

Organise students into pairs and give each student a number: 1 or 2. Number '1's are going to play the part of Kelvin Doe and number '2's are going to interview him. Ask number '1's to think about why they like inventing things, what inspires them, information about their childhood, and things they used to do. The interviewers should work together to write questions. Give students time to practise their roleplays, circulating and offering support where necessary. Ask a couple of students to perform their roleplays to the rest of the class.

Homework
MyEnglishLab

SPEAKING (SB page 27)

To start

Organise students into pairs. Tell them they have one minute to remember as many facts as they can about Kelvin Doe. When the time is up, ask students to tell you how many facts they remembered. Go around the class, collecting facts and focusing on correct use and pronunciation of vocabulary. The pair who collects the greatest number of correct facts is the winner.

Power up

1 Focus students' attention on the photographs and ask them to describe what they see (an astronaut with Earth in the background; a woman interacting with a robot). Ask students to discuss the questions in pairs, giving reasons for their answers, e.g. *I think it would be exciting to travel in space because I'd like to see if there really is life on other planets!* Open this up into a whole class discussion. Generate as much new vocabulary as possible and write it on the board.

Students' own answers.

2 Ask students what they might expect to find at a technology workshop, e.g. gadgets, computers, robots. Tell students that they are going to listen to two friends talking about technology workshops. They should write down three things they say they could learn.

Play the recording. Allow students to check their answers with a partner and think of some more ideas. Conduct class feedback and write students' ideas on the board.

➤ Tracks 2.4 and 2.5

Jason: Hi, Anna. Have you heard? The headmaster is organising some technology workshops and he wants to know what we would learn from them. Then he's going to decide which ones we'll have.

Anna: Cool! So what's the first workshop?

Jason: Er ... the first one is about robots.

Anna: Great! Well, we could learn about the history of robots and how they have developed over the years.

Jason: Yes, that's true. We could also learn about the use of robots in films – you know, *Star Wars* and so on.

Anna: I think that would be fantastic! I'm sure everyone would be really interested in that. And there's also the use of robots in medicine and in scientific research. I think that's a topic we could learn a lot about.

Jason: You're right there. OK, so shall we move on to the next workshop? This one's about some of the ...

history and development, robots in films, robots in medicine and scientific research

3 Read the Language XP box with the students. Focus on natural sounding pronunciation and intonation. Tell students that they are going to listen to the recording again and note down the phrases from the box they hear being used. Check answers around the class.

Expressing agreement:
Yes, that's true. You're right there.
Speculating or discussing a possibility:
We could learn about … , I think that would be fantastic! Everyone would be really interested …

Speak up

4 Read the task aloud to your students. Ask students to match the points with the different types of workshops in the spidergram. Check answers orally, writing the workshops and points up on the board. Give students one minute to work in groups and think of a few more ideas. Conduct class feedback.

web-based businesses: a, c
new technologies: g, i
digital photography: d, j
space exploration: b, h
inventions: e, f

5 Read the Exam advice with the students. Ask how they can react appropriately to what their partner says (by listening and using the language in the first Language XP box) and elicit why it is important to do so (because it shows that you are polite and that you respect the opinion of your partner). Organise students into groups and ask them to discuss the question in Exercise 4. Monitor as they complete the task, checking that they are using the target language accurately. Conduct class feedback, focusing on good examples of language you have heard, and addressing any problems.

Students' own answers.

6 Read the language in the second Language XP box with the students. Drill the phrases, focusing on natural sounding pronunciation, e.g. *I would definitely choose* /aɪwʊdefɪnətliːtʃuːz/. Ask students to discuss which two workshops they find most interesting, using the phrases from the second Language XP box. Monitor, offering support as necessary.

Students' own answers.

7 Ask students to turn to page 152 of the SB. Give them five minutes to jot down notes, making sure that they answer both parts of the task (how the developments will affect our daily lives and which developments are the most important). Stress that they will need to be able to give reasons for their answers, and remind them to use the language from the Language XP boxes on page 27. Students complete Part 1 of the task. Circulate as students do this, listening and noting down any issues and any good examples of target language use.

Give students a couple of minutes to read the discussion questions in Part 2 of the task and think about their answers. They should then discuss the questions, using the target language from the Language XP boxes where appropriate. Circulate, noting down accurate use of the new technology lexis as well as language for agreeing, speculating and expressing preferences.

Students' own answers.

To finish

Think of something technological which you can't do, but think your students can, e.g.
I don't know how to upload music to my phone.
Tell your students that you would really like to be able to do this thing. Ask them to write instructions for you. Choose the instructions you find most useful.

Homework
MyEnglishLab

WRITING (SB pages 28–29)

To start

Write the following sentence on the board:

Robots should replace human teachers in the school.

Organise students into two groups: *for* and *against*. Give students a minute to work with a partner and prepare their arguments. Students should take it in turns to give their opinions and respond to each other's comments using the language they learned in the Speaking lesson.

Power up

1 Focus students' attention on the photographs. Ask them to tell you what they see (a polar bear; a car accident). Organise students into small groups and ask them what they would do in these situations and how they could use a mobile phone. Open this up into a whole class discussion and write any new language on the board.

Students' own answers.

Plan on

2 Focus students' attention on the question. Ask them to read the article quickly and find out why the writer loves her mobile phone. Conduct class feedback and write students' answers on the board. Ask: *Do you like your mobile phone, Rafal? Why? What do you use it for?* Write down anything your student says which is different from the article.

It's the way she keeps in touch with her friends; it's her 'personal toy', with her own ringtone, address book and special wallpaper; she uses it to take photos and videos, and listen to music

3 Read the items on the checklist aloud with the students. Students find an example of each point in the article in Exercise 2. Elicit examples during class feedback.

your personal opinion: I don't think I'll ever get tired of my mobile.
anecdotes: There was a man in Canada who ...
your personal experience of the subject: It's the way I keep in touch with my friends; I take photos and videos on it and I listen to music.
direct reference to the reader: Do you love your mobile? How about you?
an interesting title: Mobiles rule OK?
rhetorical questions: Why is my mobile so important to me?

4 Read the Skill advice with the students. Elicit how many paragraphs the article has (3). Ask students to identify the topic sentences in paragraphs 2 and 3. Check answers orally.

Paragraph 2: Why is my mobile phone so important to me?
Paragraph 3: Not only that, mobiles can also save lives – and in unusual ways!

5 Elicit the name of the kind of questions used in the article (rhetorical). Ask students to find the questions and elicit why the writer has used them (to involve the reader). Stress that rhetorical questions are a really good way to make writing more interesting and engaging for your readers.

Do you love your mobile?
Why is my mobile so important to me?
How about you?
The writer has used the questions to make the article more interesting and keep the reader involved.

Language XP

Read the rhetorical questions in the Language XP box with the students. Tell them they will refer back to this box later on in the lesson when they come to do their writing task.

6 Students complete the rhetorical questions with phrases from the Language XP box. Check answers orally. Elicit answers to the questions they have formed.

1 Have you ever
2 What do you think
3 Are you
4 How about you
5 Do you (ever)

Write on

7 Read the announcement aloud with the students. Ask them to tell you which gadget they would choose to write about and write their suggestions on the board.

Students' own answers.

8 Tell students they are going to write an article about the gadget they chose in Exercise 7. Read the three questions aloud and give them a few minutes to brainstorm some ideas with a partner. Circulate, offering support where necessary.

Students' own answers.

9 Students plan their writing, using the article in Exercise 2 to help them. Ask them to show you their completed plan before they go on to write their essay.

Students' own answers.

10 Students write their article. After they have been writing for about ten minutes, ask them to stop and exchange their work with a partner. Encourage students to offer their partner some constructive support and feedback, before continuing to work on their article. Tell students to use the check list in Exercise 3 to assess their work before bringing it to you. Read a few of the articles aloud to your students and display them on the wall.

Students' own answers.

Model answer

My Incredible ipad!

Are you crazy about your ipad? I am! I spend lots of time on it and I am always getting into trouble from my mum and dad who say I spend far too much time on it!

So why do I love it so much? Well, I do everything on it: listen to music, check out social networking sites – I even do my homework on it! Not only that, I also use my ipad for lots of really creative stuff. There is a really cool music-making app you can buy and I've already recorded lots of tunes on it. I also use it to make short movies with my friends and family – it's got a great movie-making app which gives really professional results. I entered a short movie I made on my ipad to a local film festival – and it won second prize!

I could never get bored with my ipad. It's a really useful gadget which helps me to make amazing things. What do you think?

To finish

Put students into small groups and ask them to design a vocabulary activity for another group. Circulate to ensure that your students are designing doable activities. They can be straightforward translation from L1 if this is easiest, or students can make simple sentence gap fills or word searches. Ask groups to swap their activities and complete them.

Homework

MyEnglishLab

SWITCH ON (SB page 30)

A handy app

1 Read the question aloud to your students. Organise students into pairs and ask them to choose the most common reasons why teenagers have problems with their friends. Monitor as students talk through their ideas, offering support where necessary. Nominate a few students to report back on their discussion. Read the second part of the question aloud to your students. Ask your students to predict what Sean's problem with his friend is. Play the video so that students can check their predictions.

Students' own answers.

Sean's friend Ben misinterpreted something he said.

2 Give students a minute to read the sentences. Play the video again, and ask students to decide whether the sentences are true or false. Give them a few minutes to discuss their answers with a partner before checking answers around the class.

A F   **B** T   **C** F   **D** T   **E** F

3 Read the questions aloud. Ask students to tell you how Petri thought the app might be useful. Organise students into pairs and ask them to discuss whether or not they agree with Petri. Conduct class feedback.

Students' own answers.

She says the app might help people to communicate in a more positive way.

Project

4 Organise the class into small groups. Read both options (A and B) and tell students that they need to choose an option. Monitor as students prepare their presentation, making sure that everyone in the group is participating equally. Bring the class together to watch the presentations and encourage students to offer constructive feedback about each other's work.

Students' own answers.

REVISION (SB page 31)

1

1 B **2** C **3** A
4 C **5** B **6** B

2

1 was doing, rang
2 got off, waited
3 used to
4 was watching, was chatting
5 would ask
6 were living

3

1 amplifiers
2 scanner
3 collector
4 disconnect
5 competitors
6 redo

4

1 herself
2 themselves
3 each
4 his
5 myself
6 yours

5

1 mine
2 was
3 herself
4 own
5 hers
6 used

Homework
Workbook pages 14–15

True story?

READING (SB pages 32–33)

To start

Focus students' attention on the title of the unit: *True story?* Tell students a true story from your life, e.g. a time you met someone famous, a funny thing which happened to you, or an adventure you have had. Say something like:

I was on holiday in Budapest one time when I saw a big crowd of people standing around. I walked over to see what was happening and in the middle of the crowd I saw Nelson Mandela – he was walking around and meeting people and I even got to shake hands with him!

Tell students to share a true story from their own lives with a partner. Circulate as students tell their stories, offering support where necessary. Nominate a few students to tell their true stories to the class.

Power up

1 Focus students' attention on the advert and elicit the meaning of the word *audition* (an opportunity to show what you can do as a singer, musician, actor, etc.) Check understanding by asking: *What is this advertisement looking for?* (people to audition for a TV talent show); *How would you feel if you saw this advertisement?* Ask students to give you examples of acts from talent shows in their country and encourage them to give examples of each type.

Students' own answers.

2 Ask students to discuss in pairs which acts are usually most/least popular. Open this up into a class discussion, encouraging students to give reasons for their answers, e.g. *People usually love performing animals because they're funny.*

Students' own answers.

Background

Britain's Got Talent is one of the most popular TV shows in Britain. Simon Cowell is a judge who is sometimes famously rude to the contestants. Other famous people on the show include TV celebrities Ant and Dec. Anyone of any age can audition to appear on the show and the show has included a wide variety of acts from singers to people dancing with their pet dogs.

Read on

3 Focus students' attention on the photograph of Jack. Read the title of the article aloud and ask students to predict what they think Jack's act might be. Elicit the fact that Jack has a walking frame to support his legs. If necessary, pre-teach the following: *gigs* (performance or concert), *in the wings* (at the side of the stage, but where the audience can't see you), *aired* (been shown on TV), *backstage* (the place where actors and performers wait before they perform), *grinning* (smiling). Check understanding by asking concept questions, e.g. *Do you like going to gigs? Tell us about the last gig you went to. When you're in the wings, can the audience see you?* (no) *Can you see the performers on the stage?* (yes) *If a show airs, is it on TV?* (yes) *If you're backstage, can the audience see you?* (no) *Are you waiting to perform?* (yes) *If I'm grinning, do I feel happy or sad?* (happy). Ask students to read the list of events and predict the order in which they happen and to note the date of each event. Students then read the article quickly and check to see if their predictions are correct. Conduct class feedback.

2 d, 2 February　3 e, 3 March　4 a, 13 April　5 c, 6 June

4 Read the Exam advice and then focus students' attention on the sentences. Students read the diary again more slowly and decide which sentences fit the spaces. Remind students that one of the sentences is not needed. Allow students to check their answers with a partner before conducting class feedback.

1 b　2 g　3 d　4 f　5 a　6 c

5 Tell students that they are going to learn some common idioms. Elicit the meaning of an idiom (a phrase where it is not always possible to know the meaning by understanding the separate words which make it up). Do the first question together. Ask students to find the phrase *steady my nerves* in the article (2 February paragraph). Read the whole sentence and see if they can guess the meaning of the phrase from the context (*make me feel calmer*). Then ask them to match the idiom with its definition. Ask students to complete the rest of the task in the same way. Check answers around the class.

1 b　2 c　3 e　4 d　5 f　6 a

Sum up

6 Ask students to discuss the questions with a partner. After students have had a few minutes to do this, open it up into a class discussion. Generate as much vocabulary to do with character and feelings as possible.

Students' own answers.

Suggested answers

1 Jack is unusual because he wants to be on stage although he has a disability.

2 Jack feels quite nervous before he performs, but when he hears that he has got through to the semi-finals he feels really excited. At the semi-finals he feels nervous and when he gets through to the finals he feels very happy.

Speak up

7 Organise students into small groups and focus their attention on the example. Give students a time limit to think of as many qualities and jokes as they can. Bring the class together again and write students' suggestions on the board, e.g. qualities: think quickly, be funny, have a good imagination.

Students' own answers.

To finish

Think of a simple joke to tell your students, e.g. **Q**: *What is orange and sounds like a parrot?* **A**: *A carrot!*

Organise students into small groups. Give them a time limit to think of as many jokes or funny stories as they can. Monitor as students complete the task, offering support as necessary. Ask each group to share their best joke/amusing story with the rest of the class and vote for the funniest one.

Homework

MyEnglishLab

VOCABULARY 1 (SB page 34)

A personal story

To start

Refer students back to the text they read about Jack Carroll. Organise students into groups and ask them to write five things they remember about Jack. Some of the statements should be true, and some should be false. When students have written their statements, ask them to swap with another group. The group should read the statements and decide whether they are true or false (without referring back to the text). Conduct feedback and find out which group got all of the answers correct.

1 Ask students to read the text quickly. Ask questions to check understanding, e.g. *What is Alessandra's talent?* (singing) *How did she feel before she went on stage?* (very nervous) *What do people remember about Alessandra?* (She gave some of her prize money to the guitarist who came second in the competition.).

Ask students to read the text again and choose the correct answers. Read the story around the class.

1 hoped **2** shaking **3** felt **4** stared **5** voted **6** achieved **7** offered **8** experiencing **9** recognise **10** shared

2 Ask students to read the verbs in the box around the class. Check that students pronounce *recognise* with the stress on the first syllable. Ask students to work in pairs to write down the nouns for each verb.

experience – experience
feel – feeling
grin – grin
hope – hope
offer – offer
recognise – recognition
refer to – reference (to)
shake – shake
share – share
stare – stare
vote – vote

3 Play the recording so that students can check their answers in Exercise 2. Write the nouns on the board, marking the stressed syllables in each. Drill the nouns chorally and individually.

> **Track 3.1**

achieve, achievement
experience, experience
feel, feeling
grin, grin
hope, hope
offer, offer
recognise, recognition
refer to, reference to
shake, shake
share, share
stare, stare

4 Students complete the sentences with the nouns in the box. Read the sentences around the class.

1 weakness **2** nerves **3** relief **4** strength **5** feats

5 Read the adjectives in the box with the students. Drill pronunciation, focusing on any potentially tricky words, e.g. *sweaty* /ˈsweti/. Elicit that all of the two-syllable words are stressed on the first syllable. Students complete the sentences using the adjectives. Check answers around the class.

1 sweaty **2** tense **3** negative **4** positive **5** massive

Word XP

Read the information in the Word XP with the students. Elicit why it is important to use time words and phrases when you're telling a story (it makes it easier for your listener to follow the events you are talking about).

6 Ask students to look at Jack's diary on page 32. Tell them they have two minutes to find and make a list of all the time words and phrases they can find there (in both the main text and the missing sentences). When the time is up, ask students to read you their lists. Write the time words and phrases on the board.

....

for once, since I was a little boy

It's the big day, It takes a couple of seconds, at the outset

yet, for the past month, now, a few moments later, just, until May, for TWO whole months

tonight

afterwards, it's the first time, Overnight

as, after a tense hour, Just a few minutes later

the best day (of my life), ever, when I was born

....

7 Students complete the time phrases. Allow students to check their answers with a partner before conducting class feedback.

1 a   **2** the   **3** an   **4** the   **5** a   **6** the   **7** the

Game on

Nominate a confident and able student to demonstrate how this game works. Ask the student to choose a verb from Exercise 1. Write it on the board. Now ask them to choose one of the time phrases from Exercise 7. Tell them to think of a sentence which includes both the verb and the time phrase, and write this sentence on the board. Organise your students into pairs. Explain that they have two minutes to write as many sentences as they can using verbs from Exercise 1 and time phrases from Exercise 7. When the time is up, ask students to add up their sentences and tell you how many they have written. Ask the students with the most sentences to read them out. Deduct a point for any inaccurate or repetitive sentences. Then ask the student with the second largest amount of sentences to read them out and repeat the process. Continue until you have established who has the largest number of accurate sentences.

To finish

Refer students back to the story of Alessandra Aguirre. Elicit the names of some talent show celebrities from your students' own country/countries. Ask students to work in groups to note down everything they know about a talent show celebrity from their country. Circulate as students do this, offering help where needed. Nominate a student from each group to tell the rest of the class about their chosen celebrity. Encourage the rest of the class to ask questions, and encourage students to use the target vocabulary from the lesson.

Homework

Workbook pages 16–17

MyEnglishLab

GRAMMAR 1 (SB page 35)

Present perfect tenses

To start

Tell students that this lesson will focus on present perfect tenses. Elicit that we use the present perfect to talk about experiences. Choose a topic which you know your class are interested in, e.g. *travel*. Ask students to write as many questions as they can for their classmates about their experiences with this topic. Elicit that the questions will start with the words *Have you ever ... ?*. Organise students to work in pairs and give them a minute to collect some questions, e.g.

Have you ever flown on a long haul flight?

Have you ever been to Australia?

Have you ever stayed in a really expensive hotel?

Have you ever eaten anything really unusual in a foreign country?

Elicit ten questions and write them on the board. Students circulate, asking each other about their experiences. Encourage them to ask follow-up questions.

Grammar XP

Illustrate the concept of the present perfect with a timeline and some sentences about yourself. Think of a few events in your own life, e.g. the year you started teaching, the first time you travelled to France, the year you passed your driving test.

Write the dates these events occurred along the bottom of your timeline. Write a couple of sentences about these events using the past simple, e.g.

I went to France in 2001.

Underneath this write the sentence:

I've been to France.

Elicit the difference between the two sentences (the first refers to a specific and complete time; the second refers to experience in general and does not have a specific time so the present perfect is used). Now ask students to tell you when you started teaching and elicit the answer:

You started teaching in 2003.

Ask students:

How long have I been a teacher?

Elicit the answer:

You've been a teacher since 2003.

Stress that the second sentence links the start of your career as a teacher with the present day. Write the word *Now* at the end of your timeline. Ask students: *Do we use the present perfect to talk about the past or the present?* (we use the present perfect to talk about things which are relevant to the present, but also connect with the past).

Elicit how we form the present perfect: *has/have* + *been* + past participle and how we form questions and negatives.

Elicit the difference between the present perfect and the present perfect continuous (the continuous shows that the activity is still continuing: it hasn't been completed yet).

Finally, ask students to draw their own timelines and to make sentences about their own lives using the present perfect and the present perfect continuous.

1 Students complete the jokes and then check their answers and practise telling their jokes with a partner. Ask students to tell you which joke they think is the funniest. Do they know any similar jokes in their own language?

1 b   2 c   3 a   4 d

2 Students complete the sentences with the words in the box. Read the answers around the class.

1 since   2 for   3 ever   4 never   5 just   6 already/just
7 yet   8 still

3 Students complete the conversations with the correct forms. Ask students to check their answers with a partner by practising the conversations. Circulate, focusing on the natural sounding pronunciation of present perfect auxiliaries and past participles, e.g. *I haven't finished /aɪhəvənfɪnɪʃt/.*

1 I've seen   2 I've read   3 I haven't seen   4 I've ever watched
5 We've been reading   6 I haven't heard of   7 I've ever read
8 I've been listening   9 I haven't finished   10 I've ever heard

Write on

4 Tell students about a book you've read or a film you've seen recently and tell them a little about the plot and your opinion of it, e.g. *I've been reading the Da Vinci code recently. It's amazing! It's a detective story about a murder, but there's lots of interesting information about history and art in it, too. It's one of the most interesting books I've ever read!*

Ask students to write three sentences about a book/film they have read/seen. Circulate, offering support where necessary and focusing on accurate use of the present perfect simple and continuous. Display students' work on your classroom wall and encourage students to read each other's sentences and mingle, asking questions and swapping opinions about the books and films. Conduct class feedback.

Students' own answers.

To finish

Tell students something you've never done. The sentence can be true or false, e.g.

I've never failed an exam.

Ask students to tell you whether they think your statements are true or false (encourage them to give reasons for their answers).

Student should write an *I've never ...* statement of their own. Ask them to take turns reading their statements to a partner and guessing whether their partner's statements are true or false. Ask students to read their statements to the class.

Homework
Workbook pages 18–19
MyEnglishLab

VOCABULARY 2 (SB page 36)
Describing actions

To start

Tell students that they are going to read a story about a mythical creature. Ask them to work with a partner and make a list of as many different types of mythical creature as they can think of. After a minute, ask students to share their lists with the rest of the class. Write suggestions on the board and generate as much discussion and language as possible, e.g. *sea monster, mermaid, goblin, unicorn, centaur, faun, incubus, elf.*

1 Ask students to quickly read the article. Check understanding by asking: *What did Estella see?* (a small ugly creature with red eyes) *Why was she frightened?* (It was very ugly and it was looking at her.) *What is a chupacabra?* (It's a legendary creature which people say kills goats and other animals.). Ask students if they believe that chupacabras exist. Students read the article again and replace seven of the verbs in bold with the verbs in the box. Allow students to check their answers with a partner before reading the story around the class. Elicit the meaning of the two remaining verbs by asking students to think of sentences which contain them. Write sentences on the board.

saw = spotted
was moving = was creeping
was looking = was staring
shouted = yelled
moved = waved
stayed = remained
disappeared = vanished
noticed = realised)
dropped = let go of (her phone); let (her phone) fall

Word XP

Read the information in the Word XP box with the students. Generate some example sentences and write them on the board. Encourage students to create personalised sentences wherever possible.

2 Students read the text in Exercise 1 again and find examples of each type of adverb. Conduct feedback and write students' answers on the board.

How: suspiciously, anxiously, mysteriously, nervously
Where: at the end of her street, there
When: a few minutes later, finally

3 Students complete the table with the missing nouns, adjectives and adverbs. Monitor as they do this, checking that they are spelling the words accurately.

nerve(s), nervous, nervously
mystery, mysterious, mysteriously
hope, hopeful, hopefully
truth, truthful, truthfully
noise, noisy, noisily
suspicion, suspicious, suspiciously
–, immediate, immediately
–, final, finally

4 Students rewrite the sentences with the adverbs in brackets in the correct place. Encourage them to refer to the Word XP box to help them complete the task. Read answers around the class.

1 She answered all the questions truthfully.
2 We were waiting for the boy band outside./We were waiting outside for the boy band.
3 They called for help and eventually someone heard them./They called for help and someone heard them eventually./They called for help and someone eventually heard them.
4 The children danced happily when they heard the song.
5 I phoned my parents immediately to tell them the good news./Immediately, I phoned my parents to tell them the good news./I immediately phoned my parents to tell them the good news.

5 Focus students' attention on the article and ask them to complete the gaps with the correct form of the words in capitals. Read the article around the class, focusing on the pronunciation of the target words.

1 strength   2 competition   3 immediately   4 hopefully
5 weakness   6 achievement   7 suspiciously   8 feeling   9 happily
10 professional

To finish

Organise students into small groups. Ask students to write a short paragraph about a mythical beast from their local area or their country. Ask questions like: *What does it look like? Where does it live? Is it friendly?* Students tell the rest of the class about their creature. Ask students to illustrate their writing and display the work on the classroom walls.

Homework
Workbook page 17
MyEnglishLab

GRAMMAR 2 (SB page 37)

Verbs with direct and indirect objects

To start

Play *In the manner of the word*. Write the following on the board: *I walked into the party.* Then mime walking *happily* into a party, greeting other guests, saying hello, etc. Ask students: *How did I walk into the party?* Elicit the adverb of manner *happily* and then elicit the sentence: *I walked happily into the party.*

Whisper an adverb of manner to one student. They have to think of an activity and mime it according to the adverb. The rest of the class have to guess the adverb of manner and provide the sentence.

Suggested adverbs: *quietly, anxiously, carefully, noisily, shyly, suspiciously, mysteriously, nervously, angrily, bravely.*

Grammar XP

Read the information and examples in the Grammar XP box with the students. Tell them to think of three things which happened in the last English class, e.g. *The teacher gave us a test. Paulo told Roberto a rude joke. Suki brought in cake for everyone.*

1 Students find the indirect objects in each sentence. Check they have done this correctly by eliciting a brief feedback session. Then ask them to put the words in the correct order. Read the sentences around the class.

2 Lorenzo brought some comics for Carla.
3 Lauren paid Jack for the tickets.
4 Mrs Gibbs teaches me and Ella Spanish.
5 He's never given his brother a birthday present.
6 We've written an email to the TV producers.
7 Edith made a card for you.
8 They've found Adam a job.

2 Students rewrite the sentences in Exercise 1 using personal pronouns (not *for* or *to*). Check answers orally.

2 Lorenzo brought her some comics.
3 Lauren paid him for the tickets.
4 Mrs Gibbs teaches us Spanish.
5 He's never given him a birthday present.
6 We've written them an email.
7 Edith made you a card.
8 They've found him a job.

3 Elicit what a *fancy-dress* party is (a party where you dress up as, e.g. an animal or a famous person). Ask students to read the text quickly. Ask questions to check understanding, e.g. *What kind of costume did Antonia make for her boyfriend?* (a Batman costume); *What did she wear?* (a Superwoman costume); *Who was Antonia talking to at the party?* (Marco's friend, Robbie); *Who did she think she was talking to?* (Marco). Students read the text again and complete it with the words in the box. Read the text around the class and check students' answers. Ask students to find examples of verbs which have both direct and indirect objects.

I her boyfriend **2** for **3** me **4** me
5 Marco **6** them **7** to **8** an amazing girl **9** her
Verbs with direct and indirect objects: she <u>made</u> a batman outfit for him; she <u>sent</u> me a text message; (Antonia) <u>gave</u> me a birthday present; she didn't <u>tell</u> him who she was; I <u>lent</u> my Batman outfit to Robbie; He <u>told</u> her all his funniest jokes

4 Students rewrite the sentences using the words given. Do the first question together as an example. Allow students to check answers with a partner before conducting class feedback.

I time I have (ever) been
2 you English
3 lent/gave this Superwoman outfit to
4 sold the concert tickets to
5 you show me our
6 have been learning Spanish for

Write on

5 Tell students about a surprising thing which someone has given you, bought for you or made for you, e.g. *My best friend bought me a ticket to see my favourite singer in concert.* Give students a minute to write their sentences and share them with a partner. Circulate as students complete this activity, checking for accurate word order. Nominate a few students to read their sentences aloud to the rest of the class.

Students' own answers.

To finish

Play a memory game around the class and practice verbs with indirect objects at the same time. Begin by saying: *It was my birthday and my friend gave me a cake.* The student on your left must repeat what you have said and add another item, e.g. *It was my birthday and my friend gave me a cake and a pair of trainers.*

Continue around the class until you get to the last student, who must try to remember every item on the list.

Homework
Workbook page 19
MyEnglishLab

LISTENING (SB page 38)

To start

Ask students to choose and write down four words they have learned in this unit so far. Put students into pairs and ask them to test their partner by reading out a word and asking them to spell it.

Power up

I Read the question and situations with the students. Give students an example for one of the situations, e.g. *I think it's acceptable to tell a white lie so you don't hurt someone's feelings. For example, if my friend gives me a birthday present which I think is awful I will probably lie to her and say 'I love it!'* Ask students to work in pairs and decide whether the situations are acceptable or not, making sure to give real examples of situations to back up their ideas. Open this up into a whole class discussion, generating as much language as possible.

Students' own answers.

2 Read the question and the caption above the pictures with the students. Students work in pairs and match the pictures with the words and phrases in the box. Check answers around the class and ask students if they can think of any more signs of lying.

A look away guiltily
B rub your nose
C touch your mouth
D go red
E speak quickly
F laugh nervously
G hesitate
H sweat

Listen up

3 Tell students that they are going to listen to the beginning of a game show and they need to identify the three signs of lying which are mentioned by the TV presenter. Play the recording and ask students to check their answers with a partner before conducting class feedback. Elicit if they know of any other game shows similar to this one.

> **Track 3.2**

Presenter: Welcome to *Truth or Lie?*, the game show where a contestant on one team gives us a statement which may or may not be true.
The other team will be watching each speaker carefully. Will the speaker sweat, hesitate or look away guiltily? Afterwards, the other team can ask *one* question. Then they have to guess if the person is telling the truth or if it's a lie.

sweating, hesitating, looking away (guiltily)

4 Read the Exam advice with the students and then give them time to read the statements. Explain that they need to match the statements (a–f) on the SB page with the speakers they will hear in the recording. Remind them that one statement will not be used. Play the recording, twice if necessary. Allow students to check their answers with a partner before conducting whole class feedback.

> ► **Track 3.3**

1
Presenter: Right. Let's start with Nicole.
Nicole: OK. My statement is: '*I named my pet cats after TV comedy characters.*' Right ... um, I've always wanted to have pet cats and these two are really lovely. I wanted to call my cats Homer and Marge, but I couldn't because they're both boys. So in the end, I called them, Sheldon and Leonard, after the guys from *The Big Bang Theory*! They're so cute! Leonard's grey and quite shy, and Sheldon's black and white and very intelligent.

2
Presenter: Now we move on to the other team. Enrique.
Enrique: Right. My statement is: '*I've had a cup of coffee every day since I was four years old.*' I tried some of my mum's coffee one day and I liked it. So then she gave me some every morning. Of course, coffee is quite strong for young kids, so Mum always put a lot of milk in the coffee when I was little. And I've never had a day without coffee since then, honestly.

3
Presenter: So, back with Team 1. It's Cliff's turn.
Cliff: My statement is: '*My grandfather was the guitarist of a well-known rock band.*' His name was Cliff Burton – a really great guy. Everyone in our family believes he was really special. Of course, I haven't got the same surname as him because, he was from my mum's side of the family. He died before I was born, but my mum has always told me that I'm named after him and that's very important to me. Oh, and the name of the band was ... *Metallica*!

4
Presenter: Team 2 again. It's Sandra's turn.
Sandra: My statement is: '*I've fallen off my bike more than twenty times.*' Of course, your first question will be 'Have you ever broken anything?' The answer is, 'Yes, I have.' I've broken my arm twice, so I had to stop cycling for a while. Last week, I hurt my leg really badly because I had to leap off the bike when I crashed. In fact, the doctor said it wasn't broken, but I've damaged the muscles. I know it's hard to believe. Actually, I'm a very good cyclist. Honestly!

5
Presenter: OK. Time for both teams to guess if *I'm* telling the truth. My statement is: '*A monkey has been to our house for dinner.*' I know, it was quite a shock for me, too! Actually, the monkey belongs to a good friend. She made the arrangement with my wife. I didn't know about it. Our friend dropped her monkey off at our house and then she came to join it later. Well, of course, the monkey didn't have spaghetti and meatballs! It ate some tomato and an apple.

1 f **2** b **3** e **4** c **5** a

5 Write the numbers 1–5 on the board and ask students to remind you what each of the anecdotes was about in Exercise 4. Write brief notes on the board with their ideas. As you work through the anecdotes, ask students to tell you whether they thought the anecdote was true or not, and encourage them to give reasons for their answers. Then ask students to vote for the funniest, most boring and strangest anecdotes they heard.

Students' own answers.

6 Tell students that they will now find out which anecdotes were true and which were not. Play the recording while students note down T (truth) or L (lie). Check answers orally. Ask students: *Were you surprised by what you heard? Why/Why not?*

> ► **Track 3.4**

1
Presenter: OK, you can ask Nicole one question about her cats.
Enrique: I know Nicole enjoys comedy, so that's quite believable, but I didn't know she had any cats. When did you get your cats, Nicole?
Nicole: Oh, not long ago. I've had them about two months now.
Sandra: Right, we think it's true.
Presenter: Nicole? Are they right?
Nicole: I was telling ... a lie! I haven't got any cats. I don't really like them and I'm actually allergic to them.

2
Presenter: It's time to ask Enrique about his coffee-drinking habit.
Cliff: Why did your mum give you coffee? You were only four!
Enrique: I'm not sure. She thought it was OK.
Nicole: I don't know. Is he going red? Yes, I'm sure that's a lie.
Presenter: Enrique?
Enrique: It's ... the truth.

3
Presenter: What are you going to ask Cliff about his grandfather's name?
Enrique: What was your grandfather like?
Cliff: That's a silly question. I told you he died before I was born!
Sandra: He hesitated there. Anyway, we can't believe that's true.
Presenter: Cliff?
Cliff: It's ... a lie.

4
Presenter: Let's ask Sandra about falling off her bike.
Nicole: Nobody falls off their bike so many times! Why are you so bad at cycling?
Sandra: I've told you I'm good at cycling. I just have accidents sometimes.
Cliff: Hmm ... she's looking away. That's not true. We agree that's a lie.
Presenter: Sandra?
Sandra: The truth is that I ride a mountain bike as a hobby and I take part in competitions.
Cliff & Nicole: Ah!

5
Presenter: So, now ask me about the monkey!
Cliff: Well, you know some celebrities who might own a monkey. Why did they leave it with you?
Presenter: Because they thought it would be fun for the children.
Sandra: You're touching your mouth nervously. I'm sure that's false.
Presenter: Are you sure? It's actually ... the truth!
Cliff & Sandra: No!

Speak up

7 Read the example statements together. Write three statements about yourself on the board and make one of them a lie, e.g. *I've been playing the violin since I was three. I've been learning Chinese for one year. I climbed Mount Kilimanjaro three years ago.*

Ask students to guess which is false. Students then write their own statements. Circulate as students do this, offering support where necessary.

Students' own answers.

8 Organise students into two teams. Students take it in turns to read out their statements from Exercise 7. The opposite team are allowed to ask two questions about each statement. Award points to any student whose lie goes undetected. The winning team is the one whose students have the most undetected lies

Students' own answers.

To finish

Think of a time when you have needed to tell a lie and tell your students about it, e.g.

I went shopping with my friend. He tried on a T-shirt which really didn't suit him and asked me for my opinion. I didn't want to hurt his feelings so I said it looked good.

Ask your students if they think this lie is acceptable or not and encourage them to give reasons for their answers. Organise students into groups. Ask them to think of a time they have told a lie and tell the people in their group about it. The rest of the group should listen and decide whether they think the lie is acceptable or not, giving reasons for their answers.

Conduct class feedback and nominate a few groups to report back on the lies they discussed.

Homework
MyEnglishLab

SPEAKING (SB page 39)

To start

Play a game of *Truth or dare* with your class. Before you begin, prepare some forfeits, e.g.

Hop on one leg around the room.

Spell 'psychological' aloud or write it on the board.

Count to twenty backwards as fast as you can.

Pretend to be a monkey.

Give students one minute to think of some 'truth' questions. Encourage them to use Have you ever questions to practise the present perfect, e.g. *Have you ever cheated in a test? Have you ever lied about your homework to our English teacher?*

Circulate as students prepare their questions, making sure that they do not ask anything inappropriate.

Go around the class, asking students to choose *truth* or *dare*. If they choose *truth*, they must answer one of their classmates' questions. If they choose *dare*, they must do one of your forfeits.

Power up

1 Read the questions and experiences with the students. Ask them to work with a partner and ask and answer questions about their experiences. Encourage students to include details in their answers and focus their attention on the examples in the speech bubbles. Elicit that we use the present perfect to refer to a general experience and the past simple to be more specific about the time we did something. Nominate a few students to report back about their partners' experience.

Students' own answers.

Speak up

2 Ask students to describe the two photos, asking questions, e.g. Photo A: *What kind of ride are they on?* (rollercoaster); Photo B: *How do you think the people watching the movie are feeling?* (terrified). Now ask them to match two questions from Exercise 1 with the photos.

Photo A = Question 5; Photo B = Question 1

3 Ask students to think of two more *Have you ever... ?* questions that relate to the photos. Give them time to compare questions with a partner before conducting class feedback. Elicit and write their questions on the board.

Students' own answers.

4 Tell your class that they are going to listen to a student in a speaking exam talking about the two photos (A and B). Read the Exam advice with the students, then focus their attention on the task. Play the recording while students choose the correct answers. Check answers orally.

41

Examiner: Here are two photos of leisure activities. Can you compare them, then talk about the advantages and disadvantages of each leisure activity?

Student: Yes, well, the main similarity between the two photos is that they both show groups of friends spending their free time together. In Photo A, they look as though they're having fun. However, in Photo B they look scared.

1 the main similarity
2 as though
3 However, look

Language XP

Focus students' attention on the Language XP box. Practise the language using pictures on the classroom wall, or ask students to find and compare pictures on their mobile phones/computers.

5 Students work in pairs and discuss more similarities and differences between the two photos. Encourage students to use the language in the Language XP box.

Students' own answers.

6 Nominate a student to read the questions aloud. Students work in pairs to choose and discuss one of the questions. Alternatively, they can add a question of their own. Try to ensure that each pair discusses a different question. Monitor as students discuss their question, checking that they are using the language to compare pictures from the Language XP box. During feedback, ask students to discuss their chosen question in front of the class. Encourage students to add their own comments and generate as much discussion and new language as possible.

Students' own answers.

To finish

Tell students about your favourite photograph, e.g.
It's a photo taken of me and my family when I was about ten years old. I'm at the beach with my parents and brothers and we're all eating ice cream. I really like it because it reminds me of a great holiday.

Ask students to work in pairs. Tell them to make a quick sketch of their favourite photograph and tell their partner about it. Alternatively, they can find a photo that they really like on their mobile phone and tell their partner about it.

Homework
MyEnglishLab

WRITING (SB pages 40–41)

To start

Organise students into small groups and write the following on the board: *A great day at the beach.*

Elicit a couple of things which people might do at the beach, e.g. swim, eat ice cream, build sandcastles. Tell students that they are going to work in groups and use their bodies to make a three dimensional photograph, showing a great day at the beach. Give them a minute to position themselves and then ask the rest of the class to describe the 'photograph' and compare it with other 3-D 'photographs' in the class.

Power up

1 Focus students' attention on the photos. Ask them to describe what they see. Read the questions with the students and ask them to discuss them in small groups. Nominate a student from each group to report back on a different photo.

Students' own answers.

Plan on

2 Read the advertisement with the students. Check students' understanding by asking questions, e.g. *What is the magazine looking for?* (a story which ends with the words 'I've never felt so stupid'); *What is the prize?* (£100). Ask students to read the story in silence and ask them to tell you which photo the story is about.

Photo C

3 Write the following headings on the board: *Adjectives, Adverbs* and *Interesting verbs*. Give students one minute to find as many examples of each in the story. When the time limit is up, nominate three confident students to come up to the board. Give each student a heading and ask them to write down the words they collected. The rest of the class can add any further suggestions.

1 Adjectives: organised, tense, stupid
2 Adverbs: eventually, hopefully, unfortunately, nervously
3 Interesting verbs: was hanging, grabbed, leapt, knocked

4 Write the first sentence on the board. Ask students: *How can we make this sentence more interesting?* Listen to their suggestions and rewrite the sentence accordingly. Students rewrite the rest of the sentences to make them more interesting, using at least one adverb and one adjective.

Possible answers

1 I got up *quickly*, picked up my *heavy* school bag and left the house *immediately*.

2 He sat down *tiredly* in the armchair and read a(n) *old* book.

3 She walked *anxiously* to the park, where she talked to her *best* friends.

4 They watched a *terrible* film on TV while they waited *hopefully* for the phone to ring.

5 Read the definition of a simile with the students and write the word *simile* on the board. Ask students to find the simile in the story. Write the sentence on the board and underline the word *like*. Explain that similes often include the words *like* or *as*.

I felt as though a cloud was hanging over me.

6 Ask students to read the similes and decide what feelings are being described. Give students the chance to discuss their ideas in small groups before conducting whole class feedback.

Possible answers

1 happiness, sadness, shock

2 excitement, satisfaction, happiness, pride

3 deep friendship, love

4 stress, panic, excitement

7 Give students a minute to read the suggestions for writing a story. Explain that these will be very useful when they come to write their own stories later on in the lesson. Students match the suggestions with the paragraphs in the story. Check answers around the class.

1 B **2** A **3** D **4** C

Write on

8 Tell students they are going to write a story for the competition in Exercise 2. Direct their attention to the Skill advice and read through the different ways in which students can get and develop their ideas. Give students a minute to think about their silly mistake and jot down a couple of notes. Then give them a chance to tell their partner about their mistake. Nominate one or two students to share their ideas with the rest of the class.

Students' own answers.

9 Students plan their story using the questions to help them. Encourage them to also refer to the suggestions in Exercise 7. Circulate as students plan their essays, trying to spot any potential flaws in their plans which might affect the writing of the essay.

Students' own answers.

10 Give students five minutes to write the title of their story and their first paragraph. When the time is up, ask students to exchange their work with a partner, read it and comment on their ideas. Ask students: *Does the beginning get your attention? Is there a question or an unusual statement? Has your partner explained the main situation and/or problem?*

Students' own answers.

11 Students write the rest of their story. Encourage students to self-assess their work using the questions in Exercise 9 and the suggestions in Exercise 7. Organise students into small groups and ask them to exchange, read and comment on each other's stories. Nominate a couple of students to read their stories out to the rest of the class.

Students' own answers.

Model answer

What an idiot!

Have you ever wished you could turn back time? That's exactly what I wished I could do last week when I gave my baby brother my mobile phone to play with. My baby brother is so cute: he is two years old and has big blue eyes like saucers so it's impossible to say 'no' when he asks for something. I was in the kitchen at home. I was trying to finish my homework: I had a project due in for the next day and I was rushing to get it finished. My brother was making a terrible noise with some pots and pans so when he put his hand out and said 'Phone!' I gave it to him immediately.

After that, I carried on working on my project. I was feeling really pleased that it was nearly finished. Suddenly, I remembered my brother had my phone – but it was too late! 'Photos all gone!' he said proudly. Yes, that's right. All my photos were gone – deleted by my brother!

I felt as if I couldn't breathe. I've just come back from a school trip to Japan – all my holiday photos were on it! In future, I'll download my photos to my computer immediately – and I'll never lend my baby brother my mobile phone again. I've never felt so stupid!

To finish

Elicit why it is a good idea to use similes in descriptive writing (it makes writing more colourful and interesting to read). Write the following on the board:

I felt as hungry as …	I felt as tired as …
I felt as angry as …	I felt as sad as …
I felt as timid as …	I felt as hot as …
I felt as cold as …	I felt as happy as …

Organise students into pairs. Challenge them to see who can be the first to complete all eight similes. Collect similes around the class, writing the most imaginative examples on the board.

Homework

MyEnglishLab

SWITCH ON (SB page 42)

Jack's big moment

1 Remind students of the article they read at the beginning of the unit. Elicit some facts about Jack Carroll, e.g. *What is his special talent?* (He's a comedian.). Focus students' attention on the questions and ask them to predict the answers. Play the video and allow students to check their ideas.

1 A   2 C

2 Give students a moment to read the statements. Play the video again while students watch and decide whether the statements are true or false.

A T
B F (He writes in his bedroom.)
C T
D T
E F (He was in the audience two years ago.)
F T

3 Read the question with the students and ask them to discuss their ideas in small groups. Monitor as they complete the task, offering support as necessary.

Students' own answers.

Project

4 Read the ideas with the students. Organise students into groups and ask them to choose one of the ideas to make a poster presentation. Monitor as they discuss their ideas, distributing paper and pens to students who are ready to make their poster. When students have made their poster, give them a few minutes to prepare what they are going to say. Groups should then take it in turns to talk about their poster to the rest of the class. If you prefer, the presentations can be filmed and watched as a class.

Students' own answers.

REVISION (SB page 43)

1

1 an hour later

2 an attack of nerves

3 an amazing achievement

4 a couple of seconds/minutes

5 at the outset

6 a (great) relief

2

1 I've been calling

2 have you been doing

3 I've been reading

4 Have you ever read

5 We've never seen

6 I've been sitting

3

1 creep

2 remain

3 immediately

4 finally

5 vanish

6 afterwards

4

1 My uncle brought us some sweets./My uncle brought some sweets for us.

2 Mandy didn't offer Luke a piece of cake./Mandy didn't offer a piece of cake to Luke.

3 Mr Allen teaches young children extra maths./Mr Allen teaches extra maths to young children.

4 Have you ever given your teacher a present?/Have you ever given a present to your teacher?

5 I've just found you a great website./I've just found a great website for you.

6 They've written their cousin a letter./They've written a letter to their cousin.

5

1 C **2** A **3** A **4** B **5** C **6** B **7** A **8** C

Homework

Workbook pages 20–21

MyEnglishLab

04 Things they don't teach you

Unit objectives

Reading:	multiple-choice questions
Vocabulary:	money; learning skills
Grammar:	relative clauses; reduced relative clauses
Listening:	multiple-choice questions
Speaking:	collaborative task
Writing:	writing a semi-formal email/letter

READING (SB pages 44–45)

To start

Give students one minute to brainstorm as many school subjects as they can. Write their ideas on the board. Draw their attention to the title of the unit *Things they don't teach you* (i.e. at school). Organise students into small groups and ask them to think of things which they would like to learn at school, but don't. Circulate as students discuss their ideas, offering support as necessary and encouraging them to produce as much language as possible. Conduct class feedback and discuss the different groups' ideas. Which subject does the class think would be the most useful?

Power up

1 Read the questions aloud to your students and ask them to match three of the subjects with the photos. Allow students a couple of minutes to discuss the questions with a partner. Nominate a few pairs to report back on their choices and encourage them to give reasons for their answers. Write any useful new words/phrases on the board and generate as much language as possible.

A money management
B first aid
C safety in the home

Read on

2 If necessary, pre-teach: *voucher* (a piece of paper which allows you to get money off things or get them for free), *tough* (hard/difficult) and *economise* (to save money). Check students' understanding by asking questions, e.g. *If you have a voucher, will your shopping be cheaper or more expensive?* (cheaper); *If something is tough is it easy?* (no); *Is it difficult?* (yes); *If I want to economise, will I go out and buy an expensive pair of trainers?* (no); *Will I try to save money?* (yes). Students read the blog and find which subject in Exercise 1 is mentioned. Elicit the correct subject.

money management

3 Read the Exam advice to your students. Then ask students to read the blog again more slowly and then choose the correct answers to the multiple-choice questions.

1 C **2** D **3** B **4** D **5** A **6** B

4 Do the first question as an example. Ask students to find the words *struggle* and *improve* in the blog. Then ask them to read the sentences which the words are found in. Elicit the meaning of the words, encouraging students to use the context of the surrounding words to help them. Finally, elicit the correct answer. Ask the class to complete the rest of the task alone. Allow them to check their answers with a partner before conducting whole class feedback.

1 Struggle
2 grim
3 unexpected
4 alien
5 impulse

Sum up

5 Nominate a student to read the questions aloud. Students note down answers to the questions about Jordan. Check answers around the class.

1 Because he and his mum were struggling to pay the bills.
2 From a TV show about extreme couponing.
3 He had coupons for the things he bought.
4 He never buys things they don't need. He doesn't allow his mum to go shopping on her own because she often spends money on impulse.

Speak up

6 Read the questions to your class and organise students into groups to discuss. Circulate as students complete the task, offering support as necessary. Then bring the class together again and nominate a student from each group to report back on their ideas. Write ideas on the board.

Students' own answers.

To finish

Tell students that the school is having money problems at the moment. Explain that if students don't think of ways for the school to save money it might need to close down. Organise the class into small groups and tell them that their job is to save the school. Allocate students within each group specific roles, e.g. chairperson, note taker, reporter, timekeeper. Give students a time limit and tell them that they have to think of five ways in which your school can manage its money better. Circulate as students complete this activity, offering support where necessary and noting down any examples of good language you hear. Ask one student from each group to report back and ask the class to decide on the best ideas they heard.

Homework

MyEnglishLab

VOCABULARY 1 (SB page 46)
Money

To start

Tell students about a problem you have with money, e.g. *I am always buying things I don't need.* Ask students to think of a money problem of their own and write it down. Organise the students into pairs: one should have money problems and the other should be a financial advisor. Elicit advice from a confident student about your money problem, e.g. *Try to stay away from shops. Don't spend time near shops at the weekend; go into the countryside instead.* Ask students to talk about their money problems and get advice from their financial advisors. Then ask students to swap roles. Circulate, noting down good language you hear.

1 Read the words in the box to your students and drill pronunciation chorally and individually. Students match the words to the definitions. Check answers around the class.

| voucher | **2** total cost | **3** bargain | **4** discount | **5** bill | **6** cash

2 Students choose the correct words and complete the sentences. Check answers orally.

1 a borrow, **b** lend
2 a spend, **b** pay
3 a worth, **b** cost
4 a save, **b** economise

3 Tell students that they are going to listen to a boy and his mum at the supermarket. Focus students' attention on the picture and tell them that they need to match the items in the picture with the words in the box. Play the recording, twice if necessary. Ask students questions to check their understanding, e.g. *Was the supermarket busy?* (yes); *Why weren't the customers happy?* (because there was a massive queue); *What was Ben looking for?* (crisps). Allow students to check their answers with a partner before conducting class feedback.

> **Track 4.1**

Ben: OK, the trolley's full of food now. Is that everything we need for the party?

Mum: I think so. Let's go to the checkout and pay for all this.

Ben: Oh my word! Look at the queue. It's massive!

Mum: The other customers are looking fed up!

Ben: Mum, we haven't got any crisps. Do you know which aisle they're in?

Mum: I'm not sure. You'll have to ask an assistant. Hurry up!

| aisle | **2** assistant | **3** checkout | **4** customer | **5** trolley | **6** queue

Word XP

Elicit what an *uncountable* noun is (a noun which does not have a plural form). Read through the headings and the uncountable nouns. Ask students to think of more examples for each heading.

4 Students choose the correct answer for each question. Elicit answers around the class.

I B   2 A   3 C   4 B   5 C

5 Focus students' attention on the adjectives in the box. Students complete the sentences with the adjectives. Then ask students to write down their answers to the questions. Organise students into pairs and ask them to take it in turns asking and answering the questions. Nominate a student from each pair to report back.

I personal   2 practical   3 general   4 common   5 money   6 higher
Students' own answers.

To finish

Ask students to think of ways to live on a budget in their city. Tell them you have a friend who is moving to the area and needs to save money. Ask students what tips they can offer your friend. Organise students into pairs. Tell them to discuss:

– budget places to shop in your town
– where to find good bargains
– cheap ways of travelling
– ways to enjoy yourself on a budget
– Conduct class feedback and list your students' tips on the board.

Homework
Workbook page 22
MyEnglishLab

GRAMMAR 1 (SB page 47)
Relative clauses
To start

Tell students to pick five words they learned from the vocabulary lesson and write them down. Ask them to take turns to describe their words to their partner, who must guess the words. Students get one point for each word they manage to guess. Conduct class feedback and ask students which words they included in their game. Award extra points for students who can make sentences out of their words.

Grammar XP

Read the information and examples in the Grammar XP box to your students. Then write the following sentence on the board:

My sister who is a writer lives in France.

Ask students to tell you whether this is a defining or a non-defining relative clause (it is a defining relative clause). Ask students: Does the writer of this sentence have one sister or more than one sister? (more than one sister). Draw three stick women on the board and draw a circle round one of them. Read the sentence again. Elicit that a defining relative clause tells us exactly which sister the writer is talking about (perhaps the writer has several sisters, but only one lives in France). Then write the following sentence on the board:

My sister, who is a writer, lives in France.

Ask students to tell you whether this is a defining or non-defining relative clause (it is a non-defining relative clause). Elicit that the words inside the commas provide extra information about the writer's sister.

I Students read the sentences and decide whether the relative clauses are defining or non-defining. Check answers around the class.

I N   2 D   3 N   4 N   5 D   6 D

2 Do the first question with your students as an example. Check answers around the class and write the sentences on the board. Ask students to tell you the sentences where the relative pronoun can be left out.

2 I have a friend who/that studies child care.
3 My dad's got a TV which/that he paid for with vouchers.
4 On Sundays, when they went to the shopping centre, they used to meet./On Sundays, when they used to meet, they went to the shopping centre.
5 My sister's friend, whose name is George, is learning first aid.
6 The jeans which/that I bought yesterday were a bargain.
We can leave out the relative pronoun in 3 and 6.

3 Tell students to read the article quickly. Ask questions to check understanding, e.g. *What two different ways of making money are mentioned?* (taking part in online surveys, selling old gadgets); *What does Conrad do with the money he makes?* (He buys music downloads and games.). Students then complete the article with the correct relative pronouns. Allow time for them to check their answers with a partner before reading the article around the class.

1 who/that
2 which/that
3 whose
4 where
5 who
6 when
7 which/that
8 which

Write on

4 Demonstrate the activity by writing two sentences of your own on the board, e.g. *My best friend, who is a famous actress, lives in LA. The house where I grew up is just beside the sea.*

Ask students to pick the false sentence. Students then write two sentences of their own. Circulate as your class does this, offering support where necessary. Students work in pairs and take it in turns to read their sentences, deciding which are true and false. Conduct class feedback.

Students' own answers.

To finish

Write the following sentence beginnings on the board:
I have a friend who ...
I live in a house which ...
I live in a town where ...

Ask students to complete the sentences with ideas about themselves. When students have written their sentences, ask them to share their sentences with a partner.

Homework
Workbook pages 24–25
MyEnglishLab

VOCABULARY 2 (SB page 48)
Learning skills

To start

Write the following sentence beginnings on the board:

Happiness is a time when ...

Love is a thing which ...

A rich person is someone who ...

Ask students to discuss their ideas about possible endings for these sentences in small groups. Conduct class feedback and write the most interesting ideas on the board.

1 Students choose the correct preposition to complete each phrase. Check answers around the class. Personalise the language by asking questions, e.g. *Do you have a good memory for faces, Jimena? Do you find it easy to learn things by heart, Alex? How do you cope with exams, Sasha?* Encourage students to answer with full sentences.

1 on 2 for 3 to 4 by 5 with 6 on
Similar meaning: concentrate on, pay attention to, focus on

2 Students complete the sentences with the words in the box. Check answers orally.

1 spider diagram
2 study method
3 learning style
4 study space

3 Students work with a partner to ask and answer the questions. Circulate as students complete the task, checking that they are using the target language accurately. Open this up into a class discussion and collect as many different student perspectives as you can for each question. Encourage students to give reasons for their answers. Write any new language on the board.

Students' own answers.

Word XP

Focus students' attention on the phrasal verbs in the Word XP box. Explain that it is a good idea to group phrasal verbs together according to topic, to make them easier to learn. Ask students to tell you which of the phrasal verbs they already know and elicit sentences using these phrasal verbs. Write the phrasal verbs on the board and elicit which parts are stressed (in most cases the particle is stressed, with the exception of *look through*.)

4 Students complete the sentences with phrasal verbs from the Word XP box. Check answers around the class, focusing on natural sounding pronunciation of the phrasal verbs.

1 look through
2 keep up
3 write down
4 mess about
5 look up
6 get ahead
7 get on with
8 set up

5 Tell students to read the text quickly and ask questions to check understanding, e.g. *What kind of learning style does the writer have?* (She learns best when she listens.); *How did finding out about her learning style help this student?* (She joined a discussion group and she started getting much better grades at college.). Students choose the correct answers to complete the text. Allow students to check their answers with a partner before reading the text around the class.

1 B   2 C   3 A   4 D   5 B   6 D   7 A   8 C

Game on

Organise students into pairs. Give them one minute to list as many phrasal verbs as they can. When the minute is up, shout 'Stop!' Award points for every correct phrasal verb. The pair with the most points wins.

To finish

Write the following phrasal verbs on the board:

get on (with)

keep up (with)

mess about

give up

find out about

Organise students into small groups. Tell them they have one minute to think of a story on the theme of school life containing all of these phrasal verbs. Circulate as students make notes for their stories, offering support where necessary. Ask students to act out their stories to the rest of the class and give them a minute or two to rehearse how they are going to do this. Students perform their phrasal verbs stories. The rest of the class should note down the phrasal verbs in the order they occur. Conduct class feedback, asking students to retell the stories they have watched.

Homework

Workbook page 23

MyEnglishLab

GRAMMAR 2 (SB page 49)

Reduced relative clauses

To start

Ask students to tell you the word to describe a study technique which helps you to organise your ideas (spider diagram). Tell students that they are going to make a spider diagram about the best way to learn English. Ask them to think about the following things:

how to learn new words

how best to practise grammar

how to get good at speaking and listening

Circulate as students work on their spider diagrams, helping them to see connections and generating as many suggestions as possible. Display the best spider diagrams on the classroom wall.

Grammar XP

Read the information and examples in Grammar XP box aloud to your students. Think of some sentences about your school and your class. Write them on the board (answers in brackets below). Use relative pronouns, e.g.

Mrs Frank is a teacher who is loved by all the students.

(Mrs Frank is a teacher loved by all the students.)

Students who study at this school usually get good grades.

(Students studying at this school usually get good grades.)

Students who live in the country can take the school bus home.

Students living in the country can take the school bus home.)

English is a language which is spoken all over the world.

(English is a language spoken all over the world.)

Ask students to work in pairs to shorten the sentences. Conduct feedback, writing the shortened sentences on the board beside the longer versions.

1 Direct students' attention to the map. Ask them to read the questions and choose the correct answers. Remind them that in some questions, both answers are possible. Check answers around the class, and elicit if they have visited the places on the map of Brazil.

1 where you're studying
2 taking part/who were taking part
3 who discovered
4 born/who was born
5 using/which uses
6 that we learnt

2 Ask students if they know of any famous teachers and write down any names on the board. Students match the sentences with the famous teachers (1 Comenius, 2 Aristotle, 3 Gene Simmonds, 4 Marie Curie, 5 Confucius). Ask students to check their answers before they go on to replace the underlined phrases with reduced relative clauses. Conduct class feedback.

....

1 known   **2** learning   **3** playing   **4** made   **5** written

....

3 Do the first question together as a class. Tell students that they need to rewrite the sentence using the word *WHICH*. Ask students to identify whether the verb is active or passive (passive). Elicit the answer (*which has been taken*), reminding them we use the past participle when the verb is passive. Students complete the rest of the task alone. Allow them to check their answers with a partner before conducting whole class feedback.

....

1 which was/has been taken

2 who/that pay attention

3 whose teachers give them

4 that are used

5 buy things I don't

6 where I/you can buy

....

To finish

Refer students back to the *Famous teachers quiz* in Exercise 2. Tell students that they are going to make their own famous teachers quiz using reduced relative clauses. Their quiz should focus on teachers in the school.

Organise students into groups to prepare their questions and circulate, offering help as necessary and making sure the questions are appropriate. When they are ready, the groups take it in turns to ask their questions. Award points to each group for correct answers. The group with the most points at the end of the game is the winner.

....

Homework

Workbook page 25

MyEnglishLab

....

LISTENING (SB page 50)

To start

Write *stressed out at school* on the board. Organise students into groups and ask them to make a list of situations which are stressful at school. Conduct class feedback. Ask them to say which situations are the most stressful and elicit different ways of dealing with stress.

Power up

1 Organise students into pairs and tell them to each choose a list (A or B). Give them one or two minutes to discuss their three questions. Nominate one or two pairs to report back what they discussed. Conduct class feedback and discuss how similar/different their answers about the photos were.

....

Students' own answers.

....

Listen up

2 Tell students that they are going to listen to a recording about a very interesting kind of school lesson. Focus students' attention on the words and their definitions and tell students that they will find out the meanings of these words as they listen. Play the recording, twice if necessary. Check answers around the class, and elicit if the students have ever heard of these things.

▶ **Tracks 4.2 and 4.3**

Teacher: Close your eyes, everyone. Hold your hands out in front of you. Imagine you are holding your attention in your hands. Really focus on your hands. And breathe slowly.

Reporter: I'm in a special mindfulness lesson at Highfield Academy. The Year 11 students are taking their GCSE exams at the moment. It's a very stressful time. But at this school students have a course of lessons in mindfulness, which is basically learning total relaxation. Mindfulness is a way of thinking which involves paying complete attention to the present moment. It's popular in some UK and American schools as it helps students to find a calm moment in a busy school day. Students feel more positive afterwards, ready to focus on their work or their exams.

2

Reporter: Danny, who has just done a maths exam, described his state of mind to me.

Danny: I was dead nervous – like, really bad – so I did about twenty or thirty 7/11s.

Reporter: Hang on, what's a 7/11? It sounds weird.

Danny: Oh, it's this breathing exercise we learnt in our mindfulness lessons. It helps you relax when you feel stressed. What you do is, you count to seven when you breathe in. Then you count to eleven when you breathe out. You do it a few times to calm yourself down. It stopped me panicking in the exam and then I could think about my maths more clearly.

3

Reporter: Well, Danny seemed happy with his relaxation technique. Anything that helps exam nerves must be good. Earlier I watched a class of students learning 'beditation'. If you've ever felt tired at school, this is the lesson for you. Basically, the teacher set up the lesson in the hall, where he covered the floor with gym mats. So when the students came in, they didn't sit at desks. Instead, they lay down on the mats, which were nice and soft.

4

Reporter: Last week an instructor from a local activity centre came to the mindfulness class in order to help with new ideas. Mr Browne used to teach a type of meditation related to yoga, where students usually concentrate on their breathing or sometimes on certain thoughts or phrases. Now he prefers to teach mindfulness because it helps students to be more in touch with the present moment. He suggested that the students put together a 'mood board' with ideas that make them feel calm and thoughtful – maybe a colour, a picture or a quote.

5

Reporter: This week's beditation lesson began with students switching off their mobile phones. No iPod or TV, no console games, no chatting or laughing, no phones, no texting. It's extremely quiet for a school lesson. The teacher was walking slowly around, giving instructions quietly. At one point, another teacher walking in looked pleasantly surprised by the students' silence. Is it just an excuse for a nap? No, of course not. It's a chance to stop thinking about your problems and just be.

6

Reporter: A lot of mindfulness teaching is simply common sense. If your mind is able to pay full attention to your lessons, your memory will improve. Students practising mindfulness are almost always positive about the experience. As Jasmine, another student, reported: 'Where else can you get twenty minutes of quiet? It doesn't give me answers to questions or anything, but it helps me somehow.'

1 c **2** a **3** d **4** b

3 Focus students' attention on the Exam advice and elicit why it is important to stop thinking about difficult questions. (Because if you are worried about a question you can't answer, you won't be able to concentrate on the next question.) Students listen to the recording again and choose the correct answers. Allow students to check their answers with a partner before conducting class feedback.

1 A **2** C **3** C **4** A **5** B **6** B

Speak up

4 Students discuss the questions in small groups. Monitor as students complete this task, offering support where necessary. Ask a student from each group to report back on their group's ideas, and encourage them to give reasons for their answers, e.g. *I'd like to try beditation because it sounds really relaxing and I often feel tired at school.*

Students' own answers.

To finish

Tell your students about something which is making you feel stressed, e.g.

I have a lot of work to prepare before the exams and I don't have enough time to do it.

Ask students to write on a piece of paper something which is making them feel stressed. They should then scrumple the paper up. Conduct a 'stress ball' fight where the students throw their paper balls at each other. After a few moments, tell students to stop and open up any one of the balls. They should read out the stressful situation to the rest of the class and think of a way of dealing with it.

Homework

MyEnglishLab

SPEAKING (SB page 51)

To start

Write the phrase *after school activities* on the board. Ask students to tell you about activities which are available for them to do after school. Ask: *What do you do? Where do you do it? Why do you like it?* Generate as much discussion as possible and write any new language on the board.

Power up

1 Focus students' attention on the photos and ask them to tell you what they see (a self-defence class; a student learning how to change a light bulb). Ask them to put their hands up if they have done these things. Ask students questions, e.g. *What type of self-defence did you learn? Did you enjoy it? Where did you learn it? Would you like to do it again? Who taught you to do it? Was it easy to learn?* Ask students who haven't tried these things to put up their hands. Ask them if they think they could do these things and encourage them to give reasons for their answers.

Students' own answers.

2 Organise students into pairs and ask them to discuss the things in the photos in Exercise 1. Circulate as students discuss, taking a note of interesting ideas and offering support as necessary. Bring the class back together and ask: *Which is the best way to learn self-defence? Which is the best way to learn home maintenance?* Encourage as much discussion as you can.

Students' own answers.

3 Focus students' attention on the conversation. Explain that they are going to listen to two people talking about self-defence, and they need to put the conversation in the correct order. Play the recording, twice if necessary. Nominate two confident students to read the conversation aloud to the rest of the class in the correct order.

➤ Track 4.4

A: Some people say self-defence is a useless subject, but my cousin did a self-defence course at her school and she says it's really helped her.

B: Really? Why does she think that?

A: Because you learn to be strong and look after yourself. It's given my cousin confidence, too. You can't always rely on other people to help you, especially if you live in a big city.

B: Hmm ... well, I think it depends on your situation. For example, I don't really travel around on my own because it makes more sense to go with my friends in a big group.

A: Yes, I think so too, but what about people who don't live near their friends? For example, sometimes I go out with friends who live a couple of kilometres away and my house isn't near a bus stop, so it's impossible to avoid walking home on my own – unless my parents come and pick me up every time I go out.

B: Yes, that's true. But I think self-defence classes would also be useful because you can protect yourself and keep fit at the same time.

1 **A:** ... helped her.
2 **B:** ... think that?
3 **A:** ... a big city.
4 **B:** ... a big group.
5 **A:** ... time I go out.
6 **B:** ... keep fit at the same time.

4 Read the Skill advice with the students. Stress that the world would be a very boring place if everyone had the same opinion and encourage your students to feel confident about expressing their opinion and explaining it in detail. Explain that this lesson will help students to do this. Students then match the words and phrases in bold in Exercise 3 with their functions. Check answers orally.

1 Some people say; I think it depends
2 (but) what about...?
3 that's true; (Yes) I think so too...
4 Really?...
5 because ...
6 so
7 for example, especially

Language XP

Focus students' attention on the phrases in the box. Ask if they can think of any more phrases which can be used to exchange opinions and add these to the list.

Speak up

5 Focus students' attention on the diagram and the subjects around the central question. Read the prompt and the question aloud and explain that students are going to discuss this with a partner. Encourage students to use the phrases in the Language XP box. Remind them to express their own opinions and explain them in detail. Circulate as students discuss the question, noting any particularly good examples of the target language and jotting down any interesting and well expressed opinions which you hear. Use these during class feedback.

Students' own answers.

6 Ask students to discuss this question in small groups. Stress that they need to give reasons for their answers and remind them to use the phrases in the Language XP box to help them. Continue to circulate and conduct class feedback until the students in each group have all had a chance to talk.

Students' own answers.

7 Organise students into pairs. Ask them to turn to page 153. Focus students' attention on the diagram and the question. Give students a couple of minutes to jot down ideas. When the time is up, ask them to start discussing the task. Remind them to use the new language they have learned this lesson. Circulate, listening and noting down any good examples of language and any problems.

For Part 2 of the task, ask students to read the discussion questions and give them a minute to jot down their ideas. They discuss the questions in pairs. Circulate as before. Conduct class feedback, raising any issues, giving examples of good language you heard and nominating a few students to feed back their opinions.

Students' own answers.

To finish

Tell your students that due to financial cuts one subject is going to be dropped from their timetable. Ask students to work with a partner to decide what this should be. Circulate as students have this discussion, encouraging them to use the language they have learned this lesson. Conduct class feedback, find out which subject has been chosen and ask students to explain their choice.

Homework
MyEnglishLab

WRITING (SB pages 52–53)

To start

Find out if your students think they could improve their study skills. Ask: *Do you often get distracted? Do you find it hard to study?*

Draw a line on the board with *study skills* written underneath and the numbers 1–5 written along the top with 1 = *not good at all* and 5 = *very good*.

Ask students to rate their study skills and discuss their choice with a partner. Conduct class feedback.

Power up

1 Focus students' attention on the photos. Ask them to tell you what lessons they can see (archery and harp). Read the question aloud to your students, and allow them the chance to discuss their ideas with a partner for a minute before opening it up into a whole class discussion. Generate as many ideas as possible and write lesson ideas on the board.

Students' own answers.

Plan on

2 Give students a minute to read the leaflet in silence. Ask them to tell their partner which activity would be the most fun/least fun. Remind students to use the language they learned in the Speaking lesson to help them express their opinions. Nominate a few students to report back on their ideas.

Students' own answers.

3 Direct students' attention back to the leaflet. Elicit what Mrs Johnson wants from the students and why she wants this.

She wants an email from students, saying which two lessons would be most useful and why, and she wants extra suggestions too, so that they can plan the best timetable for the students.

4 Ask students to quickly and silently read the email and answer the questions. Give them a minute to compare their answers with a partner before conducting whole class feedback.

1 B   2 B   3 A

5 Focus students' attention on the table. Ask students to find words in the table which Pavel uses to give reasons and add ideas in his email in Exercise 4. Check answers around the class.

Giving reasons: as, because

Adding ideas: also, as well, too

6 Read the Exam advice to your students and elicit why it is important to check your spelling, grammar and punctuation carefully (Because careless mistakes can cost you a lot of marks in an exam.). Students read the sentences and decide whether the errors are to do with missing words, punctuation, grammar or spelling. Allow them time to check their answers with a partner before they rewrite the sentences correctly.

1 <u>Firstly</u> (P) I think the suggestion of sudoku and puzzles would be <u>intresting</u> (S).

Firstly**,** I think the suggestion of sudoku and puzzles would be **interesting**.

2 I believe yoga, which <u>it</u> (G) is very relaxing, will help me <u>to attention</u> (M).

I believe yoga, **which is** very relaxing, will help me **to pay attention**.

3 It's a test <u>used</u> (M) <u>improove</u> (S) learning skills.

It's a test **used to improve** learning skills.

4 Classes like <u>this</u> (P) which are <u>free</u> (P) will help all students.

Classes like this**,** which are free**,** will help all students.

5 I hope <u>so</u> (G) you <u>are liking</u> (G) my suggestions.

I hope (**that**) you **like** my suggestions.

6 <u>Also</u> (P) we could put some puzzles in the school newsletter (P)

Also**,** we could put some puzzles in the school newsletter**.**

Write on

7 Ask students to tell you which two subjects Pavel has chosen and elicit his reasons for doing so. Tell students that they are also going to choose two subjects and write a sentence for each.

Students' own answers.

8 Ask students to read each other's sentences and check that their partners' reasons are clear and sensible. Circulate as students do this, checking that you agree with their feedback. Nominate a couple of students to read their sentences to the rest of the class.

Students' own answers.

9 Read the Language XP box aloud to your students. For each point, ask them to refer to Pavel's letter and tell you whether he has done this, giving examples of the exact language he has used. Students then write the email to Mrs Johnson, using the Language XP box to help them. Ask students to check their partners' work for errors. Nominate a few students to read their emails to the rest of the class.

Students' own answers.

Model answer

Dear Mrs Johnson,

I am writing to let you know my top two ideas for the new Wednesday afternoon lessons.

Firstly, I think the suggestion of a yoga class is an excellent one because there are several students in my class who become ill with nerves around exam time and often get poor grades as they are too nervous to perform well in exams. Yoga would be a great way for these students to relax and would probably help them to do better in their other subjects, too.

Secondly, I would also find 'food for thought' really useful, especially if we could also learn some simple and healthy recipes. I know that my classmates and I often eat lots of chocolate and drink sugary drinks for energy at exam time, so it would be really good to find some alternative exam time snacks.

Finally, I would like to suggest music lessons. I have read that learning music is very good for the brain, and I think that it would also be relaxing and a nice way to make new friends. I know someone in town who teaches African drumming and who might be happy to teach an extra lesson at our school.

I hope you like my suggestions.

With best wishes,

Maria Elena

To finish

Play a game of *Pictionary* to practise the new words students have learned the unit. Ask them to write down five new words they have learned.

Then organise students into two groups. Students take it in turns to come up to the front of the class, and quickly draw a picture or mime their word to the rest of their team who must guess the word or phrase. The team with the most points at the end of the game is the winner.

Homework

MyEnglishLab

SWITCH ON (SB pages 54)

Get creative

1 Give students time to read the options and predict which of the ideas Petri and Ben will mention. Play the video so that students can check their predictions. Conduct class feedback.

They talk about B.

2 Give students a minute to read the questions and options, allowing them to check the meaning of any words they are unsure about. Play the video while students choose the correct answers. Allow them to compare their answers with a partner before checking answers orally.

1 C   2 B   3 A

3 Ask students to tell you whether or not they think Ben and Petri's idea is a good way to save money and encourage them to give reasons for their answers. Discuss the second question as a class, listing students' ideas on the board and generating as much vocabulary as possible.

Students' own answers.

Project

4 Organise students into small groups. Read options A and B aloud to your students and ask them to choose which they would like to do. (Alternatively, individual students can choose first and then work with people who have chosen the same option.) Give students time in class to discuss their project with the rest of the group. Group A can work through the bulleted instructions together. Group B will have to do some of their work out of school, but can make a start in class by describing the clothes they are going to customise and how they are going to go about doing this. Afterwards, bring the class together to do their presentations/play their videos and show their before and after videos. Generate as much discussion as you can and encourage students to offer constructive feedback on their classmates' work.

Students' own answers.

REVISION (SB page 55)

1

1 is saving

2 spend

3 borrowed

4 paid

5 cost

6 will lend

2

1 whose

2 which

3 who

4 where

5 when

6 that

3

1 look up

2 get on

3 keep up

4 look through

5 mess about

6 give up

4

1 A **2** C **3** B **4** B **5** C **6** A

5

1 money

2 who

3 personal

4 higher

5 whose

6 attention

Homework

Workbook pages 26–27

MyEnglishLab

05 Green world

Unit objectives

Reading:	multiple matching
Vocabulary:	the environment; food and water
Grammar:	the future; *so, such, too, enough*
Listening:	multiple-choice questions
Speaking:	discussion questions
Writing:	writing an essay

READING (SB pages 56–57)

To start

Focus students' attention on the title of the unit and ask them to tell you what they think they will be learning about. Then write the following question on the board:

Will there still be life on earth in the year 3000?

Give students a few moments to think about their answer. Conduct a show of hands to see what students believe. Ask students who have answered yes to sit together and share their reasons for answering in this way and ask students who have answered *no* to do the same.

Circulate as students discuss their reasons, offering support where necessary. Open this up into a class discussion, generating as much vocabulary as possible and writing students' ideas on the board.

Power up

1　Read the question aloud to your students. Elicit that *being green* and *being environmentally friendly* mean the same thing. Tell students one green thing that you do, e.g. *I switch electrical things off when I'm not using them*.

　　Organise students into small groups to make their lists of environmentally-friendly things to do. When the minute is up, find out how many ideas students collected and ask them to read their ideas aloud to the class. Write students' suggestions on the board, generating discussion by asking questions, e.g. *Do you also do this, Maria? Is this an easy way to be green or does it take a bit of effort?*

Students' own answers.

2　Focus students' attention on the photos and ask them to describe what they see. Tell students that they are going to read a discussion forum where teenagers discuss green issues. Ask students to work with a partner and use the photos to predict what they think the teenagers will say. Nominate a few students to report back their ideas, e.g. *They might talk about how dolphins are in danger from fishing nets.*

Students' own answers.

Read on

3　If necessary, pre-teach the following words and phrases: *excursion* (trip), *rural* (to do with the countryside), *self-sufficient* (when you grow enough food to feed yourself) and *endangered species* (an animal type which is in danger of dying out). Check understanding by asking questions, e.g. *Where did you go on your last school excursion? Is London a rural place?* (no); *Is the countryside rural?* (yes); *If you are self-sufficient do you spend a lot of time at the supermarket?* (no); *Why not?* (Because you grow your own food.); *Are tigers an endangered species?* (yes); *What other endangered species do you know?*

　　Ask students to read the forum posts quickly. Tell them that they need to check their answers and also find out each teenager's special 'green' interest. Ask them to check their answers with a partner before conducting class feedback.

A Felipe – ocean wildlife
B Pilar – ecotourism
C Jeni – guerrilla gardening
D Levent – wildlife corridors (for wild bears)

4　Focus students' attention on the Skill advice and then tell students to read the forum posts again more slowly and answer the questions. Allow them to check their answers with a partner before checking answers orally.

1 A　2 D　3 C　4 B　5 B　6 D　7 C　8 A　9 B　10 A

5　Students match the words from the forum posts with their meanings. Check answers around the class.

1 g　2 a　3 f　4 e　5 c　6 h　7 b　8 d

Sum up

6 Read the question aloud to your students. Ask students to choose which teenager they would like to speak about and give them a minute to think about what they are going to say, using the headings to help them.

Organise students into small groups to complete this activity (preferably group students so that they are talking about different teenagers) and monitor as students complete the task. Check students' understanding of what they have read and encourage them to use new language from the text in their answers.

Students' own answers.

Speak up

7 Ask students to discuss the question with a partner for a minute. Then ask pairs to compare their ideas with another pair. Finally, open this up into a whole class discussion. Encourage them to give full and detailed reasons for their choices, e.g. *I'd like to be involved in guerilla gardening, because I love the idea of making a grey concrete area look more beautiful.*

Students' own answers.

To finish

Tell your students that you think that their school should be a greener place. Tell them one idea you have for making the school more eco-friendly, e.g. *I think I should photocopy less.*

Organise students into groups and tell them that they are each class eco-committees. Ask them to think of at least five suggestions for making the school a greener place. Nominate a student from each group to report back their ideas. Conduct a class vote, where students vote for the best idea from each group, e.g. *I think we should encourage more students to walk to school, students who walk or cycle to school could get paid a small bonus, we should learn online more, we should use less paper, etc.*

Homework

MyEnglishLab

VOCABULARY 1 (SB page 58)

The environment

To start

Ask students to close their SBs. Write the following jumbled up words on the board (solutions in brackets):

tromino (monitor)

bledei (edible)

dedesat (sedated)

egallyill (illegally)

sreevonc (conserve)

Organise students into pairs. Tell them that they are going to race to see which pair can be first to unjumble the words to find vocabulary from the reading lesson. They must then write a sentence containing each word. The first pair to unjumble the words and use all four words accurately and sensibly in four separate sentences is the winner.

1 Focus students' attention on the words in the box. Drill pronunciation chorally and individually, focusing on any potentially tricky words, e.g. *self-sufficient* /selfsə'fɪʃənt/ and *ecological* /ˌiːkə'lɒdʒɪkəl/. Write the words on the board and elicit where the stress lies in each. Students then complete the sentences with the words in the box. Check answers around the class, focusing on the pronunciation of the new language.

1 Protected 2 urban 3 rural 4 ecological 5 Organic
6 self-sufficient, dependent 7 recycled

2 Read the phrasal verbs in the box aloud to your class. Students rewrite the sentences, replacing the underlined words with the phrasal verbs. Allow students to check their answers with a partner before conducting class feedback.

1 catch on 2 pick up 3 be into 4 die out 5 go towards
6 report back

Word XP

Read the information and the examples aloud to your students. Encourage them to learn collocations as one unit rather than separately. Ask students if they can think of any more environmental collocations and write their suggestions on the board, e.g.

ozone layer, endangered species, compost heap, sustainable energy, etc.

3 Focus students' attention on the words in the box. Do an example together as a class before asking students to complete this task with a partner. Check orally that students have collocated the words correctly.

1 waste 2 panels 3 species 4 habitat 5 energy 6 spaces

4 Direct students to the environmental campaign poster. Ask students to tell you what the aims of the *Better city campaign* are (they want to stop traffic in the town centre, improve public transport, make the air cleaner and the town more peaceful and beautiful). Students then complete the poster with the words in the box. Play the recording and allow students to check their answers.

➤ Track 5.1

Lucy: I think this poster looks good, Ollie, don't you?

Ollie: Yes, even though I say it myself, I think we did a good job on that! I'm pretty sure we mentioned all the important points like moving industries outside the town and improving public transport.

Lucy: And having more recycling bins and reducing air pollution. I hate all those traffic fumes, especially in the centre of town! We definitely need more streets in the centre that are only for pedestrians.

Ollie: Yes, sometimes it's tough living in a concrete jungle, but there's so much we could do to improve things. If only people listened to us!

Lucy: Well, I hope that at least this campaign will help to improve our neighbourhood. You know I love the idea of rooftop gardening; it would change the way the buildings look. Everything would be so much greener!

Ollie: I agree. And having some more cycle paths would be great. We could cycle to school and we wouldn't have to wait for the bus every day for ages.

Lucy: OK, so let's make those points our first priority. It's always easier to get people interested in the local area where they live.

Ollie: You're right. We can start going around the houses in our street this evening!

1 fumes   2 pollution   3 pedestrians
4 concrete   5 rooftop   6 transport
7 neighbourhood   8 recycling   9 paths
10 industries

Game on

Read the instructions aloud to your class and choose a student to demonstrate the activity with. Start with a letter and say a word of phrase about the environment starting with the letter, e.g.

E = energy, eco-friendly, eco-tourism, ecological, ecologist, environmentally-friendly, endangered

G = green, greenery, garden

P = pedestrian, pollution, path, public spaces, public transport

R = recycled, rural

S = species, snorkelling, solar

W = wildlife, wild dolphin, wild bear, waste

Monitor as students play the game, checking their pronunciation of the target vocabulary. Encourage the students who are guessing the words to play the game with their books closed as this will increase the level of challenge.

To finish

Organise students into pairs. Give students one minute to think of as many things as they can which would improve their town/city. Write the following heading on the board:

Better (students' home town/city) campaign

Go around the class, collecting students' ideas and generating as much discussion as possible. Write students' ideas on the board and ask students how possible they think these ideas would be to achieve. Ask students to choose their favourite ideas from the list.

Homework
Workbook pages 28–29
MyEnglishLab

GRAMMAR 1 (SB page 59)

The future

To start

Write the phrase *time capsule* on the board and ask students to tell you what this is (it is a small tin or box which you bury underground containing information about you and your life. People buy time capsules in the hope that they will be dug up many years into the future).

Tell students they are going to make a time capsule. Ask them to write three sentences about themselves in the present (e.g. their name, where they live and something they like doing). Then ask them to write three predictions about the future. Ask students questions to generate ideas, e.g. *What will the world look like? How will we travel?*

Students write their predictions on a piece of paper. Nominate a few students to read their predictions aloud, making a note of their use of future forms. Bury the time capsule with your students somewhere in the school grounds.

Grammar XP

Read the information in the Grammar XP box aloud to your students. Ask students to read the examples aloud, focusing on natural sounding pronunciation of the future forms, e.g. *I'm going to* /əmɡ'əʊn/ *I'll* /aɪl/.

Drill the pronunciation of the future time clauses and adverbs of likelihood, focusing on word stress, e.g. *as soon as* /əzsu:næz/.

Write some sentences about your class. Ask students to read the sentences and elicit why particular future forms have been used, e.g.

This time next week you'll all be enjoying the spring holiday.

We're going to learn some new vocabulary tomorrow.

I think I'll open the window. This classroom is getting a bit stuffy.

By the time we finish this student book, it will be the summer holidays!.

1 Students choose the correct answers. Check answers around the class, asking students to justify their answers.

1 A **2** B **3** B **4** B **5** A **6** B

2 Focus students' attention on the photo and ask them to describe what they can see (school pupils with their teacher working in a garden). Ask them to quickly read the conversation and ask: *How does Harry feel about the project?* (he isn't interested because he doesn't like gardening).

Students read the conversation again and choose the correct answers. Play the recording and allow students to check their answers.

► Track 5.2

Layla: Hi, Harry. Have you heard the news? Some people from *Edible Playground* are coming to our school later this morning!

Harry: Oh. Who are they?

Layla: They give advice about growing vegetables at school. It'll be fun!

Harry: Why? I'm not into gardening at all. And neither are my friends. They won't get me involved. I'm telling you that now!

Layla: Oh, don't be so boring, Harry. I've heard that next month we are going to plant vegetables. Then, when they are ready, we'll pick them. So in three or four months' time, we'll be cooking them in the school kitchen!

Harry: Hmm ... I tell you what – when I see a plate of spaghetti and vegetable sauce in front of me, I'll believe you!

Layla: OK, but I forgot to tell you something: according to the headmaster, the students who don't do the gardening will have to do the cooking!

Harry: Hey, that's not fair!

1 are coming
2 'll be
3 won't
4 are planting
5 are
6 pick
7 we'll be cooking
8 see
9 'll believe
10 will have to

3 Read the task and the example aloud to your students. Students discuss what they think they will be doing in ten years' time. Monitor as students complete this activity, checking that future forms are being accurately used and noting down any problems to raise in class feedback. Nominate a few students to report back on their partners' ideas.

Students' own answers.

Write on

4 Model the activity by writing three sentences about yourself on the board, e.g.

In two weeks' time I'll be spending time with my sister in France.

In six months' time I'll be getting married.

In five years' time I'll be working in a different country.

Ask students to write their own sentences. Monitor as they do this, offering support with future forms where necessary. Ask students to read their sentences to a partner. Nominate a few students to share their sentences with the rest of the class.

Students' own answers.

To finish

Collect some of the students' sentences from Exercises 3 or 4 which have one small mistake. Ideally choose sentences where the writer has made an error in using future forms. Organise the groups into two teams. Tell students that you are going to read out sentences which contain one error. Teams must confer and rewrite the sentences. When the team members all agree that the rewritten sentence is correct, they can raise their hands and read out the rewritten version. If the sentence is correct, award the team a point. The team with the most points at the end of the game is the winner.

Homework

Workbook page 30

MyEnglishLab

VOCABULARY 2 (SB page 60)

Food and water

To start

Write the following sentence beginnings on the board. Put them inside a speech bubble so that the students know that the sentences are all part of the same speech.

I am pessimistic about the future of our planet.

In fifty years' time we won't ...

We'll be ...

By the time the century is over ...

We're definitely going to ...

Ask students to work in pairs to complete the sentences with pessimistic predictions about the future. Circulate as students complete this task, offering support where necessary. Ask a student from each group to read their sentences. Award praise for interesting and accurate sentences.

1　Tell students that they are going to find out how good their environmental vocabulary is. Organise students into pairs and ask them to take turns reading and answering the questions. Check answers around the class and award a small prize or bonus to the pair who managed to answer most prizes correctly.

1 a　2 b　3 a
4 b　5 a　6 a
7 b　8 b

2　Write the following sentences on the board:

There has been an increase in the number of students cycling to school. The number of students cycling to school increases every year.

Read the sentences aloud and ask students to tell you what they notice about the word *increase*. Elicit that in the first sentence (where increase is a noun) the stress is on the first syllable, whereas in the second sentence (where increase is a verb), the stress is on the second syllable.

Play the recording. Students should listen and repeat. Ask students to check the meanings of the words in their dictionaries and check understanding by asking questions such as: *What is this country's largest export? What do we need to import? What is the most popular mode of transport in this town?*

➤ **Track 5.3**

trans**port**	**trans**port
in**crease**	**in**crease
ex**port**	**ex**port
im**port**	**im**port

transport (v) = to carry things around in a car, lorry, etc.
transport (n) = a way of travelling around
increase (v) = to get higher, more
increase (n) = when something gets higher, more
export (v) = to send products from your country to a foreign country
export (n) = the products you send to a foreign country
import (v) = to bring products into your country
import (n) = the products you bring into your country

Word XP

Read the information and examples in the box. Personalise the new language by telling students something you couldn't do without, e.g. *I couldn't do without my laptop. What could you not do without?*

3　Students complete the sentences with the phrases in the box. Check answers around the class.

1 make sense
2 make do with
3 do my bit
4 do without
5 do with
6 Make sure

4　Read the title of the article and elicit the meaning of the phrase *food miles* (it is the distance which our food travels to get to us). Ask students to read the article quickly. Ask questions to check understanding, e.g. *What does the writer want us to do?* (eat food which is produced locally) *Why?* (because the food is fresher and it's better for the environment). Students read the article again and choose the correct answers. Allow students to check their answers with a partner before conducting whole class feedback.

1 C　2 A　3 D　4 B　5 C　6 C　7 B　8 A

To finish

Ask students to write down what they ate for dinner yesterday. Ask them: *Do you know where your food came from?* Ask students to think about how many food miles their last night's dinner had travelled to get to them.

Organise students into pairs. Ask them to make a list of food that can be (and is) grown in their local area. Bring the class back together and nominate students to share their lists. Challenge pairs to design a delicious menu made from purely locally sourced ingredients. Ask students to share their menu with the rest of the class and vote for the most delicious sounding meal.

Homework
Workbook page 29
MyEnglishLab

GRAMMAR 2 (SB page 61)

so, such, too, enough

To start

Remind students of the phrases with *make* and *do* which they learned in the last lesson and write them on the board:

do with

do my bit

make do with

make sense

make sure

do without

Say a few sentences which are true about you using the phrasal verbs, e.g. *I can't do without sugar in my tea. I always make sure I've locked the door when I've left home.*

Challenge students to see who can be the first to make sentences which are true for themselves using all six phrases. The first student who manages to use all six accurately is the winner.

Grammar XP

Read the information and examples in the Grammar XP box aloud to your students. Generate some personalised examples of the language with your students by writing the following sentence beginnings on the board, e.g.

It was such lovely weather outside that our English teacher …

We've worked so well in class recently that our teacher …

The exercise was too hard to …

There aren't enough _ in this classroom.

Encourage students to complete the sentences with their own ideas. Write students' suggestions on the board, focusing on form. Ask students to read the sentences aloud, drawing attention to sentence stress.

1 Students complete the sentences with *so*, *such*, *such a/an*, *too* or *enough*. Check answers around the class.

1 so

2 such a

3 enough

4 such

5 too

2 Students complete the sentences with *so much*, *so many*, *too much* or *too many*. Conduct class feedback.

1 so many

2 too much

3 so much

4 too many

5 so much

3 As students to rewrite the sentences, referring to the information in the Grammar XP box for help. Allow students to check their answers with a partner before conducting class feedback.

1 fast enough to

2 so much ice cream

3 tired to finish

4 such a fantastic

4 Read the title of the article to your students. Focus students' attention on the photo and ask them to predict what they think the article will be about. Ask students to read the article quickly and check if their predictions were correct. Students then read the article again and complete it with one word in each space. Monitor as students complete this activity, offering support where necessary. Allow students to check their answers with a partner before reading the article around the class.

1 so **2** such **3** many **4** not **5** is **6** will **7** next **8** be

To finish

Write sentences about your students' town on the board. Choose famous buildings and places which all of your students will know, e.g.

The best cake shop in the town is Gianetti's.

The most beautiful park in our area is the city park.

The quietest place in the school is the library.

Generate more information about each sentence using language from the lesson, e.g. *The best cake shop in town is Gianetti's. It's so popular that I can never get a seat!*

Ask students to work with a partner and give more information about each place using the target language. Circulate as students complete the task, offering support where necessary. Conduct class feedback and ask students to report back on their ideas.

Homework

Workbook page 31

MyEnglishLab

LISTENING (SB page 62)

To start

Write the following question on the board:

How green is our town?

Underneath the question write headings:

transport

restaurants

clothes shops

schools

(You could also ask students to add one more category of their own choosing.) Ask students to work in small groups and answer the question, discussing each of the points as they do so. Bring the class back together again and ask groups to report back on their ideas.

Power up

1 Organise students into pairs. Give them a minute to discuss their ideas to the questions. Conduct class feedback. Check that students are comfortable with the meaning of the new words by asking questions, e.g. *In which part of the world might you find a water buffalo?* (rural Asia) *Do you have a juice maker at home? Is there a vegetarian restaurant in this town? What's it called?*

1 a place where stray or badly-treated animals are taken in and looked after temporarily

2 a large Asian animal similar to a cow, used for farm work, particularly rice growing

3 a piece of equipment for making fresh fruit or vegetable juice in

4 a line of hard rocks formed by coral found in warm sea water (coral is a hard red, white, or pink substance formed from the bones of very small sea creatures)

5 a restaurant that serves non-meat dishes (it might not serve fish either)

2 Students match the photos with the items in Exercise 1. Check answers orally.

Photo **A** 2

Photo **B** 4

Listen up

3 Read the Exam advice aloud to your students. If necessary pre-teach the following words: *demonstration* (an organised event where people protest about something they disagree with), *community* (a group of people who live in the same area) and *depressing* (making you feel sad). Tell students that they are going to listen to people talking in different situations. Allow students a minute to read the questions before playing the recording. Play the recording again and ask students to check their answers. Conduct class feedback.

➤ Track 5.4

1

Announcer: *Veggies* is a new addition to our town's wide variety of eating places. Now, all of us know that eating too much red meat isn't that healthy for us. And we know that we should increase the amount of fruit and vegetables we eat. *Veggies* has an interesting menu with lots of great new dishes. This Saturday we are offering a Saturday organic special! Bring along your friends and families and have a really healthy lunch! Very reasonable prices, too!

2

Girl: I'm going to ask my mum if we can buy one of those new juice makers – they're great!

Boy: They're pretty expensive though.

Girl: Yes I know, but you can make different vegetable juices and fruit juices in it and they're much healthier than the ones you buy in the shops.

Boy: Well, I always make a fresh orange juice when I get home from school and I don't need a juicer!

Girl: Ah, but with this one you can make a lot very quickly, so it saves time – *and* it keeps for two days in the fridge!

Boy: Hmm, not sure about it, really.

3

Boy: Hi, Dad. Just to say that I won't be going to football practice this afternoon because the coach is off sick, so I'm going to have tea at Ben's house. Then we're going to take part in a demonstration. It's against that new motorway they're going to build through a protected area. I know you didn't really want to go to it, did you? I won't be back late – probably around nine. Ben's dad will bring me home, so tell Mum not to worry! See you!

4

Interviewer: What do you remember about your childhood in Vietnam?

Woman: I grew up in a rural community where each family had an animal called a water buffalo to do the heavy work. Every day, we children took the water buffalo into the fields to eat grass and then we'd bathe it in clean water. After that, we used to play a ball game standing on the animal's back. The picture of that has always remained in my memory very clearly. We'd shout at the water buffalo to try and get it to move, but it didn't seem very interested!

5

Boy: Hi, where are you right now? OK, look, how about a change of plans 'cos I don't fancy going swimming at the pool today. Can you come to the animal shelter instead? I'm going to look for a dog! Great! Then we could go round to Mike's house later and have a game of football. Oh yes, I forgot he's away. Oh well, never mind. Anyway, the bus is coming now, so I'll be there in about twenty minutes! See you!

6

Girl: Did you see that programme on TV last night – *Our World*?

Boy: Yes, most of it. What did you think?

Girl: Well, some of it wasn't bad. I loved the underwater photos of coral reefs, but nothing much else was new. I also thought there was such a lot about problems that there wasn't time for them to talk about the solutions!

Boy: Yes, I wonder why they didn't mention the environmental organisations we've learnt about at school.

Girl: I agree. And I wonder why people make such depressing programmes!

I B   2 C   3 A   4 C   5 A   6 B

Speak up

4   Model the task by telling students which aspect of the environment you would like to learn about, e.g. *I'd like to learn about food production and healthy eating because I think that food is becoming more and more tasteless and I don't like shopping in the supermarket.*

Organise students into pairs and ask students to tell their partner about their choice. Circulate as students complete this task, encouraging them to give full and detailed reasons. Note down any particularly interesting choices. Conduct whole class feedback.

Students' own answers.

To finish

Ask students to work in groups and choose an issue they think it would be most important to make an environmental campaign clip about. Collect students' ideas around the class.

Possible ideas

ocean life

endangered species

healthy eating

animal welfare

food miles

Encourage students to give reasons for their choices and to describe any interesting environmental campaigns they have seen or heard about.

Homework

MyEnglishLab

SPEAKING (SB page 63)

To start

Tell your class that they are going to make a class survey about responsible shopping habits. Ask your students this question:

You want to buy a pair of jeans. Which do you choose?

the cheapest

the coolest

the pair made of organic cotton

Nominate one or two students to tell the class their answers, giving reasons for their choices.

Now organise students into pairs and ask them to write one similar question (with three optional answers) for the survey. Collect questions around the class. Ask students to mingle with their classmates, asking and answering the questions. Conduct class feedback: *Are your students responsible shoppers?*

Power up

1   Focus students on the questions. Write *consumer society* on the board and elicit a definition (buying more than you really need, buying without considering other possibilities, e.g. *sharing/swapping unwanted things or using simpler things that are more eco-friendly*). Organise students into pairs and ask them to brainstorm the problems which might occur as a result of consumerism, e.g. *wastage, 'keeping up with the Joneses' attitude, pollution, loss of spiritual values, environmental damage.* Conduct class feedback, organising students' responses into a spidergram.

Students' own answers.

2   Give students a few seconds to read the leaflet. Ask them to close their books and remember as many of the points as they can. Students open their books again and listen to the recording, noting down all the points on the leaflet which are mentioned. Check answers orally.

> ➤ **Tracks 5.5 and 5.6**

Interviewer: So, when you go shopping, how do you think you can shop more responsibly in order to look after the environment?

Girl: Well, ... concerning food, I think we should buy more organic food products from organic farms, which don't use any chemicals.

Boy: Yes, so do I, because the chemicals that are used to grow other food products get into the rivers and contaminate the water. And the chemicals are bad for our health, too! Also, I don't like using plastic bags when I go shopping.

Girl: Neither do I! It's horrible how so many of them end up polluting the sea. We should re-use bags ... and I'm keen on buying second-hand clothes. You know – vintage clothes, for example.

Boy: Oh, I'm not. Although it is a good way of being responsible, and not wasting things. But I always try to buy recycled paper and notebooks for school.

Buy second-hand clothes.

Don't use plastic bags – or re-use old ones.

Buy organic products.

3   Read the Language XP box aloud to your students. Play the recording again and ask them to note down the phrases they hear the speakers use. Check answers around the class.

(Yes,) so do I.

Neither do I.

(Oh,) I'm not.

Language XP

Practise the phrases in the Language XP box by making statements to your students, and asking them to agree or disagree using the target language. For example:

I think it's important to shop responsibly. I don't like shopping in supermarkets. I love the countryside, etc.

Keep the activity fast paced and encourage snappy responses from your students.

4   Students complete the conversations with phrases from the Language XP box. Check answers by reading the conversations around the class.

1 I don't
2 Neither/Nor have I
3 So would I
4 So am I
5 Oh, I would
6 Neither/Nor do I

Speak up

5   Read the Exam advice aloud to your students. Organise students into pairs and ask them to discuss the questions. Monitor as students complete this activity, encouraging them to use the target language. Note down any problems which you can address in class feedback.

Students' own answers.

To finish

Tell students to write down five personal opinions of their own. Organise students into pairs. Ask students to take it in turns to share their opinions with their partner. Students must use the language in the Language XP box to agree or disagree. They should also give a reason for their agreeing or disagreeing. Circulate as students complete this activity, offering support where necessary.

Homework

MyEnglishLab

WRITING (SB pages 64–65)

To start

Organise students into two groups. Within each group, ask students to work in pairs and make a list of three problems they think will face our planet in the future. Write an example on the board, e.g. *There won't be enough food for everyone to eat.* Elicit a solution for this problem from your students, e.g. *We can start to eat insects.*

When both groups have written their problems, they need to swap their lists with a pair from the other group. They should read the problems on the list and write a possible solution for each problem.

Nominate a student from each pair to talk about a problem they received and ask them to describe the solution they came up with.

Power up

1   Focus students' attention on the pictures and ask them to describe what they see (*travelling using a jetpack, personal submarine*). Ask students if they would like to travel by these methods. Encourage students to give reasons for their answers.

Students' own answers.

2   Organise students into pairs. Ask them to brainstorm the ways in which they think life might be different in the future. Write headings on the board to help them: *food, fashion, school, family life, entertainment, homes, jobs.*

Open this up into a whole class discussion. Generate as much new language as possible and write it on the board.

Students' own answers.

Plan on

3   Nominate one student to read the problems aloud to the class. Nominate a different student to read the solutions. Ask students to match the problems with the solutions. Conduct class feedback.

1 c   2 a   3 d   4 b

4   Read the essay prompt aloud to your students. Organise students into small groups to discuss the headings. Circulate, offering support where necessary. Bring the class back together and ask a student from each group to share what they discussed and to suggest ideas for the third point. Write their ideas for the third point on the board.

Students' own answers.

5 Give students a minute to read the essay in silence and compare the ideas in the SB with the ideas which they came up with in Exercise 4 (on the board). Conduct class feedback.

Students' own answers.

6 Direct students' attention to the introduction and the conclusion. Ask students to read the essay question again and then compare this to the introduction. Elicit that the writer has rephrased the essay question and stress that this is a very useful way to begin an essay.

1 'our life in the future could improve'   **2** B

Language XP

Direct students to the Language XP box and stress that this is very useful language to use when writing an essay. Ask students to look at the essay again and tell you which of these linking words the writer has used (In the first place, Another idea is, Secondly, Finally).

7 Students complete the paragraph with language from the Language XP box. Point out that there may be several possible answers for each gap. Allow students to check their answers with a partner before reading the paragraph around the class.

1 Firstly/In the first place/To begin with/To start with
2 Secondly/Another point is
3 As a final point/Finally/Lastly

8 Tell students that they are going to write an alternative paragraph for the essay they read in Exercise 5, using their own idea. They can also use the ideas in the box to help them. Monitor as students write their paragraphs, encouraging them to use words and phrases from the Language XP box. Nominate one or two able students to read their paragraphs aloud to the class.

Students' own answers.

Model answer

Finally, technology is constantly improving the way we live. Thanks to technology, the number of people working from home has increased. This means that fewer people are driving to work and the roads are cleaner and the air is less polluted as a result. Technology is also helping doctors find new solutions to help seriously ill people: new cures are invented every day with the help of sophisticated computer systems.

Write on

9 Focus students' attention on the photo and ask them to describe what they see (an area in a town – a square – littered with rubbish). Read the essay prompt aloud and brainstorm solutions as a class. Write students' suggestions on the board.

Students' own answers.

10 Organise students into groups. Ask them to discuss the problems and choose which one they would like to write about in their essay. Encourage them to come up with their own ideas, too.

Students' own answers.

11 Draw students' attention to the Skill advice and stress the importance of giving specific examples when writing essays. Students continue working in their groups. Ask students to read the solutions and match them to the problems they discussed in Exercise 10. Students should then think of a couple of examples to illustrate each solution. Discuss one solution as a class, before asking students to complete the rest of activity with their group. Circulate, offering support where necessary.

Students' own answers.

12 Students write their essay. Ask students to swap their work with a partner after ten minutes. Ask students to check each other's work for a clear introduction and good use of linking words. Students should then continue writing their essay. Choose the best essay to photocopy and distribute to the rest of the class.

Students' own answers.

Model answer

My town attracts a great number of tourists each year. Although this is good for the economy, the number of tourists also causes problems. However, I believe that we should not stop welcoming our summer guests, as there are solutions to these problems.

In the first place, many people complain about new accommodation buildings for tourists. It is true that these are ugly and spoil the look of our town. However, if we were strict about new buildings and only allowed beautiful buildings which fitted in with the surrounding area, I don't think that this would be a problem.

Secondly, crowded beaches can be annoying in the middle of summer. However, there are many beaches in the area which tourists don't know about. We should arrange transport to nearby beaches so that tourists can explore the area and our local beaches will be less packed. Lastly, noise late at night disturbs many people. We could build a disco on the outskirts of town and provide a free all night bus service to get to it. That way, holiday makers could enjoy themselves late and night and we could all sleep peacefully.

In conclusion, tourism does bring problems, but if we all think carefully and positively about solutions we should be able to have the best of both worlds.

To finish

Tell students that they are going to design an eco-hotel for tourists visiting their town. Write the following headings on the board and ask students to consider these features in their eco-hotel design:

food

energy supply

décor

Organise students into groups. Give them a few minutes to discuss what their eco-hotels would be like. Nominate a student from each group to report back on their group's ideas.

Homework

MyEnglishLab

SWITCH ON (SB page 66)

A good deed every day

1   Read the question aloud to your students and ask them to predict what happened next. Allow students to share their ideas before playing the video so that they can check their predictions. Conduct class feedback and ask students whether or not they were surprised by what happened.

B

2   Give students a minute to read the question and the options. Play the video again while students select the ideas which are mentioned by Petri and her friends. Check answers around the class.

A, D, F

3   Organise students into groups and ask them to think of three ways in which they could carry out a *random act of kindness* in their school or local area. Monitor as students complete this activity, offering support where necessary. Conduct class feedback and list students' suggestions on the board.

Students' own answers.

Project

4   Read options A and B aloud to your class. Ask students to choose which option they like best and organise students into groups who have the same preference. Give students some time in class to prepare their ideas: Group A can begin to list people who need help while Group B can decide who they are going to interview and what questions they are going to ask. Students can complete the activity for homework and come together in the next class to prepare their presentations or their videos. Monitor as students do this, offering support where needed. Bring the class together to watch the presentations/videos. Generate as much discussion as possible and encourage students to give constructive feedback to their classmates.

Students' own answers.

REVISION (SB page 67)

1

1 urban
2 wildlife
3 endangered
4 alternative
5 public
6 toxic

2

1 'll be watching
2 'll tell you
3 going to say
4 is helping
5 gets
6 will be

3

1 B
2 C
3 B
4 A
5 C
6 A

4

1 so clean
2 such a hot
3 too fast (for us)
4 so much rain
5 enough parks for
6 too heavy (for us)

5

1 do
2 switch
3 die
4 report
5 catching
6 is

Homework
Workbook pages 32–33
MyEnglishLab

06 Before time

Unit objectives

Reading:	multiple-choice questions
Vocabulary:	actions and reactions; describing places and experiences
Grammar:	past perfect simple; comparatives and superlatives
Listening:	sentence completion
Speaking:	comparing photos
Writing:	writing a story

READING (SB pages 68–69)

To start

Write the word *Dinosaur* on the board. Organise students into small groups and tell them they have one minute to collect as many facts about dinosaurs as they can. When the minute is up, ask groups to report back on the facts they have collected. If possible, quickly check any facts you are unsure of online. The group with the greatest number of correct facts about dinosaurs is the winner. During feedback, generate as much discussion as you can. Find out which students in your class are most interested in dinosaurs and ask them to tell you where they learned their facts.

Power up

1 Read the question aloud to students. Elicit what a fossil is (the remains of a prehistoric plant or animal which are embedded in rock). Ask students to tell the class about fossils and dinosaur skeletons they have seen. Generate as much language as possible by asking questions, e.g. *Were you allowed to touch them? What did they look like?*

Students' own answers.

2 Ask students to read the questions and discuss them quickly with a partner.

Students' own answers.

Read on

Background

The Natural History Museum is a huge museum in London. It exhibits a very wide variety of exhibits from the natural world and has about 75 million items. Many of its exhibits have historical significance too, as it also contains specimens which were collected by Charles Darwin.

3 If necessary, pre-teach the following words and phrases: *frost* (the thin white layer you find on the ground on cold nights and mornings), *display* (when things are in a place where they can be easily seen), *shivers down somebody's spine* (a tingling feeling you get when you are excited or afraid about something) and *enthusiast* (someone who is passionate about a particular thing). Check understanding by asking questions, e.g. *Would I find frost on the ground on a warm day?* (no); *On a cold morning?* (yes); *If I display something, do I want people to see it or not to see it?* (you want people to see it); *If I have shivers down my spine, am I feeling angry?* (no); *Am I excited?* (yes); *Are you a grammar enthusiast, Marcus? Are you a football enthusiast?*

Focus students' attention on the photos and ask them to describe what they see. Ask students to read the story quickly and find the names of the two films which are mentioned, and what happened in each. Allow students to check their answers with a partner before conducting class feedback

Night at the Museum: museum displays come to life
Jurassic Park: dinosaurs are brought back to life from DNA in fossils

4 Students read the story again and choose the correct answers. Draw their attention to the Exam advice. Give them time to check their answers with a partner before conducting class feedback.

1 B 2 A 3 C 4 D 5 D 6 A

5 Students match the words from the story with their meanings. Check answers around the class, drilling the pronunciation of any tricky words chorally and individually, e.g. *palaeontology* /ˈpælionˈtolədʒi/ and *herbivore* /ˈhɜːbəvɔː/. Write the words on the board and elicit where the stress lies in each.

1 e 2 f 3 h 4 d 5 a 6 b 7 j 8 i 9 c 10 g

Sum up

6 Organise students into groups. Ask them to summarise what they have learned, using the questions to help them. Nominate a student from each group to answer each question.

Students' own answers.

Speak up

7 Read the question aloud to your students. Ask them to share their thoughts with a partner before opening this up into a whole class discussion. Encourage students to provide full reasons for their answers, e.g. *I wouldn't like to spend a night in a museum. I think it would be really creepy and probably cold and uncomfortable, too!*

Students' own answers.

To finish

Write the following sentence on the board: It was the best birthday present they'd ever had. Ask students: *Why do you think this was such a good birthday present?* Elicit that it suited the twins' interests perfectly and was a really memorable experience. Ask students to write down something they really like or are really interested in on a piece of paper. Collect the papers in, jumble them up and redistribute them making sure that no one gets their own piece of paper back.

Get students to read what is written on the piece of paper and think of a really creative and exciting gift for this person. Go around the class, finding out what people had written on their paper and eliciting present ideas. Conduct a class vote for the most original and exciting present idea. Ask students: *What's the best birthday present you've ever had?* Generate as much language and discussion as possible.

Homework

MyEnglishLab

VOCABULARY 1 (SB page 70)

Actions and reactions

To start

Organise students into two teams. Choose one of the words from the Reading lesson and mime it to your students, e.g. *snoring*. Ask students to tell you the word without looking at their books. Students take it in turns to mime words they learned in the reading lesson to the other team, who must guess the word being mimed. The team with the most points at the end is the winner.

1 Students match the sentence halves. Allow them to check answers with a partner before conducting class feedback. Write the phrases in bold on the board and elicit their meaning. Check understanding by asking students to give examples of times they have experienced these feelings, e.g. *My mouth went dry before my English exam.*

1 f **2** g **3** d **4** a **5** b **6** h **7** i **8** c **9** j **10** e

2 Focus students' attention on the picture. Ask them to match the body parts with the words. Check answers around the class.

2 brain **3** skull **4** lungs **5** heart **6** stomach **7** bones
8 muscles

3 Challenge students to see how quickly they can answer the quiz questions. Play the recording so they can check their answers.

► Track 6.1

Presenter: In today's *Quick Quiz* here on Radio Five, we have Sophie on Line 1.

Sophie: Hi!

Presenter: And David on Line 2.

David: Hello!

Presenter: As usual, the questions are easy, but you must answer as fast as you can. The person with the most correct answers wins two cinema tickets. Your time starts now! Question One: Which joint is in the middle of your arm?

Sophie: Elbow!

Presenter: Correct. Two: Which joint is in the middle of your leg?

David: Knee!

Presenter: OK. Three: What joins your head to your body?

David: Neck!

Presenter: Yes! Four: What covers the whole human body?

David: Skin!

Presenter: That's right. Come on, Sophie. Question Five: Humans have fingernails, but animals have what?

Sophie: Claws?

Presenter: Yes! Six: What joins your arms to your body?

Sophie: Er ... shoulders!

Presenter: Correct. That's three points each. Four more questions. Seven: Humans have arms, but birds have what?

David: Legs!

Presenter: No! Wings!

David: Oh yes. Duh!

Presenter: Eight: What covers many animals' bodies?

Sophie: Fur!

Presenter: Good! Nine: A long extension to an animal's backbone is a what?

David: Erm, tail?

Presenter: Correct! Last question. Ten: Your top half, behind you, is your what?

Sophie: Your back?

Presenter: Well done! David has four points, but Sophie is today's winner, with five points.

Sophie: Yay!

1 elbow **2** knee **3** neck **4** skin **5** claws **6** shoulders **7** wings
8 fur **9** tail **10** back

Word XP

Read the information in the Word XP box aloud to your students and generate some examples, e.g. *They dug some dinosaur remains up. They dug up some dinosaur remains. They dug them up.* (NOT *They dug up them.*)

4 Students complete the sentences and check their answers quickly with a partner. Read answers around the class.

1 out **2** up **3** back to **4** up **5** across **6** out **7** on **8** up with

5 Remind students of what they learned in the Language XP box and elicit what the arrow symbol means (If the object of the verb is a pronoun it must come before the particle.). Students then rewrite the sentences.

2 Before the band could perform, we had to set <u>it</u> up.
4 They've just dug <u>them</u> up.
6 The guide pointed <u>them</u> out.
8 How did you come up with <u>it</u>? It's amazing!

Game on

Nominate a confident student to demonstrate the game with you. Tell the student that you are going to say a body part from Exercise 2 or 3 and they must quickly point to the correct part of their body or say 'Animal!' Keep the pace fast so that students are sufficiently challenged. Students play the game with a partner. Circulate, checking for accurate pronunciation.

To finish

Organise students into pairs. Give them a few minutes to invent and draw their very own, newly discovered dinosaur. Students then exchange drawings with another pair who must neatly label the appropriate body parts. Conduct class votes for the cutest, scariest, funniest and most realistic looking dinosaurs. If time permits, ask your students to add colour to their dinosaurs and display their creations on the wall.

Homework
Workbook pages 34–35
MyEnglishLab

GRAMMAR 1 (SB page 71)

Past perfect simple

To start

Revise the past tense by telling a story round the class. Write the title of your story on the board, e.g.
The worst day of my life.

Begin the story by saying something like:

When I woke up, it was raining. I knew it was going to be a terrible day.

Nominate a confident student to continue the story and continue around the class until everyone has had their turn. Conduct class feedback, addressing any problems with past simple and continuous.

Grammar XP

Read the information and examples in the Grammar XP box aloud to your students. Demonstrate the meaning of the past perfect by drawing a line on the board. Explain that this line represents the past and a sequence of events which happened in the past. Write a short anecdote of a few sentences on the board, e.g.

Mimi woke up feeling very nervous. Today was the day of her exam. She took the bus to school as usual. She felt really tired because she hadn't slept at all the night before.

Ask a student to come up to the board and underline all the verbs. Elicit which tense most of the verbs are in (past simple). Underline *hadn't slept* and ask: *Why is this different? When did this happen?* (the night before). Write the past simple verbs along the time line sequentially and draw an arrow to show that Mimi not sleeping happened before the other events in this story (that is why the past perfect is used). Elicit the form of the past perfect simple: *had/hadn't + past participle*

1 Students complete the sentences with the words in the box. Check answers around the class.

1 since **2** just **3** before **4** already **5** when **6** for **7** because

2 Students choose the correct answers. Allow students to check their answers with a partner before conducting class feedback.

1 went, had injured
2 saw, wagged
3 had been, noticed
4 went, had ever flown
5 enjoyed/had enjoyed, decided
6 visited, had ever seen

3 Ask students to read the text quickly. Ask questions to check understanding, e.g. *What did Mary Anning and her brother find?* (the skeleton of an Ichthyosaur); *What was exciting about the diplodocus skeleton?* (It was really big.). Students complete the gaps with the correct form of the verbs.

1 dug up
2 had found
3 became
4 changed
5 had been
6 had seen
7 had already heard
8 had never come across

Write on

4 Ask students to complete the sentences using the past perfect. Monitor as students write their sentences, checking for any problems with the meaning and form of the past form. Nominate a few students to share their sentences.

Students' own answers.

To finish

Explain that we often use the past perfect at the end of funny stories to explain something or show that we have done something silly. Write the following example on the board:

I went to the supermarket. I chose lots of food and drink. My trolley was completely full. I went to the checkout to pay and looked in my bag for money. I had forgotten my purse!

Ask students to think of similar situations where they made a mistake or did something silly. Give them a minute to jot down their ideas before sharing their stories with a partner. Conduct class feedback and ask a few students to share their stories.

Homework
Workbook page 36
MyEnglishLab

VOCABULARY 2 (SB page 72)
Describing places and experiences

To start

Write the following on the board:

It was the worst birthday present …

Ask students to complete the sentence with something true for them and think of two more pieces of information about their worst ever birthday present. Allow students to share their ideas with a partner before conducting class feedback,

e.g. *It was the worst birthday present I'd ever had. I'd told my mum I that I'd really like a Brazilian football strip. She didn't buy one though – she knitted it!*

Word XP

Write the following sentences on the board:

Our English lesson was interesting today.

Our English lesson was fascinating today.

Elicit which sentence uses a strong adjective (the second) and ask students why we use strong adjectives (to make what we are saying sound more interesting and dramatic). Focus students' attention on the information in the Word XP box. Ask students to give you examples of any other strong adjectives they know.

1 Read the words in the box aloud, drilling pronunciation chorally and individually. Write the words on the board and elicit where the stress lies in each. Students replace the adjectives in the sentences with the strong adjectives from the box. Check answers around the class.

1 filthy, dreadful   2 enormous   3 packed   4 terrifying, deafening
5 marvellous   6 exhausted, horrified

2 Students write the strong adjectives under the correct headings. Draw the table on the board and nominate students to come up to the board and write their words in the correct column.

bad: awful, disgusting, horrible, terrible
big: giant, huge, massive
nice: amazing, awesome, delightful, fantastic, wonderful

3 Read the words in the box and drill the pronunciation of *civilisations* /ˌsɪvəl-əɪˈzeɪʃənz/. Students choose the words to complete the collocations in the sentences. Allow enough time for students to quickly check their answers with a partner before conducting class feedback.

1 instrument   2 sites, civilisations   3 rain   4 heat

4 Focus students' attention on the photograph and the title of the article and ask them to predict what the *Dragon Dance* is and where it takes place. Then ask them to quickly read the article and find out whether or not they were correct. Students then complete the article with the correct form of the word in capitals. Read the article around the class and check answers.

1 amazing   2 decorated   3 colourful   4 successful   5 complicated
6 fascinating   7 deafening   8 entertainment

To finish

Write the following on the board:

I had a good day. I walked to school and the weather was good. I had a good English lesson and I had a good time with my friends in class. There was a party after school. It was good too.

Tell students they have one minute to convert this story into something much more exciting by using strong adjectives. When the time is up, ask students to read their new stories.

Homework
Workbook page 35
MyEnglishLab

GRAMMAR 2 (SB page 73)
Comparatives and superlatives

To start

Ask students to think of their favourite/least favourite place and describe it to their partner. Tell them to use at least three of the adjectives they learned in the previous lesson. Nominate a few students to report back on what they learned about their partner's favourite place.

Grammar XP

Read the information and examples aloud to your students. Challenge the students by asking them to write as many sentences as they can comparing their classmates in one minute. When the time is up, ask students to count how many sentences they have collected. Write the sentences on the board. Where students have used a simple comparison, e.g. *Silva is taller than Josef*, ask students to modify their sentence using the language they have just learned, e.g. *Silva is slightly taller than Josef.*

1 Students complete the sentences with the correct form of the words in brackets. Point out that they may need to add some extra words. Allow students to check their answers with a partner before reading the sentences around the class.

1 more intelligent than
2 straighter
3 the fastest
4 less patiently
5 most famous
6 better
7 harder
8 as carefully

2 Students rewrite the sentences using the words in brackets. Check answers orally.

1 far hungrier than
2 much more slowly
3 slightly more interesting
4 the least enthusiastically
5 lot less happily

3 Students rewrite the sentences using the words in capitals. Work through the first one together as a class and ask students to complete the rest of the exercise alone. Allow students a few minutes to discuss their answers in pairs before conducting class feedback.

1 a bit more
2 the oldest (university) in
3 are less interesting than
4 as far away as
5 much more quickly (or much faster) than
6 far/a lot/much more popular

To finish

Organise students into groups. Practise comparatives by having a race to see if they can order themselves according to the following categories:

– shortest to longest hair
– shortest to tallest
– youngest to oldest
– biggest to smallest feet

Each time students order themselves correctly, ask them to explain the order they have grouped themselves in, using comparative and superlative forms.

Homework
Workbook page 37
MyEnglishLab

To start

Organise students into groups. Write the following sentences on the board and challenge students to see who can be the first to find and correct the errors:
Jenny works the most quickest in the class.
Ben is slightly more taller than Steve.
Max did a best in his geography test.
This place isn't as nice I thought.
Give them time to discuss in their groups before eliciting the answers and highlighting them on the board.

Power up

1 Focus students' attention on the photo and elicit the word *pyramid*. Ask students: *Have you ever seen a pyramid before? Where did you see it?* Read the questions aloud to your students and give them a minute to discuss their ideas. Conduct class feedback but don't give them the answers yet.

Students' own answers.

2 Drill the pronunciation in the words of the box, focusing on potentially tricky words, e.g. *descendant* /dɪˈsendənt/ and *jaguar* /ˈdʒægjuə/. Students match the words with their meanings. Check answers orally, asking students questions to check their understanding of the new words, e.g.
Tell me about a custom we have in this country. Could you survive without water? (no)

1 mural 2 survive 3 jaguar 4 descendant 5 cultivate
6 feathers 7 custom

Listen up

Background

The Mayan civilisation is famous for its art, architecture and astronomical systems. It is also well known for encouraging the development of writing and the calendar. Many descendants of the Mayans are still alive. These descendants keep Mayan traditions, beliefs and language alive.

3 Tell students that they are going to hear the first part of a talk about a Mayan exhibition. Before you play the recording ask students: *Who were the Mayans? Where did they live? When did they live?* Write students' ideas on the board. Play the recording and ask students to check their answers.

Guide: Firstly, welcome to the Mayan exhibition, part of our *Amazing Civilisations of the Past* series, and I hope you're going to enjoy our tour today! The Mayan people first arrived in the rainforests of southern Mexico and Central America around three thousand years ago. Their civilisation is a fascinating one for many reasons, as we'll see this morning. It lasted for over one thousand five hundred years and, fortunately, enough buildings and objects have survived from that time to give us a good picture of what their life was like.

Over here is a model of one of their amazing pyramids which is still standing. It's called the El Castillo pyramid. It's just under one hundred feet high – that's thirty metres in total, including the small temple on top. It has four sides, as you see from this model, and each side has a staircase with ninety-one steps. So in total, including the final sort of 'step' on top, that makes how many steps? Yes, three hundred and sixty-five – and that, of course, is the number of days in a year!

---

1 nearly 30 metres/ 100 ft high
2 about 3,000 years old
3 the Mayans

4 Read the Skill advice aloud to your students. Give them a minute to carefully read the sentences and encourage them to predict the information required for each gap. Play the recording while students complete the gaps with one or two words. Allow students to check their answers with a partner before conducting class feedback.

Guide: Firstly, welcome to the Mayan exhibition, part of our *Amazing Civilisations of the Past* series, and I hope you're going to enjoy our tour today! The Mayan people first arrived in the rainforests of southern Mexico and Central America around three thousand years ago. Their civilisation is a fascinating one for many reasons, as we'll see this morning. It lasted for over one thousand five hundred years and, fortunately, enough buildings and objects have survived from that time to give us a good picture of what their life was like.

Over here is a model of one of their amazing pyramids which is still standing. It's called the El Castillo pyramid. It's just under one hundred feet high – that's thirty metres in total, including the small temple on top. It has four sides, as you see from this model, and each side has a staircase with ninety-one steps. So in total, including the final sort of 'step' on top, that makes how many steps? Yes, three hundred and sixty-five – and that, of course, is the number of days in a year!

Here are some pictures of the type of environment the Mayans lived in. It was a difficult environment, with extremes of temperature going from torrential rain to baking heat and from floods to drought. Not only that, the Mayans lived in fear of the jaguar, the animal that was truly king of the jungle. However, despite all the hardships, they managed to cultivate the land so successfully that a population of several million people were eventually able to live there.

The Mayans developed a sophisticated civilisation. As we have seen, they built a large number of huge pyramids and palaces and they used to decorate these buildings with different sculptures – just have a look at these amazing carvings! They also painted murals on the walls and from them, we can learn a lot about their customs and ceremonies. You can still visit many of these buildings – and that's amazing when you think how long ago they were built.

From the paintings and sculptures that have survived, we can also see that the wealthier Mayans liked to wear colourful clothing made from animal skins and huge hats and headdresses made from feathers. The person who wore the tallest hat was considered the most important! In this display case are some examples of Mayan writing. The Mayans developed an advanced system of writing using hieroglyphics – that is, symbols that represent words, sounds or objects. It looks similar to Ancient Egyptian, but according to historical researchers, it is, in fact, quite different. You can compare the two here.

For relaxation, they enjoyed music and dance – as we can see from these decorated vases and sculptures – and they played a variety of musical instruments. They had hundreds of different dances, which were often given animal names, for example, the Snake Dance or the Monkey Dance. Some of these dances are still performed today.

They also enjoyed ball games and they built giant courts where they would hold special games. The Mayans made rubber balls using a substance called latex from the rubber trees that grew in the area. In the city of Chichén Itzá, archaeologists have discovered around thirteen different ball courts! You can see some photographs of them here.

The Mayan civilisation eventually collapsed around a thousand years ago, possibly because of a long period of drought. However, there are still descendants of the ancient Mayan people alive today, who carry on the traditions as best as they can. Well, I hope you enjoyed the exhibition today! Please feel free to ask any questions, and if you'd like to ...

---

1 three/3 **2** thirty/30 **3** steps **4** rain/ floods **5** palaces
6 murals **7** hat **8** (ancient) Egyptians **9** dances **10** Ball

Speak up

5 As a class brainstorm places of historical interest in your students' country. Write suggestions on the board. Ask students to choose one of the places on the board. Give them a minute to think about what they want to say. Organise them into pairs and ask them to speak about their chosen place. Circulate as students complete this task, offering support where necessary. Bring the class back together again and nominate a couple of students to talk about their chosen place.

Students' own answers.

To finish

Students write about the place of interest they presented in Exercise 5. Encourage students to illustrate their work and make it as attractive as possible. Collect students' work and make it into a leaflet. The finished piece of work can be kept in the classroom and given to students who are new to the area.

Homework

MyEnglishLab

SPEAKING (SB page 75)

To start

Organise students into pairs. Tell them they have one minute to remember and write down as many facts about the Mayan civilisation they can. When the time is up, give students a minute to work with another pair and compare their facts, adding any they have forgotten on to their own list.

Ask the groups of four to tell you how many facts they have collected. Students should then read their facts around the class. Award a point for each correct fact. The group with the greatest number of correct facts wins.

Power up

1 Give students a minute to look at the photos and discuss the questions with a partner. Then open this up into a class discussion and nominate students to answer the questions. Encourage students to talk about similar things which can be seen in their own country.

Students' own answers.

2 Explain that students are going to hear a girl answering an exam task. Ask: *Which photos is she going to talk about?* (A and B) *What two things must she do?* (She must compare the photos, say why people have chosen the places.). Tell students to note down three headings in their notebooks: *similarity*, *difference* and *reasons for visiting*. Explain that they should jot down a few notes under each heading as they listen. Check answers round the class.

► **Track 6.4**

Anna: Well, these are both photos of things in museums – different types of museums. Picture A is taken in the Natural History Museum and it shows us a model of a whale. In Picture B, on the other hand, we can see a mask which is probably from an ancient civilisation. One difference between the pictures is that the whale is a living creature while the object in Picture B isn't! I would say that the people have chosen to visit the museum in Picture A because they are interested in the natural world – and because of the size of the model! You don't often get the chance to see a whale in real life! For Picture B, they are probably interested in the history of different people and they want to learn more about their civilisation through the things they made and decorated.

similarity: both are museums

difference: Picture A show a whale, a living creature, Picture B shows a mask, an object

reasons for visiting: whale – interested in the natural world and because of its size; mask – interested in history and want to know more

3 Explain to students that when they are working with a partner in the Speaking exam, they will have to comment on their partner's photos after he or she has spoken. Students listen to the recording and note down the place the second student prefers and his reasons. Play the recording and check answers orally.

► **Track 6.5**

Eric: I'd prefer to go to a natural history museum and look at things like whales and dinosaurs. They're much more interesting than masks, in my opinion. It's great to look at these huge creatures and learn more about their habits. And for creatures like whales that still exist, it's important for us to learn how to take care of them better.

He would prefer to visit a natural history museum because it's more interesting than seeing historical exhibits and it is important to learn to take care of animals like whales.

Language XP

Read the information and examples in the Language XP box aloud to your students. Generate a personalised example of the new language by asking students a *Why?* question, e.g.

Why do you like swimming so much, Dani?

Elicit an answer containing *because* + clause or *because of* + noun, e.g.

I like swimming because it makes me feel energetic.

I like swimming because of my amazing swimming coach. She's great!

Ask students to ask each other *Why?* questions and give reasons using the new language.

Speak up

4 Read the Exam advice to the students and stress the importance of comparing rather than describing the photos. Do this by describing one of the photos, e.g. *There's a big blue whale in a museum. There are lots of people and there are other animal skeletons.* Ask students to tell you what you are doing wrong (describing one photo and not comparing both photos).

Divide the class into two groups: A and B. Tell each group to read the relevant card on the SB page. Allow them a minute to think about what they are going to say. Circulate as students prepare their ideas. Then ask students to find a partner from the other group to complete the activity with. Monitor as students complete this activity, taking note of any examples of good language and jotting down any problems which can be addressed in the class feedback session.

Students' own answers.

5 Keep students in the pairs they were in for Exercise 4. Give students a minute to work alone and prepare their answers. Then ask them to discuss their answers. Monitor as they complete the task, checking for accurate use of the target language. Conduct class feedback.

Students' own answers.

6 Ask students to turn to page 154. Give students a minute to look at their photos, read the task and prepare what they are going to say. Remind them to address both parts of the task. Students then take it in turns to speak about their photographs. Monitor as students complete this activity, offering support where necessary. Note down any incorrect sentences for use in the 'To Finish' activity for this lesson.

Students' own answers.

To finish

Use sentences you have collected to have a grammar auction. Choose five grammatically incorrect sentences you heard students say this lesson and five correct sentences. Put students into small groups. Give every group an imaginary £1,000. Nominate one student to be 'treasurer' and keep track of everybody's money.

Write one of the sentences on the board but do not tell students if it is correct or incorrect. Tell students that they can 'bid' for this sentence if they think it is worth buying. The group which offers you the highest price gets to keep the sentence. Continue in this way until you have sold all of your sentences. (If the group runs out of 'money', they have to stop bidding for sentences.) As a class, decide whether the sentences are correct or not. Groups win points for each correct sentence they bought. The group with the most points is the winner.

Homework

MyEnglishLab

WRITING (SB pages 76–77)

To start

Write the word *Egypt* on the board. Ask students to close their eyes and imagine that they are in Egypt. Ask them questions: *What do you see? What do you smell? What do you hear?* Ask students to raise their hands (without opening their eyes) and choose two or three students to describe their ideas.

Power up

1 Focus students' attention on the photographs and ask them to tell you what they see. Read the question aloud to your students and ask them to decide which of the items on this list they would include in a story about Egypt. Conduct class feedback, drilling the pronunciation of any tricky words as you do so, e.g. *Pharaoh* /ˈfeərəʊ/.

Students' own answers.

2 Ask students to discuss the elements of a good story with a partner. Encourage them to think of more items which are not included in the list. Check understanding of the various items by asking students to give you examples in stories they have read. Elicit the non-essential item on the list.

These are all important elements – only humour is not essential.

Plan on

3 Read the advertisement aloud to your students. Give students a minute to read the story alone. Ask students questions to check understanding, e.g. *Why did Amelia almost fall off her camel?* (She heard a loud scream.) *What did Amelia see later on in the afternoon?* (a mummy) *Was it a real mummy?* (No, it was an actor.). Ask students to read the story more slowly and decide which points from Exercise 2 the story includes. Conduct class feedback and ask students to explain their answers and give examples of each point from the story.

The story includes all the points from Exercise 2.

4 Students read the story again and put the paragraph headings in the correct order.

1 d 2 a 3 c 4 b

Word XP

Read the advice in the Word XP box aloud to your students. Write the following sentences on the board:

She walked over to the pyramid.

She heard a noise.

She felt frightened.

Ask students to suggest adjectives, adverbs and verbs to make these sentences more interesting and dramatic, e.g.

She crept over to the pyramid.

She heard an absolutely horrible noise.

She felt terrified.

Write students' ideas on the board.

5　Students find the adjectives, adverbs and more unusual verbs in the story. Conduct class feedback, encouraging students to check the meaning of any unfamiliar words.

adjectives: loud, shocked, baking, worried, fascinating, historical, mysterious, long, cool, strange, horrible, real

adverbs: fearfully, suddenly

verbs: fell off, sent (shivers), calmed down, hoped, were relaxing, sipping, raced out, flapping, thumped, breathed

6　Students choose the correct answers. Read the sentences around the class.

1 loud
2 splashed
3 floating
4 long
5 horrible
6 silently
7 screamed
8 drank

7　Read the Skill advice aloud to your students and elicit why time phrases and correct tenses are so important in a story (it can be very confusing if time phrases are not used and tenses are muddled because the reader will not know what order things happened in). Read the time phrases in the list aloud to your students and ask them to find more in the story. Check answers around the class.

just, when, at first, after, later that afternoon, when, suddenly, then

8　Students read the story quickly. Ask questions to check understanding, e.g. *Why did Harry and Florence go to the house?* (They wanted to see if the stories were true.); *What did they see in the house?* (something tall and thin); *What happened next?* (They ran away.). Students read the story again and complete the gaps.

1 Before
2 A few minutes later
3 At first
4 after a while
5 Then
6 Suddenly

Write on

9　Tell students they are going to write a story for a competition. Read the instructions aloud to your class.

Students' own answers.

10　Students work in pairs to brainstorm ideas for their stories and make a paragraph plan. Circulate as students do this, offering support where necessary.

Students' own answers.

11　Students write their story. When students have been writing for ten minutes, ask them to exchange work with a partner. Ask students to check each other's work, looking for interesting language and correct use of time phrases and tenses. Students complete their story. Nominate a few students to read their work aloud to the rest of the class.

Students' own answers.

Model answer

Tim and his friends were sitting in a boat going across the Nile, when suddenly, they saw a dark shape in the water. The sight sent shivers down Tim's spine. He had always been frightened of crocodiles, and many years ago his grandfather had been eaten by one. 'What are we going to do?' whispered Tim.

The friends sat very quietly in the boat, their hearts thumping. Tim's friend, Jimmy, had read a book about survival skills before coming on the trip. 'It's OK,' he said, quietly. 'Crocodiles can't swim around corners. We have to quickly steer the boat round a corner and then row towards the desert.'

The boys rowed as fast as they could towards the yellow sands in the distance. The crocodile followed close behind. They finally got to the desert, leaped out of the boat and lay on the sand, exhausted by their hard work. The crocodile stared at them for a few moments before swimming slowly away.

'Thank goodness.' murmured Tim. A minute later they heard a very loud roar. Tim opened his eyes and saw a large pair of claws. It was ... a tiger!

To finish

Organise students into groups. Ask them to read each other's stories and choose the one they like best. Students have a five minute time limit to act out the story. Give students time to prepare their short play before letting them act it out to the rest of the class. If students are writing their story as a homework exercise, then you can ask students to share their story outlines with the rest of the group. The rest of the group should give constructive feedback.

Homework

MyEnglishLab

SWITCH ON (SB page 78)

T.rex in town

1 Tell students they are going to watch a news report on an animatronic dinosaur (an animated model of a dinosaur). Ask students to read the sentences and choose the correct answer. Play the video and ask students to check their answers. Conduct class feedback.

1 tyrannosaurus 2 230 3 twelve

2 Read the questions aloud to your students. Play the video again while students watch and listen for the answers. Allow students to check their answers with a partner before conducting class feedback.

1 A 2 C 3 C 4 B

3 Organise students into groups to discuss the question. Monitor as students complete this task, offering support where necessary. Conduct class feedback.

Students' own answers.

Project

4 Focus students' attention on the question. Read the guidelines and the example aloud and then organise students into groups. Allow students time to choose their historic object and discuss what they know about it. Then give them time to prepare their talk. Circulate as students do this, offering them advice on how to structure their talk where necessary. Students should then present their talk or make a video to show to the class. Watch the talks together and encourage students to give feedback on what they have seen.

REVISION (SB page 79)

1
1 nerves
2 fur
3 skeleton
4 brain
5 heart
6 claws

2
1 had left
2 already started
3 accepted
4 had read
5 had never been
6 just begun, was

3
1 B 2 B 3 A 4 D 5 C

4
1 more
2 as
3 in
4 less
5 than
6 the

5
1 civilisation
2 baking
3 torrential
4 Colourful
5 entertainment
6 fascinated
7 decorated
8 Musical

Homework
Workbook pages 38–39
MyEnglishLab

The feel-good factor

Unit objectives

Reading:	multiple matching
Vocabulary:	people and relationships; being positive
Grammar:	modal verbs 1; *make, let, help*
Listening:	multiple-choice questions
Speaking:	collaborative task
Writing:	writing an informal email

READING (SB pages 80–81)

To start

Focus students' attention on the title of the unit and elicit what it means (a quality in something which makes people feel positive and happy). Organise students into pairs. Give them a minute to list as many activities as possible which they think have a 'feel-good factor'. Bring the class together and encourage students to share their ideas. Ask students to talk about how the activities they have chosen make them feel. Encourage them to say why their chosen activities make them feel this way.

Power up

1 Focus students' attention on the photos and elicit what they see. Ask them to work in pairs and decide what knowledge or abilities they would need to do these activities. Bring the class together and ask students to call out their ideas when you point to them. Write ideas on the board.

Students' own answers.

Read on

2 Focus students' attention on the article and the photos and names of the students. If necessary, pre-teach the following words and phrases: *class representative* (the person who speaks to teachers about the needs of his/her classmates), *peer group* (people who are the same age as you), *charity* (an organisation which makes money for good causes) and *obvious* (very clear to see or understand). Ask students questions to check understanding, e.g. *Is there a class representative in this class?; Are your peers your mum and dad?* (no); *Are they your classmates?* (yes); *Does money from a charity go to a rich business?* (no); *Does it go to help people who need it?* (yes); *If something is obvious is it difficult to see?* (no). Students read the article quickly and find out which activity each teenager chose to do. Conduct class feedback.

Naomi: chess
Leo: long-distance running
Harper: survival course
Mick: surfing

3 Read the Skill advice aloud to your students and ask them to underline the key words in each question. Briefly conduct feedback to check that students have underlined the correct words. Students then read the article again more slowly and match the questions with the people. Check answers around the class.

1 C   2 B   3 D   4 A   5 A   6 D   7 B   8 C   9 A   10 D

4 Students read the text in more detail and complete the task on their own. Allow them to check their answers with a partner before conducting whole class feedback.

1 nerdy   2 tactics   3 inseparable   4 confided   5 survival   6 tough
7 trekked   8 addicted   9 hooked

Sum up

5 Allocate students into A and B pairs. Ask them to take turns to describe each student's problem and the solutions they found. Monitor as students do this, offering support as necessary.

Students' own answers.

Speak up

6 Give students a couple of minutes to discuss which activities they would enjoy in small groups. Then open this up into a whole class discussion. Encourage students to give reasons for their answers, e.g. *I'd enjoy surfing. Unfortunately I live really far away from the sea, but I think it looks like a really exciting and refreshing sport. I'd love to try it!*

Students' own answers.

To finish

Tell students about a young person you know who has recently moved to your students' town and is feeling very lonely and unhappy. Explain that this person is very shy, doesn't speak the local language and isn't very good at sports. Organise students into groups and ask them to suggest an activity (not from the reading task) which would help the person to feel happier in their new home. Nominate a student from each group to report back on their group's ideas and decide together on the best solution.

Homework
MyEnglishLab

VOCABULARY 1 (SB page 82)

People and relationships

To start

Draw a triangle on the board and at each point write the name of a person who is/was important in your life, e.g. Kath (your grandmother), Mr Hardy (your favourite teacher) and Maya (your best friend). Ask students to guess who the people are and why they are important to you. Ask students to draw their own triangles with names of three important people. Organise students into pairs and ask them to talk about the people they have chosen. Ask a few students to share with the rest of the class.

1 Read the words in the box aloud and drill pronunciation orally and individually, focusing on any tricky words, e.g. *council* /ˈkaʊnsəl/. Students complete the sentences with the words in the box. Check answers around the class.

1 council **2** mates **3** opponents **4** peer group **5** competitors **6** coach

2 Students complete the bold phrases with the words in the box. Check answers orally. Write the phrases on the board and drill pronunciation and intonation of the whole sentences.

1 mistakes **2** direction **3** part **4** feet **5** way **6** trick **7** camp

3 Do the first item together as an example. Ask students to refer back to the reading text on page 81 and find the phrasal verb *get sb down* (it is in a past tense form in the text). Ask a confident student to read the whole sentence aloud and guess what the phrasal verb means before matching it to its meaning. Students complete the rest of the task alone. Allow students to check their answers with a partner before conducting class feedback.

1 d **2** b **3** e **4** a **5** c

4 Ask students to read the questions before listening. Play the recording, twice if necessary. Allow students to discuss their answers with a partner before checking answers around the class.

► Track 7.1

Jaci: You know, sometimes just getting away from your normal routine helps you to see things more clearly. I was a bit depressed because my sister and I had started arguing a lot about silly things. When we were younger, we were fine, but now we were both in our teens, nothing was the same anymore and it was really getting me down. Anyway, my friend Tina invited me to go away with her family for a weekend, on a farm. It was half term at school and I really needed a break. It was fantastic there. We went horse-riding and played with some kittens belonging to the farm cats. Tina cheered me up, too, by telling me about how she'd solved the problems she was having with her two brothers! So when I got back home, I talked to my sister and said I was sad about the situation. She said that she was, too, so we're both trying very hard now. Certainly, she's not going to draw me into any more arguments. I shall just walk away, if necessary. It's really not worth it!

1 getting away from your normal routine.
2 She and her sister were arguing a lot about silly things.
3 by telling her about how she'd solved the problems she was having with her brothers.
4 She talked to her sister about the situation.
5 She's certain that she is not going to have any more arguments with her sister.

Word XP

Read the information and examples aloud to your students. Model the language by giving some examples about yourself, e.g. *I'm keen on travelling. I'm addicted to coffee. I'm passionate about football.* Write one example on the board and underline the adjective and preposition.

5 Students complete the sentences with adjectives from the Word XP box. Point out that in many cases more than one adjective is possible. Allow students to compare answers with a partner before checking.

1 proud **2** afraid/frightened **3** brilliant/good **4** passionate/enthusiastic **5** keen/hooked

6 Students write three sentences about themselves using adjectives from the Word XP box. Nominate students to read their sentences aloud to the rest of the class.

Students' own answers.

Game on

Pick a confident student to demonstrate the game with you. Choose an adjective from the unit, e.g. *addicted* and tell them the first letter (a). If they can't guess the adjective tell him/her that this adjective means when you can't live without something. Students play the game. Circulate, focusing on correct pronunciation of the adjectives. Encourage students to play the game with their books closed to increase the level of challenge.

To finish

Write the following sentence beginnings on the board:
I'm brilliant at …
I'm worried about …
I'm hooked on …
I'm frightened of …

Complete the sentences with information which is true for you, e.g. I'm brilliant at baking. I'm worried about global warming. I'm hooked on learning new languages. I'm frightened of dogs.

Organise students into pairs. Tell them to complete the sentences about themselves and then predict how their partner has completed his/her sentences. Allow students to check their predictions with their partners before conducting class feedback.

Homework
Workbook pages 40–41
MyEnglishLab

GRAMMAR 1 (SB page 83)
Modal verbs (1)

To start

Tell students about a real or imaginary problem you have, e.g. *I don't know what to do about my neighbour. She's always having really loud parties in the middle of the week and I'm finding it really difficult to sleep. Then it's hard to stay awake at work the next day. I'm frightened to speak to her, because I've heard she can be violent. What should I do?*

Allow students to discuss their ideas for a few minutes before conducting class feedback. Listen to your students' advice and take a mental note of any issues with modal verbs which can be addressed in the grammar lesson.

Grammar XP

Read the information and examples aloud to your students. Generate further examples by telling your students about a real or imaginary problem you have e.g. *I can't sleep at night because my neighbour makes so much noise.* Write the advice your students give you on the board, encouraging them to refer to the examples in the box to vary the language they use, e.g. *You ought to speak to your neighbour. You'd better not put up with it any longer. You should think about moving house.*

Focus on natural sounding pronunciation, encouraging students to use contractions where possible, e.g. *you'd better* /juːdbetə/.

Generate examples of modals for permission and obligation by asking students to tell you what they are or aren't allowed to do at school. Collect as many examples as possible, e.g. *We're not allowed to wear high heels to school. We have to help clean the classroom. We've got to do our homework.*

1 Students choose the correct modal verb to complete each sentence. Check answers around the class.

....
1 Might **2** could **3** must **4** may **5** don't need to **6** you'd better **7** Would **8** needn't

2 Focus students' attention on the title and ask them to complete the text with the modal verbs. Ask: *Which of these things do you do? Which do you think you should try?* Read the text around the class.

....
1 should, can't **2** shouldn't **3** allowed **4** may, had **5** need

3 Students rewrite the sentences using the words in brackets. Allow students to check their answers with a partner before checking answers around the class.

....
1 You'd better not go running if you're not feeling well.
2 I wasn't able to walk very far because of my bad foot.
3 My parents said I wasn't allowed to go to the late-night disco.
4 You don't need to take me there – I can find my own way.
5 You ought to ask the coach before you leave training early.

Speak up

4 Model the activity by saying something like: *I agree that you need to compromise because I don't think anyone should get their own way all the time.* Organise students into pairs and ask them to discuss the rest of the points, giving reasons for their answers. Bring the class back together again and discuss, generating as much of the target language as possible.

....
Students' own answers.

5 Organise students into pairs. Tell them they are going to work together to prepare advice for parents who have teenage children. Elicit one idea and write it on the board as an example. Students then continue thinking of ideas with their partner. Monitor as they do this, offering support as necessary. Bring the group back together and write students' ideas on the board. How many of the pairs came up with the same advice?

....
Students' own answers.

To finish

Tell your class about things you had to do when you were a child, e.g. *I had to mow the lawn every Sunday and I had to keep my room really tidy.* Ask students to make a list of things they had to do when they were small children.

Write the following discussion question on the board: *Is life harder for young people today than it used to be?* Give students a minute to work with a partner and jot down some ideas. Then open this up into a class discussion and generate as many ideas as possible. Focus throughout on students' use of modal verbs.

Homework
Workbook page 42
MyEnglishLab

VOCABULARY 2 (SB page 84)
Being positive

To start

Ask students what kind of animal they would be and why. Give an example for yourself, e.g. *If I was an animal, I'd be an owl. I don't need much sleep and I can work and concentrate better at night time.*

Ask students to write down what kind of animals they would be on a small piece of paper. Collect the pieces of paper and redistribute them around the class. Students must move around the room and try to guess the owner of the piece of paper. They must give reasons for their guesses. When they are correctly identified as the writer of an animal, they must explain why they chose the animal. Elicit some of the animals and write useful language on the board.

1 Students read the adjectives in the box and decide which ones best describe them and share with a partner. Bring the class together and ask students to speak about their partner's adjectives and why they chose them. Focus on pronunciation: write longer words on the board and elicit where the stress lies. Drill the pronunciation of any tricky words, e.g. *cautious* /kɔːʃəs/, *decisive* /dɪˈsaɪsɪv/. Ask students to choose adjectives which describe their best friend and complete the process.

Students' own answers.

2 Students complete the sentences with adjectives from Exercise 1. Check answers around the class.

1 confident   2 anxious   3 supportive   4 competitive   5 protective
6 aggressive

Word XP

Read the information and examples in the Word XP box to your students. Drill the pronunciation of the adjectives ending in *-ous, -ive* and *-ent*.

3 Read the Exam advice aloud to your students. They complete the sentences with words from the Word XP box. Ask them to check that their answers are in the correct form and that they fit grammatically in the sentence. Allow students to discuss their answers with a partner before conducting class feedback.

1 furious   2 destroy   3 depend   4 suspicion   5 dependent
6 persisted

4 Ask students to complete the gaps in the article with the correct form of the words, reminding them of the Exam advice which they read earlier.

Ask questions to check understanding and practise the language of this lesson, e.g. *How did Harry and Julian get on when they were very young?* (They were very competitive.); *What was their relationship like at junior school?* (They were always together.); *How did this change at secondary school?* (They found different groups of friends.). Allow students to compare answers with a partner before reading the article around the class.

1 adventurous   2 competitive   3 furious   4 confidence
5 inseparable   6 different   7 anxious   8 aggressive

To finish

Play *The minister's cat* around the class. Begin by saying: *The minister's cat is an aggressive cat.* The next student must think of an adjective which begins with b, e.g. *The minister's cat is a bright cat.* Continue around the class, encouraging students to use the new adjectives from this lesson wherever possible.

Homework
Workbook page 41
MyEnglishLab

GRAMMAR 2 (SB page 85)

make, let, help

To start

Organise students into pairs. Ask them to choose three adjectives from the Vocabulary lesson and write definitions for them. They read their definitions to their partner, who must listen, find the word and write it down. Students get one point if they guess the word and one point if they spell it correctly.

Grammar XP

Read the information and examples in the Grammar XP box aloud to your students. Generate personalised examples of the new language by asking students to make sentences about what their parents make them do and let them do. Ask them to make sentences about when they were very young and about now, e.g. *When I was a child my mum made me have short hair. Now I'm older she lets me have it long.*

1 Students complete the sentences. Check answers around the class.

1 let   2 made   3 help   4 made   5 helps   6 made   7 made

2 Students complete the sentences. Read the sentences around the class, pausing for students to shout out the correct forms.

1 made   2 were made   3 were allowed   4 let   5 helped

3 Students rewrite the sentences. Ask them to refer to the Grammar XP as necessary and compare answers with a partner.

1 him tidy his room every week
2 allowed to go out of the school at lunchtime
3 her very upset
4 me (to) do the sports project

4 Check students' understanding of *I'm sick of* (I'm unhappy about). Students read the article and complete the task. Ask students questions to check their understanding, e.g. *What did the girl not like about being shy?* (She didn't like blushing.); *What did she do about it?* (She went up to a group of kids and started chatting.). *How had her family helped her?* (They hadn't allowed her to go to a friend's party so she was in the restaurant with them when she saw the kids from her school.). Ask students if anything similar has ever happened to them

1 makes   2 down   3 had   4 to   5 let   6 should   7 me   8 made

To finish

Write the following questions on the board:

What makes you angry?

Have you ever helped a friend to do something difficult?

What are you made to do in sports lessons at school?

Do you think that teenagers should be allowed to stay out late on school nights? Why/Why not?

Ask students to discuss their ideas with a partner. Monitor as students do this, checking that they are using the target language accurately. Conduct class feedback.

Homework

Workbook page 43

MyEnglishLab

LISTENING (SB page 86)

To start

Write the following sentence on the board:

The teenage years are the best years of your life.

Ask students to discuss with a partner whether or not they agree or disagree. Circulate, noting down any interesting language or ideas that you hear.

Power up

1 Ask students what are some typical problems for teenagers in their country. Organise students into small groups and ask them to discuss. Nominate a student from each group to report back, listing ideas on the board.

Students' own answers.

2 Focus students' attention on the words in the box and ask them to match them with their meanings. Conduct class feedback, checking that students understand the meaning of the new language by asking questions, e.g. *Who do you get on well with in your family, Anita? I have my ups and downs with my mum. Does this mean we always get on really well?* (no); *Does it mean we argue sometimes and get on well the rest of the time?* (yes).

1 make sense

2 find your own way

3 talk things through

4 can't stand

5 get on well

6 have our ups and downs

Listen up

3 Focus students' attention on the photo of Lily and her home city. Read the question aloud to your students and tell them to listen carefully and see what they can find out about Lily's family. Play the recording. Allow students a minute to compare ideas with a partner before conducting class feedback.

➤ Track 7.2

Interviewer: This month we went to sunny Greece and met Lily Manousakis, who lives in Athens. Lily, first of all, could you tell us a bit about your family?

Lily: Hi, everyone! Well, I'm fifteen and I live with my family in Athens. I suppose you could say that we're not a typically Greek family since my mum's English and my dad's Greek. Lots of my friends envy me because I grew up here being bilingual in English and Greek and we often visit England! I've got one sister, Katie, who's five years older than me, and we usually get on pretty well.

Her mum is English and her dad is Greek. They live in Athens. She has a sister who is five years older than her.

4 Read the Exam advice aloud to your students. Give them a minute to read the questions carefully. Remind them that they will not necessarily hear exactly the same words in the recording. Play the recording while students choose the correct answers. Check answers around the class. Ask: *How is Lily's family life similar to yours? How is it different?*

➤ Track 7.3

Interviewer: This month we went to sunny Greece and met Lily Manousakis, who lives in Athens. Lily, first of all, could you tell us a bit about your family?

Lily: Hi, everyone! Well, I'm fifteen and I live with my family in Athens. I suppose you could say that we're not a typically Greek family since my mum's English and my dad's Greek. Lots of my friends envy me because I grew up here being bilingual in English and Greek and we often visit England! I've got one sister, Katie, who's five years older than me, and we usually get on pretty well.

Interviewer: And how do you get on with your parents?

Lily: Oh, you know, we have our ups and downs, but generally, things are quite good. There are definite rules in our house about what time you should be back home if you go out, but I suppose that makes sense. Certainly, if I disagree with something, I'll say so, but we usually talk things through and find a solution. Dad's fairly laid-back really. It's Mum who organises us all!

Interviewer: Your sister is quite a well-known singer, even though she's only twenty. How do you feel about that?

Lily: My sister entered a TV talent show when she was seventeen and I couldn't believe it when she won! Certainly, her life changed dramatically after that and now she sings professionally. There was a period when I compared myself with her and thought I could never do something like that. You see, I'm hopeless at singing! But I know I'll find my own way in life, eventually.

Interviewer: What's your relationship like with your peer group at school, Lily?

Lily: Well, I've got a couple of close friends and we do most things together. I can't stand some people in my class and they can't stand me! However, I don't let that get me down – I just ignore them! There's a bit of pressure to look cool – you know, you must wear the right kind of clothes and so on, and that did use to make me feel anxious. But I feel more confident about that sort of thing now.

Interviewer: Do you manage to get a good balance between your schoolwork and your free time?

Lily: Not really, because we have loads of homework and I also have private French lessons. So, during term time, I can't do much apart from schoolwork. The school doesn't organise many activities outside school, but there are one or two clubs you can join. I've tried various things – gymnastics, tennis, ballet – but I'm not really very good. I'm keen on photography though.

Interviewer: How do you fill your time in the summer holidays?

Lily: Well, we have nearly three months off in the summer – fantastic if you're able to spend all that time by the sea! My parents both work most of the summer, so I've been going to a youth camp the last few years. I was a bit homesick the first time, but it's good fun and now I've made loads of friends there. I meet up with them each year. It's a bit like having a second family! Maybe I'll become a team leader there after I leave school.

Interviewer: And finally, Lily, a few words of wisdom for our teen listeners?

Lily: Well, I'd say that you shouldn't worry too much about what other people look like. Find your own style and go with it. Most importantly, you don't have to listen to people who try to make you feel bad. Just walk away and be strong in yourself. That's all that matters.

Interviewer: Many thanks, Lily. It was great talking to you.

---

1 B **2** C **3** A **4** B **5** A **6** C **7** B

Speak up

5 Elicit what Lily's advice is at the end of the interview. (Don't worry about how other people look: find your own style and go with it. Don't listen to people who make you feel bad: just walk away and be strong in yourself). Working in pairs, students discuss whether or not they think this is good advice and what other advice they would give to teenagers. Circulate as students complete this task, offering support where necessary.

Students' own answers.

To finish

Write the following headings on the board:

elderly people

parents

unemployed people

teachers

Organise students into small groups and ask them to choose one of the categories on the board. Students then have to brainstorm the problems that these groups of people typically face.

After one minute, call out 'Stop!' and ask students to think of advice they would give to this group of people. Conduct class feedback, e.g. Ideas for 'parents'

Problems: *disobedient children, unable to communicate with them, money worries, not enough time to spend at home with the family*

Advice: *try to make time to talk with your children; don't worry so much about money*

Homework

MyEnglishLab

SPEAKING (SB page 87)

To start

Ask students to think of five activities in English. Play *Hangman* with your students, asking them to take it in turns to come up to the front of the classroom and write the number of dashes on the board for their activity. The rest of the class has to guess letters until they arrive at the right word.

Power up

1 Focus students' attention on the photos and ask them to name the activities (snowboarding and horse-riding). Ask students how popular these activities are with the teenagers they know. Find out if any of your students do these activities and ask them to tell the class a little about them, e.g. *Snowboarding isn't that popular with teenagers where I live because we don't often get any snow.*

Students' own answers.

2 Focus students' attention on the five activities shown and ask students to read the question. Tell them they are going to listen to two students discussing the question. They must note down which activities are mentioned. Play the recording and check answers around the class.

> ➤ **Tracks 7.4 and 7.5**

Alice: Well, shall I start?

Tom: Yes, fine.

Alice: OK, let's see. Er ... I think all the activities can help teenagers in different ways. Firstly, to get fitter, and also to become more confident. They're all quite difficult, so if you can get good at one of them, that's quite an achievement to be proud of. Snowboarding, for example: it can't be easy to keep your balance on a snowboard, so if you did this regularly, you'd develop your muscles and get stronger, wouldn't you? And also, you'd get out in the fresh air, which everyone says is good for you. But if I tried it, I think I'd fall over all the time!

Tom: Hmm, I don't think so. Practice makes perfect, you know! Then there's street dancing. Well, that makes you really fit because you have to practise a lot. And it's something you do with other people. It's a great feeling to be part of a team and perform in front of people.

Alice: That's true. It's good to be in a team, I think, because you learn how to get along with people better and work together and performing gives you confidence. I'm not sure about the horse-riding. You know, it's an expensive hobby, but it's a skill like all the other activities and I'm sure it's not as easy as it looks! I think the benefits would be about building up a relationship with the horse.

Tom: You're right there. Lots of people are afraid of horses, but that's one place where you mustn't show your fear!

snow-boarding, street dancing, horse-riding

Language XP

Nominate students to read the Language XP box aloud. Ask students if they know any other ways of expressing agreement or disagreement and write their ideas on the board.

3 Tell students that they are going to listen to the recording again and note down the phrases from the Language XP box which the two speakers use. Play the recording, twice if necessary. Allow students to check their answers with a partner before conducting class feedback.

Agreeing: Yes, fine. That's true. You're right there.

Disagreeing: I don't think so.

Speak up

4 Organise students into pairs. Tell them that they are going to do the task in Exercise 2. Read the question carefully, making sure that students understand there are two parts to the exercise (doing the task in Exercise 2 and choosing the two most difficult activities).

Read the Skill advice aloud to your students. Monitor as students complete the activity, encouraging them to vary the ways in which they agree or disagree with their partner, and encouraging them to use the Language XP box to help them. Organise students into groups and ask them to report back on the discussion they had with their partner. Finally, conduct class feedback; discuss the benefits of each activity and ask a student from each group to say which activities they found most difficult, giving reasons for their choice, e.g. *Martial arts would be difficult because it's a very controlled and precise activity and you need to be very strong and fit.*

Students' own answers.

To finish

Ask students to think of three statements their friends and families would disagree with them about and write them down. Give them a couple of your own examples, e.g.

Maradona is the best footballer who ever lived.

Tea is much better than coffee.

Ask the students whether they agree or disagree with you. Encourage them to use the agreeing/disagreeing language they have learned in the speaking lesson. Ask students to share their sentences with a partner and agree or disagree with their partners.

Homework

MyEnglishLab

WRITING (SB pages 88–89)

To start

Give students an adjective quiz. Read out the following definitions and ask them to listen and write down the adjective.

Someone who gets angry very easily is ...

Someone who feels sure of themselves is ...

Someone who can look after themselves is ...

Ask students to think of three adjectives and write their own adjective quiz. Ask students to swap the quizzes they have written with a partner. Conduct class feedback.

Power up

1 Focus students' attention on the teenagers in the photos. Organise students into pairs and ask them to imagine what the teenagers might be like and choose adjectives to describe them. Collect adjectives around the class, asking students to give reasons for their choice of adjectives.

Students' own answers.

Plan on

2 Students read the email. Ask students to answer the two questions in pairs, and then elicit the problem and advice from the class.

The problem is that her teachers and parents compare her to her clever older cousin. She asks for advice about how to improve things at school and what to say to her parents.

3 Ask students to imagine they are Becky's friend and to think about what the reply email should include. Students select what should be included from the list of items. Allow students to talk about their choices in pairs before conducting class feedback.

1, 3, 5

4 Ask students to read Cathy's reply and answer the questions. Check answers around the class. Ask students if they agree with Cathy's advice, encouraging them to give reasons for their answers.

1 She includes points 1, 3, 5.

2 She recommends taking up a new sport or hobby and talking to her parents.

3 When the teachers see her doing it well, they'll stop comparing her with her cousin. The parents might not realise what they're doing and will understand.

5 Students match the paragraphs in Cathy's email with the topics. Check answers orally.

1 C   2 D   3 A   4 B

Language XP

Read the phrases for giving advice. Stress that if they are writing a letter of advice, they should vary the language they use. Elicit some other ideas and write them on the board.

6 Students read Cathy's email and identify the different ways in which she gives advice. Conduct class feedback, asking if they agree with the feedback she used and why/why not.

Perhaps you should ...

Why don't you ... ?

Try to ...

7 Students choose the correct answers. Allow them time to check their answers with a partner before reading sentences around the class.

1 talking   2 take   3 asking   4 make   5 explain

8 Students match the explanations with the advice from Exercise 7. Check answers orally.

1 b   2 d   3 e   4 c   5 a

9 Elicit the difference between formal and informal by asking: *Who would you write an informal letter to?* (friends, people your own age, close family members); *When might you write a formal letter?* (if you were applying for a job or a place at college, complaining about something, writing to a teacher, etc.). Students read the beginnings and endings and find the phrases used by Cathy. Ask students to tell you which other phrases would be appropriate and write these on the board.

Beginning:

Hi Becky,

Also appropriate: Dear Becky,

Ending:

Bye for now,

Also appropriate:

Speak soon, All the best,

Write on

10 Read the question aloud to your students and ask them to read Tina's email on their own. Check students' answers orally.

1 She asks for advice about making friends and dealing with her parents.

2 Students' own answers.

11 Students plan their reply to Tina, noting down the main points they want to mention. Circulate as students complete this activity, offering support where necessary.

Students' own answers.

12 Students write their email to Tina. Remind students to use the ideas and language on the page to help them. Ask students to check each other's emails. Write this check-list on the board for them to refer to:

Has he/she used different ways of giving advice?

Has he/she given explanations?

Has he/she begun and ended their letter in the right way?

Has he/she included expressions of sympathy and understanding?

Nominate students to read their emails aloud to the class.

Students' own answers.

Model answer

Hi Tina,

It was really nice to hear from you, but I'm sorry to hear things aren't going so well for you. It must be lonely not having many friends.

I think there are many things you can do to help yourself make friends though. For example, why don't you try taking up a new hobby or joining an after-school activity? That way you could meet people with similar interests to yourself. Having something in common is a good start to a new friendship. I know you're really interested in photography. Perhaps you should find out about photography clubs in your area?

As far as your parents are concerned, I think it might be a good idea to have a serious talk with them. You're seventeen years old and I don't think they've got the right to be so strict with you. If you explain that their rules are making it hard for you to make friends, I'm sure they'll see sense and try to compromise with you.

If you want me to come and stay with you for a few days, that's not a problem. Or if there's anything I can do to help – just ask.

Speak soon,

Jenny

To finish

As a class, generate a list of problems which are often experienced by teenagers, e.g.

exam worries, falling out with friends, worrying about your appearance, feeling like you don't fit in anywhere, etc.

Organise students into groups. Ask them to choose one of the problems and think about the best advice for dealing with it. If time permits, ask students to create role plays where one student explains their problem, and the rest of the group offers advice. Nominate a student from each group to report back on their discussion/perform their role play.

Homework

MyEnglishLab

SWITCH ON (SB page 90)

Smile and be happy

1 Organise students into pairs. Give them a minute to read the questions and give their opinion about the benefits of smiling a lot. Then play the video so that students can see if Petri, Ben and Sean think the same.

Students' own answers.

2 Give students a minute to read the questions and options, allowing them to check any words they are not sure of. Play the video again while students choose the correct answers. Allow them to compare their answers with a partner before checking answers orally.

1 A, C and D 2 feel, inside, face 3 D

3 Read the question aloud to your students and discuss it as a class. Generate as many different opinions and as much language as possible.

Students' own answers.

Petri wants to send a photo to her grandmother in Australia.

Project

4 Organise students into pairs. Ask students to read both options (A and B) and tell them they need to choose one of the two options. Alternatively, ask students to choose the option they like best before grouping them with students who have chosen the same option.

Monitor Group A students as they take their selfies. Bring the class together to look at the selfies and encourage students to offer their opinion about the fake and real smiles.

Group B will have to do their work out of school, but can make a start in class by discussing the form their vlog will take. In the following lesson, bring the class together to watch the video logs. Generate as much discussion as you can and encourage students to offer constructive feedback on their classmates' work.

Students' own answers.

REVISION (SB page 91)

1

1 about

2 up

3 of

4 on

5 up

6 at

7 away

8 on

2

1 won't be able to

2 aren't/are not allowed to use

3 ought to take up

4 have got to see

5 had better go

6 don't need to get/needn't get

3

1 decisive

2 dangerous

3 confident

4 adventurous

5 persistent

6 imaginative

4

1 d   **2** f   **3** a   **4** c   **5** e   **6** b

5

1 mistakes

2 self-sufficient

3 way

4 part

5 direction

6 embarrassed

7 trick

Homework

Workbook pages 44–45

08 Magic numbers

Unit objectives

Reading: multiple-choice questions
Vocabulary: maths; thinking skills
Grammar: the passive; quantifiers and pronouns
Listening: multiple-choice questions
Speaking: comparing photos
Writing: writing a review

READING (SB pages 92–93)

To start

Tell your students that this unit is going to be all about numbers. Read the following sum aloud to your class and challenge students to see who can be the first to solve it:

$12 + 3 - 4 + 5 + 67 + 8 + 9 = 100$

Write the sum on the board. Ask students to notice what is interesting about it (it has numbers 1–10 in chronological order). Ask students if they have any similar puzzles to share.

Power up

1 Ask students to name the items in the photos. Write their answers on the board.

A road sign   **B** mobile phone   **C** lift buttons

2 Ask students to work in pairs to think of places where they see numbers in everyday life, e.g. *speedometers in cars, phones, computers, clock faces*. After a couple of minutes, bring the class together again and collect ideas on the board.

Students' own answers.

Read on

3 Draw students' attention to the series of numbers in the box at the beginning of the article on page 93. Explain that this is a famous puzzle in maths (which they are going to read about). Give them one or two minutes to look at the numbers and try and work out the sequence, or what links the numbers.

Students' own answers.
Each number is the sum of adding together the number that comes before it.

4 If necessary pre-teach the following words: *reaction* (something you think or feel about an event), *eventually* (at last), *petals* (the brightly coloured parts of a flower) and *spiral* (winding around in a curve).

Check students' understanding by asking questions, e.g. *There's extra homework tonight. What's your reaction?* (I'm fed up, annoyed, etc.); *If something happens eventually, does it happen very quickly or does it happen slowly over time?* (slowly over time); *Where do you usually find petals?* (on a flower); *Can you see anything spiral in this classroom?* Focus students' attention on the title of the article and the photos. Ask them to read the article quickly and answer the questions. Check answers orally.

Name of series: the Fibonacci series (sequence)
Where you can find them: in nature, music, architecture and art

5 Students read the article more slowly and choose the correct answer for each question. Ask them to compare their answers in pairs and show each other where in the text they found their answers. Check answers around the class.

1 C   **2** B   **3** C   **4** D   **5** A   **6** B

6 Read the Exam advice to the students. Do the first question in the matching task together as a class to demonstrate how it is possible to work out the meaning of the word by the other words around it. Ask students to find the word *manage* in the text. The first student should read it out in the context of the sentence, e.g. *Well we can manage without these things, surely.* Elicit what these things are (clocks, calendars, etc.). Encourage students to guess the meaning of the word *manage* and match it to its definition. Students complete the rest of the task alone before class feedback.

1 stuff   **2** system   **3** occur   **4** missing
5 manage   **6** observed

Sum up

7 Ask students to read the list and think about their information. Organise students into small groups to discuss what they have learned, e.g. *I learned that Fibonacci numbers are found in the natural world, for example the seeds in a sunflower or in a pine cone.* Monitor as students complete this task, checking for comprehension and accurate use of new language.

Students' own answers.

Speak up

8 Write some important numbers in your life on the board and ask students to guess why they are important to you. Choose a range of significant numbers, e.g. *the year you met your best friend, the age you were when you started university, the number of times you sat your driving test.* Ask students to think of three numbers which are significant to them and to tell their partner about the numbers and why they are important. Nominate a few students to report back.

Students' own answers.

To finish

Tell students that they are going to write a questionnaire for the other students. The aim is to find out about important numbers for the class. Every question they write should have a number in its answer. Give students a couple of example questions, e.g. *When's your birthday? How many hours do you sleep every night?* Organise students into pairs and ask each pair to think of five questions. When students have had the chance to ask and answer their questions, bring the class back together again and discuss the results of the survey.

Homework
MyEnglishLab

VOCABULARY 1 (SB page 94)

Maths

To start

Organise students into two teams. Tell them that you are going to write some really long numbers on the board. The first student who reads out the number correctly wins a point for their team. Write the numbers on the board, one at a time and award points to students who can read them correctly, e.g. *2035* (two thousand and thirty five)

999,573 (nine hundred and ninety nine thousand, five hundred and seventy three)

1000001 (one million and one)

1 Ask students to match the sentences with the sums and then choose the correct answers. Check answers around the class.

1 E, divided by
2 C, minus
3 F, plus
4 A, add, to
5 D, multiplied by
6 B, subtract, from

2 Organise students into pairs. Challenge students to see who can be the first to do the sums in Exercise 1.

A 110   B 1,250   C 1,000   D 1,000   E 50   F 3,000,000

3 When students have completed the sums, play the recording so that they can check their answers. Ask students to repeat the numbers they hear. Drill pronunciation of the numbers chorally and individually.

1
Boy: OK. Let's try the game on this app. The faster you answer, the more points you score, so we'll have to be quick!
Girl: OK. Go! What's seven hundred and fifty divided by fifteen?
Boy: Hang on ... seven hundred and fifty divided by fifteen equals ...
Girl: Too slow! It's fifty. Let's try an easier level!
2
Boy: Right. First easy question: four thousand minus three thousand equals ... er ... one thousand.
3
Girl: One million plus two million equals three million, of course. Simple.
4
Boy: If you add thirty-seven to seventy-three, the answer is ... umm, oh, one hundred and ten.
5
Girl: Right. What's two hundred multiplied by five? No, don't use your calculator!
Boy: It's ... a thousand.
6
Girl: OK, last one. Subtract one hundred from one thousand three hundred and fifty.
Boy: The answer is ... it's one thousand two hundred and fifty.

4 Read the words in the box aloud to your students. Write the words on the board and elicit where the stress lies in each. Drill *mathematician* /mæθəmə'tɪʃən/ and *calculations* /kælkjə'leɪʃənz/. Students complete the sentences.

1 mathematician   2 base   3 zero   4 calculations   5 patterns
6 series

5 Challenge students to see who can be the first to match the words with the pictures. Check answers around the class.

A rectangle   B square   C triangle   D circle   E line   F spiral
G pyramid   H cube   I cone   J side

6 Focus students' attention on the words in the table and point out the headings *Adjective* and *Noun*. Students fill in the gaps with words from the table. Allow students to check answers with a partner before asking pairs to read the conversations aloud in turns.

1 width, wide
2 length, long
3 depth, deep, deep
4 height, high, high

Game on

Demonstrate the activity with your students. Nominate a confident student to come up to the board and announce that you are going to give him/her a maths challenge to complete. Ask the student to measure the width of the classroom door and write the measurement on the board. When your student has managed to do this, read the instructions aloud to your students and ask them to play the game in pairs. Circulate as students complete this activity, offering support as necessary.

To finish

Organise students into two teams. Ask them to form a line at the back of the classroom (where they are furthest away from the board). Give the students at the front of the line a board pen. Tell the teams they are going to have a numbers relay race. Stand at the front of the classroom and call out simple sums. The two students at the front of the queue have to race to the board and write the answer. The first student to write the answer correctly wins a point for their team. The students next in line then have a shot. Continue until every student has had a turn. The team with the most points at the end of the game is the winner.

Homework
Workbook page 46
MyEnglishLab

GRAMMAR 1 (SB page 95)

The passive

To start

Organise students into small groups and make sure that every group has a ruler. Tell students that they are going to practise the numbers they learned in yesterday's lesson by doing a treasure hunt around the classroom. Tell students that they have to race to find all of the following items in the classroom. When they have found them, they need to write down the name of the object with that shape or measurement.

a triangle

a rectangle

a pyramid

a spiral

a circle

something which is over a metre long

something which is over two metres wide

something which is less than a metre high

When a couple of groups have found all the items on their list, conduct class feedback.

Grammar XP

Read the information and examples in the Grammar XP box aloud to your students. Write these sentences on the board:

Mobile phones should always be switched off during English class.

Marks will be taken off any student who hands in homework late.

Pens have been borrowed from the drawer and not returned.

Ask students to comment on why the passive form has been used in each case.

1 Students choose the correct answers. Conduct feedback orally.

1 is written
2 invented
3 was killed
4 didn't have
5 have not been solved
6 will never be written down

2 Students rewrite the sentences in the passive. Allow time for students to check their answers with a partner before eliciting the correct sentences around the class.

1 The maths lesson has been cancelled (by the teacher).
2 The exam papers are going to be kept in the school office.
3 The results will not be known for weeks.
4 The maths teacher was seen at the café (by Jack and Ben).
5 Our class computers haven't been repaired yet.
6 This textbook is used by most classes.

3 Focus students' attention on the title. Ask students if they know what 'the golden ratio' is. Then ask them to read the article quickly to check. Students complete the article with the correct form of the verbs in brackets. They check their answers with a partner before feedback.

1 is related
2 has been used
3 was believed
4 is divided
5 get/will get
6 is called
7 see/will see
8 appears/will appear
9 be found
10 was built

Write on

4 Read the question and the example aloud to your students. Ask students to write two sentences about the past and future using the passive. Monitor as students complete the task, checking that they are using the passive voice accurately. Ask students to share their sentences in small groups before bringing the class together and asking them to share their sentences, e.g. *In the future, lessons will be taught by robots.*

Students' own answers.

To finish

Write the following on the board:

All children must be carried.

All breakages must be paid for.

Tell students that these are notices you have seen in public places. Ask students if they can guess what the places are (the first one is escalators on the London Underground and the second is in a shop selling lots of breakable items). Elicit that both of these sentences are written in the passive voice and ask students why they think this is the case. Explain that rules are often written in the passive voice, as it is more polite and less direct than saying, e.g. *You must carry your children. You must pay for your breakages.* Organise students into pairs. Ask them to write five rules for the English classroom using the passsive voice. Conduct class feedback. Select the best rules to display on your classroom wall.

Ideas:

All conversations must be in English.

Mobile phones must be switched off.

All food and drink must be eaten outside the classroom.

Homework

Workbook page 48

MyEnglishLab

VOCABULARY 2 (SB page 96)

Thinking skills

To start

Think of some general knowledge questions to ask your students. Use the passive voice, e.g. *In which country is flamenco dancing performed?* (Spain); *In which city can the Golden Gate Bridge be found?* (San Francisco)

Ask students to work in pairs and think of a general knowledge question using the passive voice. Monitor as students do this, offering support where necessary. Organise students into two teams. Students from each team take it in turns to ask their general knowledge questions. Conduct class feedback, focusing on any issues you have noticed with students' use of the passive.

1 Students read the sentences and choose the correct answers. Check answers around the class.

1 experience   2 news   3 research   4 equipment   5 intelligence
6 advice   7 knowledge

Word XP

Read the information in the Word XP box. Elicit the different meaning of the word *experience* in each sentence. In the first sentence the word *experience* is uncountable and refers to a person's entire 'life experience'. In the second sentence it refers to 'experiences'. It is countable and refers to something separate which takes place and lasts for a specific amount of time.

2 Work through the first sentence together with your students to demonstrate the activity. Ask students to choose the countable noun (*lights*) and uncountable noun (*light*) and elicit the difference between them. Students complete the rest of the task alone. Allow them to check their answers with a partner before conducting class feedback.

1a plural countable (electric lights)

1b uncountable (the energy that allows you to see things)

2a uncountable (space)

2b singular countable (in a building)

3a uncountable (time measured in minutes, hours, days, etc.)

3b plural countable (occasion)

4a plural countable (documents)

4b uncountable (the material)

5a plural countable (particular sounds)

5b uncountable (more general)

6a uncountable (employment, a job)

6b plural countable (sth such as a painting, piece of music, etc.)

3 Focus students' attention on the article and ask them to tell you what they know about James Bond. Write down students' ideas on the board and tell them to read the article and find out more. Students read the article and choose the correct answers. Read the article around the class and ask students to tell you what they learned about the famous spy.

1 A   2 C   3 A   4 B   5 D   6 A   7 C   8 A

4 Ask students to look at the answer options for Exercise 3. Challenge students to be the first to find all the uncountable nouns in the options. Check answers orally.

2 knowledge, imagination

3 information, notice (as in 'attention')

4 advice, speech (as in 'the ability to speak')

5 exploration, research

6 knowledge, learning, education

7 luggage

8 attention, knowledge, information, advice

To finish

Ask students to choose five words they have learned in this lesson, and then put them into pairs. Ask students to take it in turns to read their words to their partners, who must listen and write the words down. Once students have written down all their words, they can look at the book and check their spelling, awarding themselves one point for every word they have spelled correctly.

Homework

Workbook page 47

MyEnglishLab

GRAMMAR 2 (SB page 97)

Quantifiers and pronouns

To start

Write the following words on the board:

bread

coffee

business

failure

success

silence

Give students a minute to look at these words with a partner and decide what the words have in common. Elicit that these words can all be both countable and uncountable. Ask students to choose one word and write two sentences illustrating the difference, e.g.

Do you like coffee? Would you like a coffee?

There was a silence. Silence is golden.

Grammar XP

Read the information and examples in the Grammar XP box aloud to your students. Think of a topic and choose questions which your students will have a range of responses to, e.g.

Who likes football?

What's your favourite team?

Who likes David Beckham?

Ask the questions around the class, ensuring students pay close attention to their classmates' responses. Then ask students to make sentences about their class, using the language in the Grammar XP box, e.g.

Every student answered the question.

Nobody thought David Beckham was a good player.

Neither Roberto nor Luca like playing football.

They both like watching football.

1 Students choose the correct answers to complete the sentences. Check answers orally.

1 a few   2 Few   3 little   4 a little

2 Focus students' attention on the words in the box. Ask students to complete the sentences with the words. Point out that there is one word which they don't need. Conduct class feedback.

1 the other one   2 both   3 None   4 Neither   5 another one
6 each

3 Students complete the sentences. Read the sentences around the class.

1 nowhere   2 anyone   3 someone   4 nothing   5 anything
6 everywhere

4 Students complete the review. Ask students if they have ever been to a museum like this. If not, would they like to.

1 Few   2 neither   3 Everything   4 all   5 another
6 everyone/everybody   7 few   8 everywhere   9 none
10 something

To finish

Tell students to think of one interesting question they would like to ask everyone in their class and give them a few moments to jot it down. Give students a minute to circulate, asking their question to everyone in the class. When everyone has had a chance to ask the questions, ask the class to report back on what they have learned about their classmates. Ask students to use quantifiers and pronouns when they are reporting back and focus on accurate production of the target language.

Homework

Workbook page 49

MyEnglishLab

LISTENING (SB page 98)

To start

Write the following riddle on the board:

A man is looking at a photo of someone. His friend asks who it is.

The man replies, 'Brother and sisters, I have none, but this man's father is my father's son'.

Ask students: *Who is in the photo? (himself)*

Organise students into pairs and ask them to discuss their answers. Conduct class feedback.

Background

The Rubik's Cube was invented in 1974 by Hungarian, Erno Rubik. It has six faces, each covered by nine stickers, which are coloured green, yellow, red, blue, orange and white. You can mix up the colours by moving the individual cubes, and then you must try and get the cube faces back to one colour again.

The aim of Sudoku is to fill a 9 x 9 grid with numbers so that every column and row contains the digits 1–9. The name *Sudoku* is Japanese and means single number.

Power up

1 Read the list of challenges aloud to your students and check that they know the meaning of each one. Students then rank the challenges in order of how difficult they find them. Students work with a partner and compare their answers. Conduct class feedback. Ask students to tell you which of these challenges they like doing and find out if any of your students do challenges like this on a regular basis.

Students' own answers.

2 Explain that the words and phrases in the box all mean either 'difficult' or 'easy'. Ask students to work with a partner and decide where each word should go. Conduct class feedback. Then ask students to describe the activities in Exercise 1 using the new language.

Difficult: fiddly, hard, tough, tricky
Easy: a piece of cake, child's play, simple, straightforward

Listen up

3 Focus students' attention on the first of the questions in Exercise 4 and ask them to identify the key words, e.g. *interviewer, what does she say, event*. Students read the rest of the questions and identify the key words throughout, thinking about the information they should be listening for. Elicit ideas.

Students' own answers.

4 Read the Skill advice aloud to your students and make sure they have a pen and paper ready before they listen. Play the recording, twice if necessary, while students answer the questions. Allow students to check their answers with a partner before conducting class feedback.

➤ Track 8.2

1

Gabriella: Hi, this is Gabriella Martinez, your reporter for YBC news. I'm here at the I-Spy Convention. It's held in Toronto every year, and it's a game-based exhibition for young people with a focus on maths and problem-solving. If, like me, you enjoy logic, tricky puzzles and mini competitions, then this is the place to get your brain working. Over ten thousand people attend this event, so things can get a little noisy. I'll be speaking to various people about their experiences here and I'm also going to ...

2

Gabriella: We'll just go back to the studio for a brief weather report for those of you who will be coming to this event in Toronto.

Reporter: Yes, Gabriella, the weather has been a bit of a problem for the last few days, hasn't it, with those very strong winds and sudden showers? Luckily for you, things are getting calmer now and the rain is clearing away to the west. We've still got those grey skies and maybe a few odd showers this afternoon, but in general, it will be brighter and a little warmer today, so not too bad!

3

Gabriella: Oh right. Can I ask where you're from, Marcella?

Girl: Sure, I'm from Ottawa. I'm here for the weekend with other people from my school.

Gabriella: Great. And what's the best thing you've seen so far?

Girl 1: I really liked the talk about Magic Squares. The speaker explained how to solve them and then she showed everyone how to make them, too. Do you know how to do them? It's a piece of cake when you know how. Why don't you go? I'd really recommend it. It's fun.

4

Boy 1: The talk about spy techniques was brilliant! We learnt how some spies used pigeons!

Girl 1: Huh? I didn't go to that talk. What were you told about pigeons?

Boy 1: Well, this was before the days of planes. So if spies needed to go somewhere new, they had to find out who was there, what it looked like, etc. They trained pigeons to fly over the place. The pigeons were so clever – they carried tiny cameras which could photo the land and the buildings.

Girl 1: Amazing!

Boy 1: It's cool, isn't it? They tried using bats to do the same job, but that was too hard. They just flew off!

5

Girl 2: Hey, did anyone see that guy solving the Rubik's cube? He was amazing!

Boy 2: Well, he wasn't *that* good. I think I can do it nearly as fast as him. It's not that hard, really.

Girl 2: Maybe not for you. I thought he was really good at showing us how to solve it – he made it look like child's play.

Boy 2: Yeah, you're right about that.

Girl 2: It really helped me because I normally find it quite fiddly. I forget where I've got to.

6

Boy 3: I like the idea of writing secret messages. I never knew that lemon juice was used as invisible ink. Can you show us how to do it? Is it difficult?

Woman: It's all quite straightforward. You need a few drops of lemon juice and a thin stick. Dip it in the lemon juice and write – just let it dry. Look, there's nothing on the paper now. So, the person who receives the message can hold it over a light bulb, or something warm, like this and the message appears like magic!

Boy 3: Brilliant! I like the way it's so simple, but really clever at the same time.

1 C 2 B 3 A 4 B 5 B 6 C

Speak up

5 Read the questions aloud to your students. Organise students into groups to discuss their ideas. Nominate a student from each group to report back.

Students' own answers.

To finish

Ask students to think of things they do in the English class, e.g. learn grammar, new words, tenses, phrasal verbs. Ask them to discuss what they find difficult and what they find easy and encourage them to use the words and phrases from Exercise 2 when talking about their choices. Conduct class feedback.

Homework
MyEnglishLab

SPEAKING (SB page 99)

To start

Tell students that this lesson is all about challenges and that you are going to give them a challenge to start things off. Tell students that they have one minute. They need to write a sentence which includes as many of the new words they have learned in this unit as possible. The sentence must be grammatically accurate, although it should be as long as possible. Read the sentences around the class. Award a small prize for the best one.

Power up

1 Give students a few moments to read and think about the questions, and ask them to jot down their answers. Allow them to check their answers with a partner before conducting class feedback.

Students' own answers.

2 Organise students into pairs. Ask them to read the list of challenges and use words from Exercise 1 to describe them. Check answers around the class.

2 outdoors, mental (and physical), team

3 outdoors, physical, team

4 indoors, physical, team

5 outdoors, physical, individual

6 indoors, mental, individual

3 Organise students into small groups to discuss which challenge they would prefer to do and why. Circulate as students do this activity, listening to their answers and providing support where necessary.

Students' own answers.

4 Tell students that they are going to listen to four people talking about challenges. Read the question aloud to your student and elicit the meaning of *paraphrase* (saying something in a different way). Play the recording while students match the words with the paraphrases. Conduct class feedback.

► Tracks 8.3 and 8.4

1

Boy: I took part in the Canoe Challenge. I had to wear a life jacket and helmet. The instructor taught me how to use the ... umm, what's it called? The thing you move with ... the paddle.

2

Girl: We were in the Obstacle Course Challenge. We had to climb up ropes and over wooden bridges. Of course, we were wearing a special type of safety belt to fix us to the rope – a ... a harness, that's it. We didn't win, but it was a good challenge.

3

Boy: Our team was in the Football Challenge. I scored four goals, which was amazing. The other people who were taking part, the ... um, participants, were all very competitive, but we came second in the end.

4

Girl: I was in the Chess Competition. The place where we went was like a big hall. I was really nervous, but I came top in my age group.

1 paddle   2 harness   3 participants   4 venue

Language XP

Ask students what they do if they have forgotten a word in English. Point out that it is not always possible to look words up in the dictionary as this can slow things down too much. Read the sentences in the Language XP box and elicit that these are all ways in which we can deal with unknown or forgotten words

5 Focus students' attention on the photos. Tell them that you will play the recording again and that they need to match the speakers with the challenges. Check answers orally, asking students to tell you how they arrived at their answers.

Photo A: Speaker 4

Photo B: Speaker 2

Speak up

6 Organise students into pairs. Tell them that they are going to compare the photos in Exercise 5, using the questions to help them. Monitor as students complete the task, providing support where necessary, and encouraging students to use the phrases in the Language XP box to help them deal with words they don't know. Conduct class feedback.

Students' own answers.

7 Read the Exam advice to your students and focus students' attention on the three questions. Give them a minute to think about their answers before organising them into pairs and asking them to complete the discussion task. Circulate, offering support where necessary and noting any problems you hear. Conduct class feedback.

Students' own answers.

8 Organise students into pairs and ask them to turn to pages 156–157. Focus students' attention on the photos and the questions. Allow them a minute to prepare what they are going to say before they start. Monitor as students complete the task, noting any issues or any examples of good language.

Students' own answers.

To finish

Organise students into two teams. Remind them of the challenge at the beginning of the lesson. Tell them they are going to think of a similar challenge for the other team to complete. It must involve English in some way. Students work in their groups to set and perform each other's challenges. Conduct class feedback.

Homework

MyEnglishLab

WRITING (SB pages 100–101)

To start

Tell students that they are going to be talking and writing about digital games in this lesson. Ask students to prepare 2 or 3 questions that they would like to ask their classmates about their gaming habits. Give students a minute to prepare their questions and then organise them into small groups to ask and answer their questions. Conduct class feedback.

Power up

1 Organise students into pairs. Read the questions aloud and focus their attention on the items in the list. Ask them to discuss their ideas for a minute or so before opening this up into a whole class discussion. Ask students to report back on their discussions, generating as much language as possible and writing new vocabulary on the board.

Students' own answers.

Plan on

2 Read the rubric and the advertisement aloud to your students. Ask students to identify the key points which need to be included in the review. Conduct class feedback.

describe a game, explain the main idea and how to play it, give details of the game, personal opinion

3 Ask students to discuss Sabrina's questions in pairs. Check answers around the class.

1 for an English language gaming website; informal language
2 a text with clear paragraphs; it's a review
3 a review, you need to describe and explain

4 Give students a minute to read Sabrina's review. When they have finished ask them if any of them have ever played this game. If not, have they played something similar? Students match the paragraphs with the topics. Allow students to compare their answers with a partner before checking answers orally.

A 4 **B** 2 **C** 1 **D** 3

Language XP

Focus students' attention on the language in the Language XP box. Ask students if they can think of any more language to express an opinion about something.

5 Draw students' attention to the Skill advice and then read Sabrina's review again. Ask students to find phrases from the Language XP box which she uses in her review. Collect answers around the class.

If you ask me, Personally, It's bright/fun/addictive!

6 Nominate a student to answer the first question using language from the Language XP box. Students answer the questions using this language. Collect answers around the class.

Students' own answers.

7 Ask students to find examples of the linkers *if*, *so* and *when* in Sabrina's review. Check answers orally.

If you want to play a great game, When you start, When you get a line of three, so you can get a massive score, If you're clever, When this occurs, If you ask me,

8 Students complete the sentences. Read the completed sentences around the class.

1 if
2 When
3 If/When, so
4 so
5 when
6 so

Write on

9 Ask students to think of a game they would like to review. They write a few sentences and give their opinion of the game using the phrases in the Language XP box. Ask students to read their sentences to a partner and circulate as students do this, checking that they are using the language accurately.

Students' own answers.

10 Students work with a partner, answering the questions about the game they have chosen. Monitor as students answer the questions, providing support where necessary.

Students' own answers.

11 Focus students' attention on the task and the questions. Ask students to write a plan for their review, thinking about these questions as they do so. Nominate a couple of students to report back on their ideas.

Students' own answers.

12 Students write their review. When they have finished ask them to check their own work. Write the following checklist on the board:
- introduction?
- conclusion?
- opinion phrases?
- linking words?
- Exercise 10 questions?

Nominate a couple of students to read their reviews to the class.

Students' own answers.

Model answer

If you want to play a game which is totally addictive, you should try *Temple Run*. It's fast and exciting and once you start you just can't stop! At the start of the game, your character runs out of a temple. There is a huge monster chasing you and you have to escape from the monster by jumping over obstacles, leaping over rocks and ducking under flaming archways. Sometimes you have the chance to collect extra lives: you can do this by jumping extra high.

You can buy extra features for this game, such as gemstones. The gemstones give you extra powers and protect you from the monster. I've never done this though, as I think the basic version of the game is good enough for me.

I think this game is great as anyone can play it and you don't need any special skills. The graphics are realistic and the monster is really scary! Personally, I'd recommend this game to players of all ages and abilities. I taught my granny how to play it and she loves it now!

Rating: 10 stars

To finish

Tell your class that they are going to create their own digital game. Organise students into pairs. Tell them to use the headings in Exercise 1 to help them to create a new digital game. Nominate a few students to report back on their ideas and conduct a class vote on the most exciting sounding game.

Homework
MyEnglishLab

SWITCH ON (SB page 102)

Fabulous Fibonacci

1 Remind students of the text they read in the Reading lesson and ask students to remember what they read about Fibonacci. Ask questions, e.g. *What did he do?* (He was a mathematician.); *Where was he from?* (Italy). Ask students to match the words 1–4 with A–D. Play the video so that students can check their answers. Conduct class feedback.

1 C   2 D   3 A   4 B

Students' own answers.

2 Give students a moment to read the sentences. Play the recording so that students can check their answers. Check answers around the class.

1 T

2 F (He travelled in Africa with his father.)

3 F

4 F

5 T

3 Organise students into groups and ask them to discuss their ideas. Monitor, offering support where necessary. Conduct class feedback, generating as much discussion as possible and writing students' ideas on the board.

Students' own answers.

Project

4 Organise students into small groups. Focus their attention on the ideas and ask them to choose the idea they find most interesting. Tell students that they are going to make a poster about the idea they have chosen. Distribute paper and pens and move around the groups, offering support where necessary. Give students a few moments to rehearse what they are going to say and give groups the option of either explaining their posters in front of the class or making a video presentation. Encourage students to give constructive feedback on the presentations they have seen.

Students' own answers.

REVISION (SB page 103)

1
1 subtract
2 rectangle
3 depth
4 pattern
5 calculation
6 triangle

2
1 can be taken
2 was used
3 been invented
4 will be performed
5 had been collected
6 you ever been told

3
1 noise
2 experiences
3 imagination
4 luggage
5 times
6 light
7 noise

4
1 C
2 A
3 B
4 C
5 B
6 A

5
1 calculation(s)
2 equipment
3 another
4 multiplied
5 knowledge
6 anyone
7 intelligence

Homework
Workbook pages 50–51
MyEnglishLab

09 All Change

Unit objectives

Reading:	gapped text
Vocabulary:	homes and furniture; going places
Grammar:	zero, first and second conditionals; third conditional
Listening:	multiple matching
Speaking:	exchanging personal information
Writing:	writing an informal letter

READING (SB pages 104–105)

To start

Give students one minute to brainstorm all the different types of homes where people can live. Conduct class feedback. Ask students: *What type of home would you most/least like to live in? What's important to you in a home?* Encourage students to give reasons for their answers and generate as much discussion as possible. Write any interesting language on the board.

Power up

1 Focus students' attention on the photos and ask them to describe the houses. Then draw the students' attention to the questions and give them a minute to discuss their ideas with a partner. Nominate students to report back on their partners' ideas. Generate as much language as you can and write it on the board.

Students' own answers.

Read on

2 If necessary, pre-teach the following words and phrases: *cosy* (warm and comfortable), *scrap wood* (unwanted wood which has been thrown away), *downsize* (when you start using something smaller and possibly cheaper), *roomy* (having a lot of space). Check students' understanding by asking questions, e.g. *Is a cosy room warm or cold?* (warm); *If I use scrap wood to build a house, will I pay a lot of money for it?* (no); *If I downsize, do I buy something smaller and cheaper or bigger and more expensive?* (smaller and cheaper); *Is this classroom roomy?* Ask students to read the articles quickly and answer the questions. Check answers orally.

1 They are both small and cost very little to build. They were built using natural/second-hand materials.
2 He couldn't live in such a small house.

3 Read the Exam advice aloud to your students. Complete the first space of the article together as an example. Students complete the rest of the task alone. Allow students to check their answers with a partner before conducting whole class feedback.

1 g   2 f   3 a   4 e   5 b   6 d

4 Students match words in the sentences and articles to the definitions and compare their answers with a partner. During feedback, personalise the new language by asking students questions, e.g. *Do you know anyone who lives in a mansion? Are there any rooms in your house/this school which feel a bit cramped? Does your house have a loft? What do you keep in it?*

1 straw   2 cramped   3 mansion   4 disclose   5 loft
6 claustrophobic

Sum up

5 Ask students to choose a house they would like to describe (either Simon's or Hari and Carl's). Give them a minute to think what they are going to say and then ask them to work with a partner who has chosen a different house. Monitor as students describe their chosen houses, offering support where necessary.

Students' own answers.

Speak up

6 Ask students to tell you whether or not they agree with Gavin. Encourage students to give reasons for their answers. Conduct a whole class discussion, encouraging students to comment on the article. Ask questions to generate as much language as possible, e.g. *Do you think that small is beautiful when it comes to houses? Have you ever seen any houses like this in your area/in this country? What do you think are the advantages of living in a small house?* (easy to keep clean, cheap to heat, environmentally friendly); *What are the disadvantages?* (cramped, perhaps not very sociable as there wouldn't be enough space to have friends round).

Students' own answers.

To finish

Tell students that they are going to design their dream house. Tell them to think about:

where it would be

what materials it would be built of

what the garden would be like

how many rooms there would be

Give students a few minutes to make a sketch of their dream house. Then organise students into groups and ask them to discuss their ideas with their classmates.

Homework
MyEnglishLab

VOCABULARY 1 (SB page 106)

Homes and furniture

To start

Ask students to choose three words they learned in the previous lesson and write them down. Students should then give their words to a partner who has one minute to write sentences using the words. Read sentences around the class and check that students are using the words accurately.

1 Focus students' attention on the picture of the house and ask them to work with a partner to match the words in the box with the numbers on the picture. Check answers around the class, focusing on the pronunciation of any tricky words, e.g. *duvet* /'duːveɪ/. Write words of two syllables and over on the board and elicit where the stress lies. Point out that *cutlery* is an uncountable noun.

---

1 sink **2** dishwasher **3** drawer **4** fridge
5 cushion **6** pillow **7** mattress **8** lampshade
9 duvet **10** washbasin **11** cupboard **12** shelf
Other items in the picture
toaster, kettle, washing machine, oven, dishes, picture, bedside table, bed, rug, bathtub, shower, toilet, taps, sofa, armchair, stool, table, chairs, curtains

---

2 Read the words in the box aloud around the class, drilling the pronunciation of any tricky words, e.g. *bungalow* /'bʌŋgələʊ/. Check understanding by asking questions, e.g. *What are igloos made of?* (snow); *If I live in a semi-detached house, do I have houses joined onto one side or both sides of my house?* (one side). Organise students into groups and ask them to discuss the questions. Circulate, offering support where necessary. Bring the class back together and find out which type of accommodation is the most popular.

Students' own answers.

---

3 Tell students that they are going to listen to a conversation about a holiday cottage in which some the items from Exercise 1 are mentioned. Ask students to listen and note down the items they hear. Check answers orally.

► Track 9.1

Lucy: Hello? Oh hi, Mum.

Mum: So, how's the holiday cottage, Lucy? Are you settling in OK?

Lucy: I really like this cottage! It's small, but there's enough room for everything we need.

Mum: Yes, well, I made sure I booked a cottage with a washing machine for the children's clothes, but I thought you'd be OK without a dishwasher. You'll eat out quite a bit, won't you?

Lucy: Oh yes, that's not a problem. We can make sandwiches if we go out for the day, and we'll have lots of picnics. There are some lovely rugs on the floor, Mum – they look hand-made! Much better than having carpets everywhere, especially on these nice wooden floors.

Mum: Oh, I'm so pleased you like everything. What are the beds like?

Lucy: The mattresses are nice and soft, but there aren't any duvets – just sheets and blankets.

Mum: Oh well, it's quite warm, so I don't think you'd need them, anyway.

Lucy: And there's one of those big fridges in the kitchen – you know, the ones that produce ice cubes.

Mum: Great! Well, my favourite TV show is just starting, so why don't you go and make yourself a nice glass of iced coffee and we'll speak again tomorrow?

Lucy: Fine. Bye for now!

Mum: Bye, dear.

---

washing machine, rugs, mattresses, fridge

---

4 Students complete the sentences with words from Exercise 1. Read the sentences around the class. Write down the phrases in bold on the board. Check understanding by asking questions, e.g. *Are couch potatoes very active people?* (no); *If you take everything but the kitchen sink with you on holiday, is your suitcase light or heavy?* (heavy).

---

1 sink **2** tap(s) **3** Couch **4** carpet

Word XP

Read the information and examples in the Word XP box. Check understanding of the terms by giving students a minute to collect as many synonyms and antonyms as they can for the word *great*.

Synonyms of 'great': *super, fantastic, excellent, awesome, wonderful, marvellous terrific, etc.*

Antonyms of 'great': *awful, terrible, horrendous, disgraceful, etc.*

5 Students find the synonyms and antonyms in the list. Allow students to check their answers with a partner before conducting class feedback.

roomy = spacious
tidy = neat
messy = untidy
cramped ≠ roomy/spacious
enormous ≠ tiny
messy/untidy ≠ tidy/neat

6 Organise students into pairs and ask them to complete the task. Circulate as they talk with their partners, making sure they are using vocabulary from the lesson. Bring the class back together and ask one or two pairs to report back on what they learnt.

Students' own answers.

Game on

Demonstrate the Game on activity with a confident student. Choose a word from the page and describe it to the student, e.g. *It's something warm and cosy and it's sometimes filled with feathers. You put it over your bed.*

Elicit the answer from the student (a duvet). Students play the game with a partner. Circulate, offering support and modelling accurate pronunciation of the new language where necessary.

To finish

Tell students to imagine that they are going to try to sell their own house. Ask students to write a short paragraph describing their house to potential buyers. Encourage students to be creative with language and to use synonyms and antonyms to avoid repeating language. If time allows, students can roleplay showing visitors around their house and describing rooms.

Homework
Workbook pages 52–53
MyEnglishLab

GRAMMAR 1 (SB page 107)

Zero, first and second conditionals

To start

Tell students that you are going to practise the furniture and house words from the Vocabulary lesson. Organise students into two teams. Nominate a student from one team to come up to the front of the class and give him/her a word from the Vocabulary lesson. Ask them to describe the word to their teammates who should call out the word which is being described. Continue until everyone has had a chance to describe one of the words from the lesson. The team with the most points is the winner.

Grammar XP

Read the information and examples in the Grammar XP box aloud to your students. Write the following sentences on the board.

If you work hard in this English class, you soon see results.

If you all pass the writing test on Friday, I'll buy you cake.

If I won the lottery, I'd take my favourite class on a trip to London.

Ask students: *Which of these sentences is about an imaginary or very unlikely situation?* (3) *Which sentence describes a future possibility?* (2) *Which sentence is talking about results?* (1)

Elicit the name of each conditional and how the conditional is formed in each case. Encourage students to generate more examples which are true for them and for the class as a whole. Drill the sentences chorally and individually, focusing on natural sounding pronunciation.

1 Ask students to choose the correct answers. Check answers around the class.

1 switch on
2 don't need
3 I'd bring
4 lived
5 wouldn't
6 reach

2 Students complete the sentences with the correct form of the verbs in brackets. Read the sentences around the class.

1 stay, will definitely have
2 wants, will have to
3 put, will never look
4 never throws, thinks
5 doesn't want, will go
6 don't take, will regret

3 Ask students to complete the conversation with the correct form of the verbs in brackets. Students check their answers by reading the conversation aloud with their partner. Monitor as students do this checking for accurate use of the conditional forms. Conduct class feedback.

1 were
2 would be
3 was/were
4 would come
5 don't find
6 will go
7 was/were
8 wouldn't have

Write on

4 Read the rubric aloud to your students. Take a minute to brainstorm some ideas with your students and write useful language on the board. Students write their short paragraphs and share them with a partner. Nominate a few students to read their work aloud to the rest of the class.

Students' own answers.

To finish

Prepare a couple of conditional questions to ask your students, e.g.

What would you do if you saw someone robbing an old woman in the street?

What would you do if someone gave you a present you really didn't like?

Ask your questions around the class. Give students a minute to prepare a similar question of their own. Organise students into groups and ask them to take it in turns to ask and answer their questions.

Homework
Workbook page 54
MyEnglishLab

VOCABULARY 2 (SB page 108)
Going places

To start

Tell students about your favourite way of travelling and explain why you like it, e.g.

I love travelling by train because I find it really relaxing and I love the sound the train makes.

Ask students their preferred way of travelling with a partner. Conduct class feedback, encouraging students to give reasons for their choices. Generate as much language as possible and write any new words and phrases on the board.

1 Focus students' attention on the photos and elicit the different ways of travelling which are shown (by train/rail, by ship/sea, by plane/air). Students copy the table into their notebooks and put the words from the box under the correct headings. Check answers around the class, drilling pronunciation where necessary. Write words of over two syllables on the board and elicit where the stress lies.

Rail: cabin, compartment, crew, dining car, guard, passenger, platform, track
Ship/Boat: cabin, crew, deck, passenger, port
Plane: cabin, crew, departure lounge, flight, passenger, pilot, terminal

2 Students complete the phrases. Check answers around the class and write the phrases in bold on the board, asking students to make a note of them.

1 at 2 on 3 for 4 into 5 of 6 for 7 after 8 through
9 On 10 to

3 Read the title of the review and ask if any of your students have heard of this train journey before. Students read the review and complete it by choosing the correct answers. Allow students to check answers with a partner before reading the review around the class. Check understanding by asking questions, e.g.
Why is this train journey called 'The Ghan'? (Because of the Afghan workers who helped the early explorers.). *What did Mattie see from the train?* (She saw amazing scenery.); *What did Mattie really enjoy about life on this train journey?* (She enjoyed the cosy cabins and the way that the beds could be folded out of the way during the day.). Ask students if they have ever been on a long train journey and encourage them to tell you about it.

1 B 2 D 3 A 4 C 5 A 6 D 7 C 8 B

To finish

Tell students to think of a great journey they have made. Organise students into groups to talk about it. Write the following ideas on the board to help your students:

Where did you travel?
How did you travel?
Who were you with?
What did you see when you were travelling?
Why did you enjoy it?

Nominate a few students to report back on their journeys.

GRAMMAR 2 (SB page 109)

Third conditional

To start

Organise students into pairs. Explain that they must rewrite the following sentences correctly (correct answers in brackets):

We *really want to keep costs at a minimum this year.* (... **to** a minimum ...)

I *can't wait to arrive in our destination!* (... **at** our ...)

I'm *just heading in the shops.* (... **to** the shops.)

I *was named of my mother.* (... **after** my ...)

I *don't like going at customs. It takes ages.* (... **through** customs.)

Do *you know her? I haven't come of contact with her yet.* (... come **into** contact ...)

When a few pairs are ready, correct answers around the class. Pairs should award themselves one point for each correctly rewritten sentence. The pair with the most points wins the game.

Grammar XP

Read the information and examples in the Grammar XP box aloud to your students. Write a personal regret of your own on the board, e.g.

If *I hadn't spent all of my money on clothes, I'd have been able to afford a roomier flat.*

Focus students' attention on the form, e.g. *if* + past perfect, *would have* + past participle

Drill natural sounding pronunciation of the sentence, paying particular attention to *I'd have been able* /aɪdəvbiːneɪbəl/.

Ask students to write down regrets that they have. Allow them to share regrets with a partner before collecting answers around the class.

1 Students complete the sentences with the correct form of the verb in brackets. Point out that students will need to use the negative form of some verbs. Check answers around the class.

1 had booked
2 would have got
3 hadn't gone
4 wouldn't have got
5 wouldn't have
6 had used
7 had been
8 wouldn't have felt

2 Students complete the sentences with the correct form of the verbs. Check answers orally.

1 had paid, would have learnt/learned
2 had kept, wouldn't have lost
3 would have got, hadn't taken
4 would have bought, had been
5 hadn't packed, wouldn't have forgotten

3 Students rewrite the sentences. Allow them to compare answers with a partner before reading the sentences around the class.

1 could have gone
2 if we hadn't gone
3 he had worn
4 might have visited
5 Lily had known Spanish
6 wouldn't have missed/would have caught

Speak up

4 Organise students into small groups. Read the question and the example aloud. Students make their own disaster stories. Circulate as students do this, checking for any difficulties in forming the third conditional. Ask groups to tell their stories to the rest of the class. Conduct class feedback.

Students' own answers.

To finish

Tell students something you regret, e.g.

If *I hadn't been lazy in science lessons, I might have been an astronaut.*

Explain to students that almost everyone has regrets, but that some people have very serious regrets. Write the following on the board:

someone *in prison for armed robbery*

someone *who doesn't speak to their family*

someone *who is bankrupt*

someone *who has split up with their partner after many years*

Organise students into pairs and ask them to think of one regret that each of these people might have. Monitor as students complete this task, focusing on accurate use of the third conditional. Nominate students to report back on their ideas.

Homework
Workbook page 55
MyEnglishLab

LISTENING (SB page 110)

To start

Write the following sentence beginnings on the board. Give students one minute to complete them with their own ideas. Encourage them to be as creative as possible.

If I hadn't been born in this country, ...

If I'd been born a boy/girl, ...

If my parents hadn't met each other, ...

Ask students to share their ideas with a partner before conducting class feedback.

Power up

1 Tell the students about a time you experienced one of the situations on the list, e.g.

When I was a teenager, the school I went to closed down and I had to move to another school. I was so nervous and worried about things but by the end of the first day I had decided that my new school was even better than my old one!

Organise students into small groups and ask them to discuss their experience of these situations. If they haven't experienced any of these situations, they might know someone else who has.

Students' own answers.

Listen up

2 Read the words in the box around the class. Drill the pronunciation of any tricky words, e.g. *bilingual* /baˈəlŋgwəl/ and *traumatic* /trɔːˈmætɪk/. Students complete the task. Check answers around the class.

1 motto
2 break the ice
3 traumatic
4 language barrier
5 bilingual

3 Tell the class that they are going to listen to five students talking about changes in their lives. Give students a minute to read the sentences and encourage them to check with you if they have any questions. Play the recording, twice if necessary. Point out that three of the statements will not be needed. Allow students to check their answers with a partner before conducting class feedback.

> **Track 9.2**

1

Man: My father got a job abroad when I was ten and the whole family moved with him. It was a bit traumatic, to say the least, and I really hated leaving my best friends at school. Still, looking back, I suppose we all settled down quite fast in our new environment. Of course, things were kind of difficult at first because of the language barrier, and some lessons were a bit tricky. After only six months though, both my brother and I were virtually bilingual!

2

Woman: I was fifteen when I first travelled abroad without my parents. I went with a friend to stay with our e-pals in Germany. We had a good time, although I felt there were times when I wanted to say something to my e-pal, Eva, but I didn't really know the right words to use. Apart from that, as teenagers, we all enjoyed similar things. You know, everyone says that people are different in other countries, but I don't think they're right!

3

Man: When I was sixteen, I went to a new school. It was a sixth form college in a different part of town and I was, well, a bit worried about meeting a whole new set of people. Anyway, it wasn't too bad as it happens because lots of other kids at the school were in the same position. So I made some really good friends. On top of that, the teachers there were brilliant and they helped me a lot with ideas about what I wanted to study. So, no regrets there at all!

4

Woman: Last year we moved house and went to live in a different town. I'd never moved before and it was horrible! If I'd had the choice, I wouldn't have left my home for anything, but we had to go. I disliked my new school at first and my parents were getting worried. But then I joined some kung fu classes. I used to take my dog along, too, and he'd sit and watch! Of course, the people in the class thought that was really funny and that kind of broke the ice. It was easier to get talking after that.

5

Man: I spent two weeks away from home last summer at an activity summer camp which was also a language school. Every morning we were only allowed to speak the language we were learning – Italian, in my case – and then in the afternoon we did an activity. My motto is that if you want to learn something properly, you have to be willing to make a fool of yourself! Well, I said lots of stupid things, but after two weeks I could see the difference. And my tennis skills improved a lot, too!

1 f   2 h   3 d   4 b   5 a

Speak up

4 Organise students into pairs. Read the question aloud. Ask students to tell you how they would feel if they needed to move to a new school. Ask: *What would you worry about?* Students complete the task. Monitor, and remind students to use the language they learned in Unit 7 for giving advice. Nominate a strong pair to perform their roleplay to the rest of the class.

Students' own answers.

To finish

Refer students back to the situations they discussed in Exercise 1. Organise students into groups and ask them to choose one of the situations to make a roleplay about. Circulate as students prepare their roleplay, offering support where necessary. Groups should then take it in turns to perform their roleplay in front of their classmates.

Homework

MyEnglishLab

SPEAKING (SB page 111)

To start

Tell students that this lesson is going to focus on asking and answering personal questions. Draw a box on the board. Inside the board, write some answers to personal questions about yourself. Make sure that your answers are a mixture of easy to guess and cryptic items, e.g. *38, 3, chocolate biscuits, Glasgow, cat, Mallorca*

Organise the class into two teams and ask them to try and come up with the questions which would elicit the answers you have written on the board. Award a point each time someone asks you a correct question, e.g.

What shoe size are you?

How many times have you taken your driving test?

What are you addicted to?

Where were you born?

What's your favourite animal?

Where are you going on your next holiday?

As you answer the questions, make sure you provide more detail, e.g. *Yes, I took my driving test three times. I was so pleased when I finally passed.*

Power up

1 Organise students into pairs and go around the class allocating students within pairs the letters A or B. Read the Exam advice aloud to your students. Focus students' attention on the questions and give them a minute or so to jot down any useful vocabulary which they might need. Circulate as students discuss the questions, offering support where necessary and noting down any issues to be covered in the class feedback.

Students' own answers.

Speak up

2 Make sure that students understand what an *avatar* is (a person who represents you in a game or computer forum). Ask the boys to read the information about Mickey and the girls to read the information about Veronica. Allow them a minute or two to think about how they would answer the questions from Exercise 1, filling in any missing details with their own ideas.

Students' own answers.

3 Ask students to work with someone who has chosen a different avatar. They take turns asking and answering the questions from Exercise 1. Monitor as students complete the task, offering support where necessary. Nominate a few students to report back on their partners' answers.

Students' own answers.

4 Students create their own avatar and write a description of him/her. Elicit one or two questions students can ask about their partner's avatar, encouraging students to make their questions as creative and as interesting as possible. Circulate, checking students' question formation and noting down any issues to be addressed in the class feedback session.

Students' own answers.

5 Students ask and answer questions about their new avatars. Remind them of the Exam advice which you read earlier. Monitor, encouraging students to give full and detailed answers to their partners' questions. Conduct class feedback, nominating a few students to report back on their partners' avatars.

Students' own answers.

To finish

Explain to students that keeping the conversation going is a very important skill. Organise the students into pairs. Ask them to choose one of the questions from the page. Choose one student in each pair to begin the conversation. Tell students that you are going to set the timer on your phone for one minute and that you want them to keep the conversation going for as long as they can using the Exam advice they have been practising in this lesson. Circulate as students have their conversations, providing support where necessary. Conduct class feedback and congratulate the students who managed to carry on their conversation for the longest time.

Homework

MyEnglishLab

WRITING (SB pages 112–113)

To start

Tell your students what you think an ingredient of a great holiday is, e.g. *A great holiday has sunshine*.

Indicate the student on your right to continue. They must say *A great holiday has sunshine and '…'* and include an idea of their own, e.g. *A great holiday has sunshine and beautiful beaches*.

Continue around the class with students adding ideas, until the last student has to remember all the ingredients of a good holiday.

Power up

1 Focus students' attention on the photos. Ask students if they know which cities the photos were taken in. Write the names of the cities on the board. Ask students: *Have you ever visited these cities? What do you know about them?*

Photo A: New York, Manhattan Bridge
Photo B: New York, Statue of Liberty

Plan on

2 Nominate a student to read out the extract from the letter and ask students to choose what they should do in their reply.

describe, give an opinion

3 Read the letter aloud to your students. Ask them to compare their ideas from Exercise 2 with what the writer has included. Conduct class feedback.

Students' own answers.

4 Students match the different parts of the letter with the topics. Check answers around the class.

1 E 2 A 3 D
4 B 5 F 6 C

5 Students complete the sentences with prepositions from the letter in Exercise 3. Allow students to check their answers with a partner before conducting class feedback.

1 to 2 on 3 in
4 for 5 at 6 on

6 Students complete the comments. Check answers orally.

1 went 2 had 3 spent 4 have/had 5 go

Language XP

Elicit the situations in which students would write a formal email or letter (to someone they don't know, for a job application, etc.) and an informal email or letter (to a close friend or family member).

Check that students understand the meaning of *semi-formal* by asking: *Who would you write a semi-formal letter to?* Elicit that if students were writing a letter to someone their age that they didn't know very well they would write a semi-formal letter. Read the information in the Language XP box aloud to your students.

7 Students complete the opening sentences from informal letters. Collect answers around the class.

Suggested answers
1 Sorry I haven't written recently
2 It was great to hear your news
3 Thanks for your letter
4 How are you

Write on

8 Read the Exam advice aloud to your students. Focus their attention on the question and nominate a student to read the extract aloud. Students plan their reply. Allow them to check their answers with a partner before conducting class feedback.

Questions to answer: What were your e-pal's family like? Did you get on well? What did you do while you were there? Did you go to any interesting places?
Background details: where your e-pen's family lives, description of e-pal and family, their home, whether you enjoyed your stay and why

9 Focus students' attention on Susie's letter in Exercise 3 and elicit how many main paragraphs it contains (3). Students make a paragraph plan. They should decide how many paragraphs their letters will contain and where they will put the information.

Students' own answers.

Word XP

Focus students' attention on the words to describe positive and negative experiences. Ask students if they can add any more words to the list.

10 Students write their letter. Write the following points on the board for students to use as a checklist:

– *points from Exercise 4*

– *semi-formal phrases*

– *structure which is easy to follow*

Monitor as students complete the task, offering support where necessary. Conduct class feedback and nominate a few students to read their letters aloud.

Students' own answers.

Model answer

Dear Jan,

Thanks for your letter. It was great to hear your news.

My trip to see my e-pal was amazing. Her name is Andi and she lives in Budapest in Hungary. She came to meet me at the airport with her mum and we went for a tour of the city before going back to Andi's house. It was night time and it looked so beautiful all lit up in the dark. It was almost Christmas time so there were lovely Christmas markets selling hot spiced drinks and bread.

We visited some really interesting places. My favourite places were the thermal baths in the city centre: they are warm baths in impressive buildings where you can soak and relax for hours. We also visited lots of cake shops and saw some really interesting museums.

The whole holiday was fantastic. I had a brilliant time, but the two weeks went too quickly! I uploaded some photos for you to look at. If I could, I would stay here for a month! Write soon,

Marina

To finish

Tell your students about a holiday you went on which didn't go well. Say something like:

I was so looking forward to my holiday in Greece with three of my friends, but it was a big disappointment. If only I hadn't eaten seafood on my first night! I hadn't ever eaten it before and I was really allergic to it, so I ended up in hospital! If I'd bought travel insurance before my trip it wouldn't have been so bad.

Organise students into pairs. Write these headings on the board:

a bad holiday

a bad night out

Ask them to think of a time they experienced one of these situations and tell their partner about it. Monitor as students talk.

Homework

MyEnglishLab

SWITCH ON (SB page 114)

Make yourself at home

1 Read the instructions aloud to your students. Organise students into pairs and give them a minute to write down the things they think they will see in Petri's room. Play the video and ask students to see how many of their predictions were correct.

Students' own answers.

2 Read the sentences aloud around the class. Play the video again and ask students to decide whether they are true or false. Check answers orally.

A F   **B** F   **C** T   **D** T

3 Read the question aloud to your class and ask them to discuss their ideas with a partner. Nominate a few students to report back on their ideas.

Students' own answers.

Project

4 Organise students into pairs. Ask them to read the three options and choose which one they would prefer. If students choose option C, they will need to prepare some of their project outside class. To make things fairer, Groups A and B can also prepare some of their presentation as a homework activity. In your next class, give students a chance to rehearse before filming their roleplay, recording their commentary or doing their presentation. Watch the finished products as a class, and use them as a springboard for further discussion.

Students' own answers.

REVISION (SB page 115)

1

1 igloo

2 cutlery

3 mattress

4 dishwasher

5 stool

6 log cabin

7 pillow

8 tap

2

1 am/'m

2 wouldn't

3 unless

4 were

5 doesn't

6 Don't

3

1 B

2 C

3 C

4 A

5 B

6 A

4

1 If we hadn't caught the train, we would have missed our flight.

2 If you'd gone on the trip, you'd have seen Paris.

3 If Jenny hadn't gone to town, she wouldn't have bought a new rug for her room.

4 If I hadn't left my bag on the seat at the airport, someone wouldn't have stolen my purse.

5 If you'd planned the holiday (more) carefully, we wouldn't have spent (such) a lot of time in the car.

6 If it hadn't been cold and rainy, we would have visited the lighthouse.

5

1 spacious

2 language

3 passengers

4 take

5 headed for

6 break

7 couch

8 well-known

Homework

Workbook pages 56–57

MyEnglishLab

10 Inspiration

Unit objectives

Reading:	multiple-choice questions
Vocabulary:	science; experiments
Grammar:	-ing forms and infinitives; have/get something done
Listening:	sentence completion
Speaking:	discussion questions
Writing:	writing an article

READING (SB pages 116–117)

To start

Focus students' attention on the title of the unit and elicit the meaning of the word *inspiration* (being stimulated to do something creative). Organise students into groups and ask them to discuss the following questions:

What inspires you?

Think of your favourite writer/film maker/ musician. Do you know where they get their inspiration?

Do you find nature inspiring? Why/Why not?

Circulate as students discuss the questions, offering support where necessary. Conduct class feedback.

Power up

1 Focus students' attention on the photos of insects. Challenge students to see who can be the first to correctly match the insect with its name in English. Check answers around the class, drilling the pronunciation of *mosquito* if necessary: /məsˈkiːtəʊ/. Ask students to tell you what insects they like/dislike and encourage students to give reasons for their answers.

A bee   **B** ladybird   **C** fly   **D** mosquito

2 Students match the insects with what they do. Check answers around the class.

bee: 1, 2, 5
ladybird: 4
fly: 3, 6
mosquito: 3, 6

Read on

3 Ask students to discuss their answers to this question with a partner, before opening this up into a class discussion. Generate as many ideas as you can and write students' suggestions on the board, e.g. ladybirds: *Because they can control other bugs which might eat food plants, useful in organic farming.*

Students' own answers.

4 If necessary, pre-teach the following words: *laboratory* (where a scientist does experiments), *durable* (something that can last a long time) and *delicate* (something which is easily broken). Check students' understanding by asking questions: *Does a waiter work in a laboratory?* (no) *Who usually works in a laboratory?* (a scientist) *If something is durable, does it break easily?* (no) *Does it last a long time?* (yes) *If something is delicate, does it break easily?* (yes). Focus students' attention on the insects in the photos. Elicit what type of insects they are and what they do. Ask students to predict why scientists are interested in these insects and write their ideas on the board. Students read the text and check their ideas. Conduct class feedback.

Students' own answers.

5 Read the Exam advice aloud to your students. Students read the article again and choose the correct answers. Allow them to check their answers with a partner before conducting class feedback.

1 A   **2** C   **3** D   **4** B   **5** C   **6** A

6 Read the words in the box, drilling the pronunciation of any which are tricky, e.g. *odour* /ˈəʊdə/. Ask students to complete the sentences with the words from the box. Collect sentences around the class.

1 smooth   **2** rotten   **3** equivalent   **4** repair   **5** spin   **6** repel
7 odour

Sum up

7 Write the headings on the board. Choose one heading (e.g. size) and ask students to compare the golden orb web spider with the blue morpho butterfly. Organise students into pairs and ask them to continue making comparisons using the headings to help them. Circulate as students complete this activity, offering support where necessary. Conduct class feedback.

Students' own answers.

Speak up

8 Elicit which item in the article is mentioned as benefiting from a waterproof coating (a mobile phone). Organise students into groups and ask them to discuss other items which would benefit from a waterproof coating. Ask students to give reasons for their answers. Circulate as students discuss their ideas, offering support where necessary. Bring the class back together. Write students' suggestions on the board and ask them to explain their ideas in more detail. Conduct a class vote for the best idea.

Students' own answers.

To finish

Organise students into pairs and tell them that they are going to be fashion designers. They are going to create an outfit *inspired by nature*. They can think of any insect, animal or natural thing to inspire their design, e.g. a dress the colour of a butterfly's wing. Ask students to sketch and label their ideas. Nominate a student from each pair to show the rest of the class their design and tell the rest of the class about it.

Homework

MyEnglishLab

VOCABULARY 1 (SB page 118)

Science

To start

Organise students into small groups. Challenge them to remember and write down three facts each about the golden orb web spider and the morpho butterfly which they learned about in the Reading lesson. When a couple of groups have collected all their facts, conduct class feedback.

Possible ideas:

Golden orb spider: they come come from Africa, they eat fruit, they spin silk which is stronger than steel, their silk can be used to make medicines.

Morpho butterfly: they come from South America, they have tiny scales on their wings, their wings are waterproof.

1 Students read the sentences and choose the correct answers. Collect answers around the class.

1 laboratory **2** cells **3** infection **4** researchers **5** species
6 medical **7** microscope

2 Read the words in the box and write them on the board. Elicit where the word stress lies in each. Ask students to complete the task. Check answers orally.

1 inspiration **2** material **3** structure **4** surface **5** properties
6 power

3 Elicit that these words describe our senses. Ask students to match the words with the parts of the body. Check answers around the class.

1 sight, vision **2** hearing, sound **3** smell **4** taste **5** touch

4 Allow students a minute to discuss this question with a partner before conducting class feedback. Write the words which can be verbs and nouns on the board. Elicit two sentences containing each word: one sentence should contain the word as a noun and the other as a verb, e.g. *There is a lovely smell in the kitchen. I can smell fresh bread.*

smell, sound, taste, touch

5 Students complete the sentences. Allow them to check their answers with a partner before conducting class feedback. Elicit example sentences containing each of the words from your students and write them on the board, e.g. *Bats have a strong sense of hearing. What an amazing sight! I love the sound of rain hitting the roof. Flies have excellent vision.*

1 sight **2** vision **3** sound **4** hearing

6 Students work with a partner. Ask them to choose which properties the animals (or parts of the animals' bodies have). Give them a minute to discuss their answers before conducting class feedback. Generate as much discussion as possible and write any new language on the board.

1 A **2** B **3** B **4** C **5** A **6** C **7** C

7 Students listen and check their answers. Ask students to note down any other interesting information they hear and ask them to contribute their ideas in the class feedback session.

> **Track 10.1**

1

Woman: In other news, a lucky tortoise has been to the vet's for a very special operation. Poor Speedy Septimus the tortoise lost his front legs when he was attacked by rats. He couldn't walk after that, so the vet has given him a man-made solution: a wheel!

2

Man: And here we see the chameleon trying to hide. Like all lizards, chameleons don't want to be seen by any insects while they're waiting for their dinner to arrive. They hide by changing colour to match their surroundings, so they're almost invisible. Look! The fly didn't see it at all!

3

Man: The cockroach may be ugly, but it's one of the most successful creatures on the planet. Its hard shell makes the cockroach very durable so it can survive in almost any conditions, from extremely hot to very cold.

4

Woman: Of course, all birds have a waterproof coating on their feathers, to keep them dry and warm in all weathers, but these penguins need to be extra warm as they sometimes swim for days in the icy waters of Antarctica.

5

Man: It's hard to believe that snakes have backbones, but they do. Humans have thirty-three small bones in their backbone, but snakes have between 200 and 400! That's what makes them so flexible and helps them move along!

6

Woman: Butterflies and moths look quite similar; they each have four wings, not two. A moth won't die if you touch its wings, but they are very delicate, so be careful.

7

Woman: There's nothing worse than swimming in the sea and spotting a jellyfish beside you, especially because they can sting you badly. The reason they can get so close is that their bodies are quite transparent, so it's really difficult to see them in the water.

Game on

Demonstrate this activity with a confident student. Choose a science word from the page, e.g. *microscope* and ask your student to make a sentence with it, e.g. *I like looking at things under the microscope.*

Ask students to continue the game, awarding themselves points when they manage to make a sentence with the word their partner gives them. Circulate, offering support and encouragement.

To finish

Organise students into small groups. Ask them to write down the names of five animals which have interesting abilities or properties. They should write a short description of each animal and what they can do, but without mentioning their names. The groups should then take turns to read their descriptions to the rest of the class, who should listen and guess the name of the animals being described. Award points for correct guesses and good descriptions. Write any new language on the board.

Homework

Workbook pages 58–59

MyEnglishLab

GRAMMAR 1 (SB page 119)

-ing forms and infinitives

To start

Students choose five words from the Vocabulary lesson and write them down. They should then read them to their partner who listens and writes them down. Students get a point for each word they spell correctly. Conduct class feedback and encourage students to make sentences with the words they have spelled.

Grammar XP

Read the information and examples in the Grammar XP box aloud to your students. Write a series of sentences on the board (ideally linked to your students and their interests in some way). Ask students to read the sentences and identify why the infinitive or the -ing form of the verb has been chosen in each case, e.g.

Learning English in this class is really fun.

(learning is the subject of the sentence)

Pablo really loves surfing.

(-ing after a verb which expresses likes or dislikes)

Julia appears to be daydreaming at the moment.

(appear is one of the state verbs which takes the infinitive)

Marta knew how to answer the most difficult question in class yesterday.

(infinitive after where, how, etc.)

Ask students to generate their own examples of sentences with -ing and infinitive forms and write students' ideas on the board.

1 Students read the sentences and choose the correct answers. Check answers around the class, asking students to tell you which of these facts they found new/surprising.

1 Killing   **2** to smell   **3** taste   **4** feeding

2 Ask students to complete the sentences with the correct form of the verbs. Allow students to check their answers with a partner before reading the sentences around the class.

1 to do

2 touch

3 working

4 to write

5 Seeing

6 meeting

7 to love

8 covering

3 Students read the article and complete the task. Allow students to compare their answers with a partner before reading the article around the class. Ask students questions about what they have read, e.g. *Why are Monarch butterflies so famous?* (because they can fly for such long distances) *What is the mystery about Monarch butterflies?* (nobody knows how they manage to pass on the information about their journey to the next generation).

1 working
2 studying
3 watch
4 look
5 to do
6 to fly
7 to become
8 (to) protect
9 make
10 to pass on
11 to discover
12 Finding out

Speak up

4 Read the rubric aloud to your students and ask them to discuss it with a partner. Circulate as students complete the task, offering support where necessary and focusing on accurate use of *-ing* forms and infinitives. Note down any issues you hear and address these in the class feedback session.

Students' own answers.

To finish

Write the following sentence beginnings on the board:
I want …
I hope …
I'm looking forward …
I'm going …
I've decided …
Tell the students some information about yourself using the phrases from the board:
I want to go to Spain on my next holiday. I hope to find the time to learn Spanish before then. I'm looking forward to trying some Spanish paella. I'm going to invite my friend to come with me. I've decided to travel there by train.
Ask students to complete the sentences with information about themselves. Allow them to share their ideas with a partner before conducting class feedback.

Homework
Workbook page 60
MyEnglishLab

VOCABULARY 2 (SB page 120)
Experiments

To start

Focus students' attention on the title of the lesson. Ask students to tell you about experiments they have done in science class. Ask them to describe the process and the result.

Now organise students into pairs. Ask them to think of what experiments they could design if they wanted to find out the following things:

Where are people most friendly: in London or New York?

Does vegetarian substitute meat taste the same as real meat?

Ask students to add one more thing that they would like to find out and design an experiment for it.

1 Focus students' attention on the table and read the headings aloud. Ask them to read the first sentence of the teacher's instructions and provide another noun, adjective or verb (biological) for the table. Students complete the rest of the task alone. Conduct class feedback. Drill the pronunciation of the nouns and adjectives the students have found, eliciting where the stress lies in each.

Noun: music
Adjective: biological, practical, basic, central, scientific, logical, inspirational
Verb: panic

Word XP

Read the information in the Word XP box aloud to your students. Ask your students if they can think of any more nouns or adjectives with *-ic* or *-all-ical* endings. Write their ideas on the board.

2 Students complete the sentences with the words in the box. Read the sentences aloud to the class, focusing on accurate pronunciation of the target language.

1 metallic   2 magnetic   3 microscopic   4 electric   5 plastic
6 scientific

3 Focus students' attention on the words. Write the word *metallic* on the board and elicit where the stressed syllable lies. Mark this on the board. Tell students they are going to listen and mark the stressed syllables. Play the recording, twice if necessary. Check answers orally.

1
me**tal**, me**tal**lic
2
magnet, mag**ne**tic
3
science, scien**ti**fic
4
drama, dra**ma**tic
5
edu**ca**tion, edu**ca**tional
6
logic, **log**ical
7
magic, **mag**ical
8
nature, **nat**ural

---

1 metal, metallic
2 magnet, magnetic
3 science, scientific
4 drama, dramatic
5 education, educational
6 logic, logical
7 magic, magical
8 nature, natural

Word XP

Read the information in the Word XP box and generate examples to demonstrate the pattern. For example, with the word logic the stress is on the penultimate syllable. In logical the stress is on the ante-penultimate syllable.

4 Ask students to read the text about bats and complete it with the correct form of the words in capitals. Allow students to check their answers with a partner before reading the article around the class. Ask students questions about the text which they have just read, e.g. *How are bats able to fly in the dark when they can't see?* (they use their sense of hearing) *What is the name to describe how bats use sound to help them know where they are?* (echolocation) *Which other animal uses echolocation?* (dolphins).

1 sight **2** magical **3** magnetic **4** hearing **5** musical **6** natural
7 electrical **8** dramatic

Game on

Nominate an able student to help you demonstrate the activity. Choose a word from the page, e.g. *dramatic*. Tell the student to give you either a definition of the word or a sentence. Award a point for a definition (*meaning 'like a drama', used to describe something exciting*) and a point for an accurate sentence (*The storm last night was very dramatic*). Circulate as students complete the activity.

To finish

Elicit how bats' senses inspired researchers to help blind people (scientists developed an electronic gadget based on echolocation). Organise students into groups and give them a few minutes to think about how animals with amazing abilities could inspire scientists and researchers. Nominate a student from each group to report back on their ideas.

Ideas:

Thick, protective sharks' skin could be used to inspire deep sea clothes.

The grips on gecko's feet could inspire no-slip running shoes.

The substance which sticks mussels onto rocks could be used to develop a very strong type of superglue.

Homework
Workbook page 59
MyEnglishLab

GRAMMAR 2 (SB page 121)

have/get something done

To start

Write the following sentence on the board:

It's totally logical that the natural magnetic qualities of this object would form the base of this very scientific and educational experiment.

Organise students into pairs. Ask them to copy the sentence into their notebooks and mark where the word stress lies. Students should practise saying the sentence aloud until they are confident that they can say it with the correct stress. When they feel ready, they can put up their hands.

Listen to a few students saying the sentence. Award a small prize or bonus to the first student who can say it correctly.

Grammar XP

Read the information and the examples in the Grammar XP box aloud to your students. Tell your class that you have just bought a new house/flat. Explain that it is very old and that no one has lived in it for many years. A lot of things are broken and there is no furniture. Tell your students:

I'm going to need a lot of things done.

Write these sentences on the board:

I'm getting the windows replaced.

I'm having new carpets put down.

Ask students to work in pairs. Give them a minute to think of as many things as possible which you will need to *get/have done*. Circulate as students complete the task, offering support when necessary. Conduct class feedback and write students' ideas on the board.

1   Students complete the sentences. Check answers around the class.

1 had a special science kit delivered

2 are having their height measured

3 is getting/is going to get his heart rate checked

4 has just had his motorbike washed

5 are getting/are going to get our hair coloured

6 had his nose broken

7 Are you getting/Are you going to get your laptop fixed

8 haven't had the new science lab painted

2   Read the title of the article aloud to your students and ask them to predict what might happen during a bad day in the science lab. Students read the article and complete the sentences with words from the box. Check answers orally and ask students whether any of their predictions were correct.

3 had

4 stolen

5 are having

6 written

7 is having

8 taken

9 is going to have/is having

10 repaired

11 is going to have/is having

12 installed

3   Students rewrite the sentences using the words given. Allow students to check their answers with a partner before conducting class feedback.

1 have had my eyesight

2 is having his hair cut

3 are having/getting

4 had her phone stolen

5 how to do

6 where to meet

Write on

4   Ask your class a question using *have/get something done*, e.g. *Has anyone had their hair cut in the new hairdressers on the main street?* Students write two questions of their own using *have/get something done*. Circulate as students write their questions, offering support where necessary.

Students' own answers.

To finish

Tell students to imagine that they have just moved house and have been given a small bedroom which is completely bare. What will they do to make their room homely? What will they have done? Organise students into pairs and ask them to discuss this. Monitor as they do this, offering support where necessary. Conduct class feedback.

Homework

Workbook page 61

MyEnglishLab

LISTENING (SB page 122)

To start

Challenge students to make a list of five things they are *going to have done* over the next month. Ask students to share their lists with a partner. Nominate a few students to report back on their partners' ideas.

Power up

1   Organise students into pairs. Ask them to look at the photos and give them a few moments to talk about any similarities they see. Conduct class feedback, asking students if they know which country the train comes from (Japan) and what kind of bird it is (a kingfisher).

Students' own answers.

Listen up

2   Read the question aloud and check students' understanding of the phrase *sources of inspiration* (where inspiration or ideas come from). Tell students that they are going to listen to a student's podcast and make a note of her five sources of inspiration from the natural world. Play the recording, twice if necessary. Allow students to check their answers with a partner before conducting class feedback.

Fiona: Hello, everyone! I'm Fiona and this is my podcast for the summer term science project, Year 9, Greenwoods High School. For my topic, I've chosen to look at different ways in which scientists have been inspired by the natural world – and I've discovered some fascinating things! Here are some of them and I hope you enjoy hearing about them.

First, I suppose you've heard of the bullet train in Japan? That's a type of train that goes very fast, over three hundred miles per hour. There was a problem with the bullet train in the early days because when it came out of a tunnel at high speed, it made an incredibly loud noise. It's quite funny that the solution to this problem was found by an engineer who used to go bird-watching. He saw how the kingfisher – a bright blue bird with a long beak – would dive into the water and hardly make a splash at all. So the design of the bullet train was changed to give it a long nose in front. This reduced the noise level – and everyone was grateful to the kingfisher!

Now, we think *we're* the clever ones on this planet, but it's amazing how animals and insects somehow know how to use nature intelligently. For example, there's a black beetle in Africa that lives in the desert, where there's not much water, of course. So, whenever the fog comes in – and yes, it *does* get foggy sometimes in the desert – the beetle puts its back up in the air so that the drops of water from the fog run down into its mouth! Designers of camping equipment have imitated this idea and have made a special bottle that can catch water from the early morning dew on the tent. This, of course, helps campers who aren't near any other water supply. The sea inspires us in different ways and there's nothing like the underwater world for amazing and unbelievable types of fish. One of these is a boxfish. Yes, there's a fish that is a sort of square shape, and it actually moves through the water at a surprising speed! This particular fish gave Mercedes-Benz, the car manufacturer, the idea for a new aerodynamic model of a small two-door car, which really moves well for its size. Incredible, isn't it?

Also, still relating to water, have you ever noticed the pattern that makes up a soap bubble? Well, it's a six-sided shape like a hexagon, and this was the inspiration for the 2008 Beijing Olympics swimming centre, which they called 'the Watercube'. The walls were made of these particular plastic shapes, which trapped the hot air from the sun and heated the pools. Quite an architectural phenomenon!

Finally, if you live in a hot country or have been somewhere hot on holiday, I'm sure you have seen a lizard running along a wall – and perhaps you've even seen one running across the ceiling! Well, lizards can do this because they have millions of tiny hairs under their toes, which means they can stick to a surface without falling off. This idea was used by scientists to develop a really strong glue which they call Geckskin, after a type of lizard called a gecko. And one day not so far in the future, we may be able to put on Geckskin gloves and climb walls, just like Spiderman!

So, those are just a few of the most interesting things I learnt while I was doing my project. Thanks for listening, everyone!

1 a bird (kingfisher)
2 a beetle/insect
3 a type of fish (boxfish)
4 a soap bubble
5 a lizard

3 Read the Exam advice aloud to your students. Play the recording again while students complete the sentences. Give students a minute to compare their answers in pairs before reading the sentences around the class.

1 noise
2 bird-watching/birds
3 water
4 campers/camping
5 square
6 car
7 soap bubble
8 swimming
9 hairs
10 glue

Speak up

4 Organise students into small groups to discuss the question. Ask a student from each group to report back on what they discussed.

Students' own answers.

5 Read the question aloud to your students and ask them to discuss their ideas in small groups. Conduct class feedback, eliciting students' ideas.

Students' own answers.

To finish

Ask students to think of things in their country which have been inspired by nature and to discuss their ideas with a partner. Write this list on the board to help them:
buildings
modes of transport
art
fashion
business ventures
Conduct class feedback, generating as much discussion as possible.

Homework
MyEnglishLab

SPEAKING (SB page 123)

To start

Write the following quote (from an anti-fur campaign) on the board: *It takes forty dumb animals to make a fur coat, but only one to wear it.*

Ask students:

What does this quote mean?

(It means that many animals die to make a fur coat, for the benefit of one stupid person).

Ask students to tell you whether or not they agree with this quote and to give reasons for their answers. Elicit other ways in which animals are used by humans and write these on the board.

Power up

1 Focus students' attention on the photos. Elicit where the photos were taken (at an aquarium and in a pet shop or pet market) and ask them to describe what they see (a seal balancing a ball on his nose and a white rabbit in a cage). Organise students into pairs and ask them to discuss the positive and negative aspects of each situation. Open this up into a class discussion and encourage as much debate as possible.

Students' own answers.

2 Organise students into pairs and ask them to discuss the different ways in which humans and animals interact, deciding which are positive and which are negative. After a minute, ask each pair to find another pair to work with and compare their answers together. Conduct class feedback, encouraging students to give reasons for their answers.

Students' own answers.

3 Read the rubric and the questions aloud to your students. Play the recording, twice if necessary. Allow students to check their answers with a partner before conducting class feedback.

➤ Tracks 10.5 and 10.6

Interviewer: Some people say that no wild animals should be kept in captivity. What do you think?

Student 1: Well, that's a tricky question because I partly agree that animals should be free and not in captivity, but on the other hand, we can learn a lot from studying animals' behaviour.

Student 2: Yes, it's difficult. We all know that animals kept in zoos can be depressed or ill and it's really cruel to take them away from their families when they are young. But it's also interesting to able to see wild animals like elephants and tigers close up and have that experience. Most of us will never see them in the wild at all.

Student 1: You're right there!

Interviewer: Thank you.

1 They are discussing the issue of whether wild animals should be kept in captivity or not.

2 They think there are both positive and negative aspects.

Language XP

Focus on a statement from Exercise 2 which your students had different opinions about. Model the language from the Language XP box, by presenting your students' ideas on one of the statements, e.g.

Ben agreed with Hans that it can be cruel to keep animals as pets, but on the other hand he thought that most pets are well looked after and love their owners.

4 Tell students that you are going to play the recording again. Ask students to listen and note down the phrases they hear from the Language XP box.

Well, that's a tricky question because … ,
I partly agree … , but on the other hand, …

5 Organise students into pairs. Ask them to discuss the questions, using phrases from the Language XP box. Monitor students as they complete the task, offering support where necessary and focusing on accurate use of the target language.

Students' own answers.

Speak up

6 Read the Exam advice aloud to your students. Organise students into pairs and ask them to discuss the questions in small groups. Circulate as students discuss the questions, encouraging them to use the phrases from the Language XP box where necessary and noting down any interesting discussions to comment on later.

Students' own answers.

7 Ask students to work with a partner and turn to page 157. Circulate as students complete the task, offering support and encouraging them to use the target language.

Students' own answers.

To finish

Organise students into pairs. Ask them to think of another topic which could be seen from two sides, e.g.

Young children and computer games
Young children and TV
Teenagers and pocket money

Students should write a question about their topic, which is similar to the questions in Exercise 6. They should then give their question to another pair, who should discuss it using the language from the Language XP box. Conduct class feedback.

Homework
MyEnglishLab

WRITING (SB pages 124–125)

To start

Write the word *Inspiration* on the board. Challenge students to make as many words as they can from this word.

Ideas: *in, spirit, trip, pan, sin, not, trap, aspirin, train, etc.*

Power up

1 Ask students to discuss the question with a partner. Conduct class feedback, asking students to tell you what they have seen in the night sky and finding out if any of your students are interested in astronomy.

The sky is clearest outside the cities, in the middle of the countryside away from any lights, or by the sea. You might see: stars, the moon, planets, constellations, shooting stars, a meteor shower, a comet (!).

Plan on

2 Read the rubric aloud to your class, and then give students a minute to read the article in silence. Allow students to discuss their answers with a partner before conducting class feedback.

1 the stars **2** He might study astronomy.

3 Focus students' attention on the list of topics. Ask students to read the article again and match the topics with the paragraphs. Check answers around the class.

A 4 **B** 1 **C** 3 **D** 2

4 Read the rubric to your students and ask them to find the writers' personal reactions in the text. Write the answers on the board.

That really made a wonderful end to the evening – and one I'll never forget.
Perhaps one day I'll study astronomy – who knows?

5 Students match the situations with the personal reactions. Allow students to check their answers with a partner before conducting class feedback.

1 c/d **2** b **3** a **4** c/d

Language XP

Read the exclamations aloud to your students. Stress that using exclamations such as these is one way of making your writing become more alive and interesting.

6 Students read the situations and write exclamations for each one, using the language from the Language XP box, e.g. *What a fantastic sight! What an amazing find! What wonderful (multi-coloured) fish we saw! What incredible animals!* Students compare their exclamations with a partner. Elicit a few exclamations from around the class.

Students' own answers.

Write on

7 Read the task aloud to your students. Nominate a student to read the magazine announcement aloud. Spend time discussing possible sources of inspiration before students start planning their article. Focus their attention on the spidergram and ask them to begin planning their article. Circulate as students do this, offering support where necessary.

Students' own answers.

8 Read the Exam advice aloud to your students. Ask students to write their article. Write this checklist on the board:
   – *correct structure?* (see Exercise 3)
   – *personal reactions?*
   – *Language XP phrases?*
   Nominate students to read their articles aloud to the rest of the class.

Students' own answers.

Model answer

Inspired by the sea!

Have you been inspired by something in nature? Sometimes all it takes is a break from the normal routine and a journey out of town for us to see things in a new way and feel completely refreshed.

This happened to me two weeks ago on a cloudy Saturday. I was really having problems with a piece of homework I had been given by my teacher. She had asked us all to write a poem. Well, I'd never written a poem before and I was in quite a bad mood about it! I decided I needed to get out of the house. I didn't know where I was going but I just got on my bike and started cycling out of town.

After an hour I came to the seaside. It was such a cloudy, misty day that the beach was completely empty. It looked amazing, all covered in mist. I walked along the sand and smelt the air and listened to the sound of the waves on the sand. What an amazing hour I spent all alone!

When I returned home, it was easy to write my poem. The silence on the beach had inspired me. Now I can't wait for the next cloudy day. Maybe I'll write another poem too – who knows?

To finish

Ask students to write three sentences about inspiring or memorable experiences, e.g.

When I was little, I went on holiday to Greece and I saw dolphins leaping out of the water behind the boat.

When they have written their sentences, organise them into pairs. Ask them to read their sentences to each other. Their partner must respond using language from the Language XP box. Circulate and make sure they are using the target language accurately.

Homework
MyEnglishLab

SWITCH ON (SB page 126)

Spider science

1 Read the rubric aloud to your students. Ask them to predict the answers with a partner. Play the recording so that students can check their answers.

If a thread in a spider's web was as thick as a pencil, it could pull an ocean liner.

2 Play the video again while students answer the questions. Allow students to check their answers with a partner before conducting class feedback.

1 C 2 A 3 B

3 Ask students to discuss the question with a partner. Monitor as students complete this task, offering support where necessary.

Students' own answers.

Project

4 Focus students' attention on the task. Organise students into groups to discuss their ideas and help students to find out about their scientist using books or the Internet. Give students time to write their interview script, offering support where necessary. When the scripts are ready, let students practise their interview before they film it. Watch the interviews together and encourage your students to offer positive feedback on what they have seen.

Students' own answers.

REVISION (SB page 127)

1
1 inspiration
2 man-made
3 natural
4 structures
5 properties
6 durable
7 material

2
1 C 2 B 3 A 4 C 5 B

3
1 magical
2 nature
3 microscope
4 dramatic
5 artist
6 logical

4
1 broken into
2 having
3 taken
4 getting
5 repaired
6 had

5
1 where
2 have/get
3 to
4 man-made
5 sight (vision)
6 getting/waking
7 waterproof

Homework
Workbook pages 62–63
MyEnglishLab

119

11 The art of make-believe

Unit objectives

Reading:	multiple matching
Vocabulary:	creative arts; live entertainment
Grammar:	reported speech; reporting orders and requests
Listening:	multiple-choice questions
Speaking:	collaborative task
Writing:	writing a review

READING (SB pages 128–129)

To start

Write the word *make-believe* and elicit what it means (to make something up, to imagine something). Ask students to make believe that they have found a genie in a bottle and that they have three wishes. Ask them to note down what they would wish for. Encourage students to be as creative and as imaginative as possible.

Power up

1 Tell students about your favourite cartoon character, e.g. *My favourite cartoon character is Garfield because he reminds me of my own cat.*

Organise students into small groups and ask them to discuss their favourite cartoon characters. Circulate, encouraging students to give reasons for their choices. Conduct class feedback.

Students' own answers.

2 Read the question aloud and ask students to discuss their ideas with a partner. Collect ideas around the class and write them on the board, e.g. *very creative, good at drawing, able to work to deadlines.*

Students' own answers.

Read on

3 If necessary, pre-teach the following words: *current* (belonging to the present), *mess around with* (to do something in a relaxing, not very serious way), *to have a vivid imagination* (to be able to picture things very clearly), *combine* (to mix together). Check students' understanding by asking questions, e.g. *Is history the study of current events?* (no); *Do we study current events in politics?* (yes); *If someone has a vivid imagination, do they find it difficult to imagine things?* (no, they find it easy); *If I combine two things do I mix them together or pull them apart?* (mix them together).

Ask students to read the article and match the headings to the paragraphs. Allow students to check their answers with a partner before checking answers quickly around the class.

1 E   2 C   3 D   4 B   5 A

4 Read the Exam advice with students. They read the article again and match the questions with the paragraphs. Check answers around the class.

1 A   2 C   3 D   4 C   5 A   6 B   7 D   8 E   9 A   10 C

5 Ask students to find words in the article which match the definitions. Check answers orally, personalising the new vocabulary by asking students questions, e.g. *Do you ever doodle when you are talking on the phone? What do you doodle? When you were younger, did you swap football stickers?*

1 issue   2 swapping   3 stain   4 doodling   5 portfolio   6 enable
7 showcase   8 bring (a drawing) to life   9 expertise

Sum up

6 Read the rubric aloud to your students and ask them to complete this task in pairs. Circulate as students summarise what they have read, offering support as necessary.

Students' own answers.

Speak up

7 Ask students to work in groups and talk about their answers to the question. Monitor, noting any good use of language which can be mentioned in the class feedback session. Nominate a student from each group to report back on their ideas.

Students' own answers.

To finish

Tell students to think of their favourite cartoon character. Ask them to tell their partner who their favourite cartoon character is and why. Ask them: *If you were a cartoon character, which would you be and why?* Model the answer, by telling students who you would choose and giving a reason for your answer, e.g.

I think I'd be Road Runner because I'm not very talkative and I'm a fast runner.

Ask students to discuss their ideas with a partner, before conducting class feedback.

Homework

MyEnglishLab

VOCABULARY 1 (SB page 130)

Creative arts

To start

Ask students to look back through their SBs and write down five words they've learned so far in this course. Organise the class into two teams. Nominate a student to come to the front of the class. Ask them to choose one of their words and draw it on the board without saying the word. Their team has to guess what the word is within a minute. The team with the most points is the winner.

1 Students complete the task. Point out that one of the words will not be needed. Read the sentences around the class. Ask them to make a sentence of their own with the word which is not needed (animation).

1 cartoons   2 artwork   3 comics
4 sketch, drawing, crayons, paints

2 Students complete the matching task. Check answers around the class. Then ask them to read out the phrasal verbs from the sentences and write them on the board. Give students a few minutes to discuss what the phrasal verbs mean before conducting class feedback.

1 c   2 d   3 e   4 b   5 a
come out = be published
throw away = get rid of as rubbish
make up = invent
go for it = try to achieve/get/win something
mess around = spend time lazily, doing things slowly

3 Read the words in the box aloud to your students, eliciting the stress patterns of the words which are longer than one syllable. Students complete the conversation with the words. Fast finishers can practise the conversation with a partner.

1 skill   2 imagination   3 world   4 characters   5 experience

4 Play the recording and ask students to check their answers. If time allows, ask students to read the conversation with a partner. Circulate as students do this, focusing on the pronunciation.

➤ Track 11.1

Lola: What's that you're reading, Jake?

Jake: It's a graphic novel. Here, have a look!

Lola: Wow! This is amazing! Look at the artistic skill in some of these drawings! It must take ages to illustrate one of these.

Jake: And you really need a vivid imagination to think up some of these plots!

Lola: Yeah, it's a real fantasy world, isn't it? If I could write, I'd write about dragons and huge monsters!

Jake: Cool! I'd make up my own cartoon characters – maybe animals with special powers.

Lola: Hey, that reminds me: there's a one-day animation course on at the Arts centre at the weekend. Shall we go? It would be an incredible learning experience. We could learn how to bring cartoons to life!

Jake: Great idea!

Word XP

Read the information in the Word XP box. Elicit that a *set phrase* or *expression* is a group of words which belong together and have a particular meaning. Tell students to look out for set phrases and expressions in the article they are about to read.

5 Students read the article and choose the correct answers. Ask them to check their answers quickly with a partner before reading the article around the class. Ask students to tell you the meaning of the phrases in the answers and stress that these groups of words need to be learned together.

1 blown   2 chances   3 nothing   4 go   5 place   6 true

Game on

Read the instructions aloud to your students and organise them into groups. Give them five minutes to come up with an idea for a new comic book or cartoon using three or four characters. Encourage students to make sketches of their characters. Monitor as students discuss their ideas, offering support as necessary. Nominate a student from each group to present their ideas to the rest of the class and have a class vote for the best idea.

To finish

Using the characters from the Game on activity organise students into groups and ask them to draw the first few frames of a comic strip. Display students' work on the wall and encourage students to offer each other positive feedback about their work.

Homework
Workbook page 64
MyEnglishLab

GRAMMAR 1 (SB page 131)

Reported speech

To start

Organise students into pairs. Write the following phrasal verbs on the board and ask students to remind you what they mean.

come out

mess around

make up

go for something

throw something out

Challenge students to choose three of the phrasal verbs and drop them into a conversation with a partner. The first student to succeed in using three of the phrasal verbs is the winner and has to perform their conversation to the rest of the class.

Grammar XP

Read the information and examples in the Grammar XP box aloud to your students.

Ask students to remind you of three things you said at the beginning of the lesson. Write these on the board using speech marks to show that they are direct speech, e.g.

'We're having a test tomorrow.'

'Why don't we open the window?'

'If you've forgotten your homework, you must do it for tomorrow.'

Working as a class, make this directed speech into reported speech. Support your students by providing the first couple of words in each sentence, e.g.

The teacher told us … we were having a test tomorrow.

The teacher suggested … opening a window.

The teacher told us we … had to do our homework for tomorrow.

Generate as many examples as possible, focusing students' attention on what happens to the verb in each case.

1 Focus students' attention on the names, speech bubbles and sentence beginnings (1–5). Ask students to rewrite the comments in the speech bubbles using reported speech, using the Grammar XP box for reference as they complete the task. Students compare their answers with a partner before class feedback.

1 Trish said that she hated TV reality shows and that we/they shouldn't waste time watching them.

2 Max told us that he was starting to get interested in traditional dances and that he was learning some that he'd never seen before.

3 Jasmine told Milly that her aunt had been a rich and quite famous film star and had never had any financial problems.

4 Leo said that there hadn't been many good films on at the cinema recently.

5 Elena said that if I wanted to be really good at playing the clarinet, I would have to put in a lot of hard work.

2 Focus students' attention on the text message and give them a minute to read it. Ask if they have ever experienced anything like this. Students then read the email and complete it with one word in each space. Give students a minute to compare notes before reading the email around the class.

1 told 2 was 3 her 4 were 5 there 6 being 7 were 8 had
9 her 10 was 11 had 12 had

3 Students rewrite the sentences using reported speech. Check answers orally.

1 he wouldn't get paint all over the floor.

2 she couldn't understand what those abstract paintings meant.

3 they had been there before.

4 went/should go to the museum.

5 the band were playing there again the following week.

Write on

4 Ask students to think about something interesting a friend told them recently. Give them an example of your own, e.g.

I met my best friend yesterday and she told me that my favourite shoe shop was having a sale. She said there were lots of great bargains!

Ask students to write a short email reporting on something a friend has told them. Ask students to read their emails to a partner and nominate a few students to read their work aloud to the rest of the class.

Students' own answers.

To finish

Tell students that we sometimes use reported speech to remind people of their promises, e.g. *If our mum says we can stay out late, and then forgets her promise we might say, 'but you said I could stay out late!'*

As a class generate some situations where people don't always keep their promises, e.g.

A boy has promised to love his girlfriend for ever (and then dumps her).

A boss has promised excellent working condition at interview (but the pay and conditions are terrible).

A clothes shop has promised a money back guarantee (but won't take back your jumper when it shrinks).

A friend has promised to go on holiday with you (but lets you down at the last minute).

Organise students into pairs and ask them to choose one of the situations and make a roleplay out of it. Monitor, as students perform their roleplays, focusing on accurate production of the target language. Nominate a few students to perform their roleplay and conduct class feedback.

Homework

Workbook page 66

MyEnglishLab

VOCABULARY 2 (SB page 132)

Live entertainment

To start

Organise students into pairs. Ask them to have a chat with their partner about anything they want or to choose something from the following topics:

the weather

their favourite food

travel

deciding what to do that weekend

Give students a minute to chat about their chosen topic. When the time is up, call the class back together. Nominate a pair of students to perform their conversation for the rest of the class. Pretend that you are having trouble hearing. After a few minutes interrupt the students and ask them to tell you what they said. Repeat this a few time, focusing on accurate use of reported speech.

1 Ask students: *Do you often go to concerts? What's the best venue you've ever experienced?*

Focus students' attention on the photos in Exercise 2 and ask them if they would like to go to a concert in these places. Encourage students to give reasons for their answers and write any new language or useful phrases on the boards.

Students' own answers.

2 Ask students to complete the texts with the words in the boxes. Allow students to check their answers with a partner before reading the texts around the class. Ask students to tell you what is special about each of the venues and to give their opinion on which venue sounds the most exciting and why.

O2 Arena

1 venue   2 acts   3 classical   4 shows   5 exhibition   6 premières

Red Rocks Amphitheatre

1 open-air   2 stage   3 settings   4 acoustics   5 music-lovers
6 background   7 Fame   8 musicians

3 Focus students' attention on the words in the box and ask them to complete the conversation using the words. Then play the recording so that students can check their answers.

➤ Track 11.2

Ben: Hi, Kim. Where are you off to?

Kim: I'm just going to join the queue outside the box office. I want to get a seat in the front row!

Ben: Cool! What play are you going to see?

Kim: Oh, it's a comedy which is really funny. My drama teacher is in one of the main roles and I hope she remembers her lines! How about you?

Ben: I'm off to our final rehearsal before the concert tomorrow. The tickets are sold out and I'm a bit nervous!

Kim: Don't worry, Ben! I'm sure the audience will love you!

1 box office   2 seat   3 row   4 play   5 comedy   6 roles   7 lines
8 rehearsal   9 sold out   10 audience

4 Focus students' attention on the title and ask: *Have you ever had a last-minute panic? What was your last-minute panic about?*

Students complete the article choosing the correct answer. Read the article around the class. Ask your students if they have ever been in a similar situation. How did they feel about it?

1 C   2 A   3 D   4 D   5 A   6 C   7 B   8 D

To finish

Ask students to write a short paragraph about a concert venue in their town. Ask them to think about the following:

Where is the venue? What kind of concerts can you see there? Is it a good venue? Why/Why not?

Ask students to share their paragraph with a partner. Nominate a few students to read their work to the rest of the class.

Homework

Workbook page 65

MyEnglishLab

GRAMMAR 2 (SB page 133)

Reporting orders and requests

To start

Write the following anagrams on the board (solutions in brackets):

eunev (venue)

claislsca (classical)

castuoisc (acoustics)

nepo-ria (open-air)

gesta (stage)

eaiednuc (audience)

Tell students that these are words they learned in yesterday's Vocabulary lesson. Challenge students to see who can be the first to solve them. When a few students are ready, check answers around the class.

Grammar XP

Read the information and examples in the Grammar XP box aloud to your students.

Think of an example where your students might have been ordered or requested to do things, e.g. *going into an exam room*, or *their first day of the course*. Elicit some of the things you asked your students to do on the first day of the course and generate sentences as a class, e.g.

You asked us to keep a vocabulary notebook.

You told us to work with a partner.

You encouraged us to speak English as much as possible.

Elicit the pattern in each of these sentences, e.g. verb + person + *to* infinitive

1 Focus students' attention on the pictures and ask them to complete the sentences to report what the people said. Do the first question together as an example.

1 the audience/the students/them to switch off their mobile phones.
2 him to practise his trumpet in there.
3 Kev/him to bring the tickets with him.
4 the boy/him not to skateboard there.

2 Ask students to rewrite the sentences in reported speech using the verbs in the box. Allow students to check their answers with a partner before conducting class feedback.

1 ordered the students not to make a sound once the curtain went up.
2 persuaded Luke to come to the party on Saturday.
3 allowed her to go to dance classes that term.
4 begged her father to let her go to the concert.

3 Students rewrite the sentences using the words given plus two to four words. Check answers around the class.

1 told us to be
2 think (that) you will become
3 had never taken part
4 the students not to be
5 encouraged me to go in
6 am not having

To finish

Write the following words on the board:

allow, beg, order, persuade

Elicit a situation for each of these verbs (e.g. *a mother might allow her teenager to borrow her car, a teenager might beg to be allowed to the party, a teacher might order her students to be quiet and a student might persuade her friend to let her copy his homework*).

Organise students into pairs and give them a minute to roleplay one of the conversations. Nominate students to report back on their conversations, using the language they have learned to report orders and requests.

Homework

Workbook page 67

MyEnglishLab

LISTENING (SB page 134)

To start

Tell students that today's lesson is going to be all about the performing arts and so you are going to do some drama warm-ups to start with. Organise students so that they are standing in a circle. Write a simple sentence on the board, e.g. *For breakfast this morning I had a fried egg.*

Go around the circle repeating the sentence. Before each student speaks, say an adverb of manner and ask students to say the sentence in this way. Encourage students to suggest adverbs of manner, too. Continue until every student has had a turn.

Power up

1 Focus students' attention on the photo and ask them to describe what they see and how they think the people in the photo are feeling, e.g. *The people are dancing. It looks like modern dance rather than traditional ballet. I think they are feeling free and energetic. They look happy.* Generate as many ideas and suggestions as possible and write new language on the board.

Students' own answers.

2 Give students a minute to discuss this question with a partner before conducting class feedback. Ask students: *Have you ever known anyone who attends a performing arts school? What kinds of things do they do there?*

Students' own answers.

Listen up

3 Focus students' attention on the words in the box. Check understanding and pre-teach any unfamiliar words. After students finish the task, collect answers around the class and drill the pronunciation of tricky words, e.g. *tuition* /tjuˈɪʃən/.

1 sound-proofing 2 tuition 3 lyrics 4 talent-spotters

4 Tell students that they are going to listen to the first part of a radio interview with a teenager called Mick who wants to have a career in the performing arts. Ask students to listen carefully to the recording and note down the performing arts he mentions. Play the recording, twice if necessary. Collect answers around the class.

▶ Track 11.3

Interviewer: Today we have in our studio Mick Rogers, a local boy from Exeter. Mick, at the age of fifteen, has recently got into a top performing arts school, Tring Park School. Mick, hello and welcome to our programme!

Mick: Thanks a lot, Becky. It's great to be here.

Interviewer: How do you feel about getting into the school, Mick?

Mick: Over the moon! It's definitely where I want to be at the moment. It will be a bit weird leaving my family and staying at the school during term-time, but I really hope I can stay in touch with my friends from home. They're important to me!

Interviewer: And in what ways will Tring Park be different from a regular school?

Mick: Well, we'll have normal lessons there, but we'll also have extra hours of tuition in music and dance – and theatrical studies, of course.

music, dance, theatrical studies

5 Give students a minute to read the questions and options. Play the recording, twice if necessary, while students choose the correct answer for each question. Give students a minute to compare their answers with a partner before checking answers orally.

▶ Track 11.4

Interviewer: Today we have in our studio Mick Rogers, a local boy from Exeter. Mick, at the age of fifteen, has recently got into a top performing arts school, Tring Park School. Mick, hello and welcome to our programme!

Mick: Thanks a lot, Becky. It's great to be here.

Interviewer: How do you feel about getting into the school, Mick?

Mick: Over the moon! It's definitely where I want to be at the moment. It will be a bit weird leaving my family and staying at the school during term-time, but I really hope I can stay in touch with my friends from home. They're important to me!

Interviewer: And in what ways will Tring Park be different from a regular school?

Mick: Well, we'll have normal lessons there, but we'll also have extra hours of tuition in music and dance – and theatrical studies, of course.

Interviewer: Tell us about your performing arts experience, Mick.

Mick: Sure, well, I started learning the guitar in my early teens and, like Eric Clapton, I picked up songs simply from listening to them. I spent hours working out the notes until they were perfect. The only thing that interested me was getting to be really good at the instrument – nothing else. Now I play lead guitar in a band. I even write the lyrics for songs sometimes, but my real love is the guitar.

Interviewer: You said you play in a band. Is it difficult to find somewhere to practise?

Mick: Well, we're lucky because my dad lets us use the garage at home. He's put soundproofing in so we can make as much noise as we like! Of course, we're only fifteen, so we've got our schoolwork to do, but we're all mad about music. It would be awesome if the band could stay together, but it might be more difficult after I go to Tring Park in September.

Interviewer: How about acting? Have you ever done much of that?

Mick: Yes, I belong to a teenage theatre group. My friend Logan persuaded me to join the group, but I wasn't sure if I'd be any good. I told Cathy, the organiser, that I hadn't had any previous acting experience, but she wasn't too worried. As it turns out, I seem to have a hidden talent! We went on a theatre trip recently. It was *A Midsummer Night's Dream*, a comedy by William Shakespeare – and we had seats in the front row! Cathy said it was going to be funny, but it wasn't only that, it was brilliant!

Interviewer: What do you like about acting, Mick?

Mick: I certainly get a buzz from the audience. I just love it when they laugh or even cry! Acting is strange: it's like a child's game of make-believe, where you pretend that you're another person for a short time. Rehearsals, of course, are hard work and tiring. But practice makes perfect, as they say!

Interviewer: That's very true. And I know you do some breakdancing. Is it really as easy as it looks?

Mick: No, it isn't! It's just as difficult as professional gymnastics and that's why I go swimming a lot to keep fit! You've got to be passionate about it, otherwise there's no point in trying! You've got to put yourself into it one hundred percent.

Interviewer: So what do you think you'll gain from your time at the performing arts school?

Mick: Well, Tring Park puts on a number of shows each year and I know for sure that talent spotters turn up to these events. Since they'll be on the lookout for promising young performers, I'm just hoping that I can improve my dance technique enough to make a good impression! I definitely think that going there will open a few doors – although my teachers have warned me that the competition is fierce, so we'll see.

Interviewer: I wish you luck, Mick, and keep in touch!

Mick: Many thanks, Becky.

---

1 C **2** B **3** A **4** B **5** A **6** C **7** B

Speak up

6 Focus students' attention on the questions and ask them to discuss their ideas in small groups. Monitor as students complete this task, offering support as necessary. Nominate a student from each group to report back on their discussion.

Students' own answers.

To finish

Play charades to finish off the lesson. Write the following categories on the board:

a film

a musical

a ballet

a play

a song

Tell students to choose one of the categories and think of an example in English. Nominate students to the front to mime their title to the rest of the class who must guess what it is. Demonstrate the activity by miming an example yourself, e.g. the ballet *Swan Lake*.

Homework

MyEnglishLab

SPEAKING (SB page 135)

To start

Write these headings in four columns on the board: *film, dance, music, art*.

Organise students into groups and give each group a different coloured piece of chalk or pen. Give them one minute to fill the columns with as many different words and phrases related to the headings as possible. When the minute is up, ask students to sit down and look at the language which has been generated. Count the words from each colour and see which team thought of the most topic related words. Generate as many words and phrases as possible.

Power up

1 Focus students' attention on the photo. Ask them to describe what they see and to suggest what they think the people in the photo are working on. Generate as much language as possible and write students' suggestions on the board.

Students' own answers.

2 Nominate a student to read the list of weekend courses aloud. Ask them to match the courses with the comments. Check answers orally, eliciting reasons for their answers.

1 c, f **2** a, e **3** h, j **4** d, g **5** b, i

3 Tell your class that they are going to listen to two students discussing how useful the 'acting as an extra' course would be. As students listen they should note down any phrases from the Language XP box which they hear being used. Check answers orally.

Student 1: What do you think about working as an extra at the film studios? I think that would be really interesting.

Student 2: Yes, I agree. Especially for any teenagers who are interested in acting and who might want a career in the theatre or films. They could learn more about how films are made. And if you're an extra, you can get experience without having to play a particular role.

Student 1: OK. Now what about the next one, creating fashion with ...

What do you think about ... ?
What about ... ?

Language XP

Nominate students to read aloud the phrases in the Language XP box. Drill pronunciation and intonation of the phrases chorally and individually. Emphasise that it is important to sound polite but firm when you are managing a discussion.

4 Students listen to more of the same conversation. This time they are going to listen to the two students deciding which course would be the most popular. Ask them to note down the phrases from the Language XP box which are used. Collect answers around the class.

➤ Tracks 11.6

Student 1: Well, a lot of teenagers are interested in tattoos, aren't they? So perhaps that one might be the most popular. What do you think?

Student 2: I'm not sure. Working with a wildlife photographer would be good, but most teenagers wouldn't like the idea of working at night very much – if that was necessary.

Student 1: So, shall we decide?

Student 2: OK then, let's say the tattoo artist.

What do you think?,
So, shall we decide?

Speak up

5 Read the Exam advice aloud to your students. Stress the importance of being able to keep the conversation going, especially in an exam situation. Organise students into pairs and read the tasks aloud. Remind students to use the language in the Language XP box and the comments in Exercise 2 to help them.

Circulate as they complete the task, offering support where necessary and noting down examples of how students have successfully managed their discussion. Conduct class feedback.

Students' own answers.

To finish

Choose a group who kept the conversation going successfully in Exercise 5. Ask them to perform their conversation again in front of the whole class. Ask the class to listen and note down strategies the students use to keep the conversation going. Conduct class feedback and write down students' observations on the board.

Homework

MyEnglishLab

WRITING (SB pages 136–137)

To start

Ask students to choose five new words they've learned in this unit. Organise students into pairs and ask them to read the words to their partner who should listen and write them down. Students should check the spelling of the words in their SB, awarding themselves points for each word they have spelled correctly.

Power up

1 Focus students' attention on the photo and ask them to describe what they see. Organise students into pairs to discuss the questions. After a minute, open this up into a class discussion. Encourage students to give reasons for their answers and write new language on the board.

Students' own answers.

2 Nominate a student to read out the first comment. Ask students whether this person was satisfied or disappointed and ask them to tell you the key words and phrases which helped them arrive at their answer (satisfied: *better than I'd expected, really brought it to life*). Students then read through the rest of the comments alone, deciding if the speakers were satisfied or disappointed with what they saw.

1 satisfied 2 disappointed 3 satisfied 4 disappointed

Plan on

3 Read the task aloud to your students. Ask students to read the review in silence and answer the questions. Check answers around the class.

1 at the end of the summer term
2 hip hop dancing, school choir singing blues, a play by the drama group, the school orchestra playing film music
3 hip hop – excellent, school choir – brilliant, drama group – OK but forgot their lines, orchestra – professional

4 Refer students to the two plans and ask them to decide which plan the review in Exercise 3 follows. Allow students to discuss their ideas with a partner before checking answers.

B

5 Ask students to complete the sentences with adjectives from the review. Read the sentences around the class.

I disappointing   2 proud   3 brilliant, great, excellent   4 nervous
5 professional

Language XP

Read the phrases out loud to the class and point out the different structures used each time. Ask students to think of a disappointing film, show or concert they have seen recently. Generate *It's a pity* phrases and write them on the board.

6 Ask students to read the situations and write sentences. Check answers orally.

Students' own answers.

7 Refer students to the linking words in the box. Challenge students to see who can be first to find three of the linking words and phrases in the model review. Write students' answers on the board. Focus students' attention on the position of the linking words in the sentences.

They were good, **but** a bit disappointing.

However, they carried on and …

All in all, it was an exciting evening … ,

8 Ask students to work in pairs to complete the sentences with the linking words and phrases from Exercise 7. Remind them that sometimes more than one answer is possible.

I although/but

2 Despite

3 but

4 Generally speaking/All in all/On the whole

5 However

Write on

9 Nominate a student to read the notice aloud to the rest of the class. Organise students into pairs to discuss what they could write about. Open this up into a class discussion. Generate as many ideas as possible and write them on the board.

Students' own answers.

10 Refer students back to the plans in Exercise 4. Tell them that they can choose either of these plans to follow and write their review. Read the questions aloud to your students and ask them to include this information in the review they write, pointing out the Exam advice as you do so. Circulate as students write their plans, offering support if necessary.

Students' own answers.

11 Students write their reviews. When they have written a few paragraphs, ask them to exchange their work with a partner. They should read the review so far and check that their partner is following the plan, and including the information in the correct order. Students should then continue writing their review, bearing any feedback from their partner in mind. Nominate a few students to read their reviews aloud to the rest of the class and display the best reviews on your classroom wall.

Students' own answers.

Model answer

This summer I went to see the youth drama group put on *A Midsummer Night's Dream* by William Shakespeare. The performance took place in the gardens of the town hall on a beautiful summer evening.

The play tells the story of a group of fairies who like to play tricks on humans, especially working magic to make people fall in love!

The acting was lively and enthusiastic. They really brought Shakespeare's play to life and made it feel fresh and modern. I was really impressed by some of the younger members of the group who remembered all their lines and showed no signs of stage fright.

It was a pity that there were no cushions on the grass. After an hour, some of the older members of the audience started to get uncomfortable and I think that we would all have enjoyed the play even more if we had had something soft to sit on. However, it was still a brilliant evening!

At the end of the play, the actors got a great round of applause. It seemed as if everyone agreed that this was a brilliant show. I'd definitely recommend going to see this performance.

To finish

Tell students that they are going to organise an English school show for the end of term. Organise students into groups and ask them to discuss the following:

What will be performed: music, dance, theatre, other?

What kind of music will there be?

How will the show be advertised?

Who will be invited?

Monitor, as students discuss the questions. Conduct class feedback and find out what your students are planning.

Homework

MyEnglishLab

SWITCH ON (SB page 138)

Can you believe your eyes?

1 Read the rubric aloud to your students. Ask them to read the definitions of stop motion animation and choose the one they think is correct. Play the video and allow them to check their answers.

A

2 Give students a few moments to read the steps. Play the video again so that students can put the steps in the correct order. Allow students to check their answers with a partner before conducting class feedback.

1 Start videoing person A.
2 Pull a piece of material up to hide person A.
3 Stop the video.
4 Swap person B for person A behind the material.
5 Start videoing again and slowly lower the material.
6 Play the final completed video.

3 Organise students into pairs. Ask them to complete the steps for the telekinesis video. Play the video one more time so that students can check their answers. Read the steps around the class.

1 Place a glass of water in the middle of the table.
2 Start videoing person A who is staring at the glass.
3 Stop the video.
4 Move the glass a bit towards person A.
5 Start videoing again.
6 Repeat steps 3, 4 and 5 until person A picks up the glass and drinks the water.
7 Play the final complete video.

Project

4 Read the options aloud to your students and ask them to choose the one they prefer. Organise students into groups so that they are working with people who have chosen the same option. Note: Part C might be slightly more time consuming than the other options, so students who choose this can complete some of the activity out of class. Monitor as students complete their projects, offering support and guidance where necessary and making sure that everyone is participating. Bring the class together to present their ideas and show their videos. Encourage students to give each other constructive feedback.

Students' own answers.

REVISION (SB page 139)

1
1 cartoon
2 crayon
3 sketch
4 fantasy
5 animation
6 imagination

2
1 (that) he couldn't find all his old comics.
2 us (that) she had bought some new drawing materials the day before.
3 we all went/we should go to the film première the following day.
4 me (that) I had quite a lot of artistic talent.
5 he wasn't really working very hard then.
6 them (that) she would meet them there in an hour.

3
1 rehearsal
2 audience
3 stage
4 musicians
5 lines
6 classical

4
1 were not allowed to take
2 ordered the fans to stand
3 begged her parents to let
4 advised Mark to buy the
5 warned the children not to

5
1 out
2 out
3 away
4 of
5 said/explained
6 to
7 us
8 for

Homework
Workbook pages 68–69
MyEnglishLab

12 Find your voice

Unit objectives

Reading:	gapped text
Vocabulary:	values; issues: fair or unfair?
Grammar:	modal verbs (2); reply questions; question tags
Listening:	multiple matching
Speaking:	making a speech
Writing:	writing an essay

READING (SB pages 140–141)

To start

Focus students on the title of the unit and ask them what it means. Then ask: *Why might someone need to 'find their voice'? Can you think of an example of someone who found their voice?* Generate as much discussion as possible and write any new language on the board.

Power up

1 Ask students if any of them have ever spoken in public. If so, find out more by asking, *Where were you? What were you speaking about? How did you feel?*

Focus students' attention on the scale and ask them to discuss with a partner how confident they feel about public speaking. Nominate students to report back on their discussion and encourage them to explain their reasons. Generate as much discussion as possible and write new language on the board.

Students' own answers.

Read on

2 If necessary, pre-teach the following words and phrases: *standing up for something* (to defend something), *shocked* (very surprised and upset about something), *stare* (to look at something for a long time), *research* (to find out more about a particular subject). Check students' understanding by asking questions: *If you stand up for something, do you say it is important or do you say it is not important?* (You say it's important.); *Would you be shocked if you got a nice birthday present from your friend?* (no); *Would you be shocked if you saw a car crash from your window?* (yes); *If you stare at something, do you look at it and then look away quickly?* (no); *Do you look at it for a long time?* (yes); *Do you research a pair of shoes you can't find?* (no); *What might you research?*

Tell students that they are going to read an article about four teenage speakers. Give the students a few moments to discuss with a partner which four topics the teenagers speak about. Conduct class feedback.

graffiti   love is bad   the right to equal pay   Greek gods

Background

Hyde Park Corner is a very famous spot in London where people are free to stand on wooden boxes (soap boxes) and speak about things which they find important. They do not need to plan or announce their speech beforehand. They do risk being 'heckled' (disagreed with) by members of the public though.

3 Ask students to read the rest of the article quickly. Ask them what they think the number at the beginning of each paragraph refers to (a reference to a piece of information in each paragraph). Find out how well the speakers do in the competition. Check answers orally.

They don't make it to the final.

4 Read the Exam advice aloud to your class. Ask students to read the article again and complete the task. Point out that one of the sentences is not needed. Allow students to check their answers with a partner before conducting class feedback.

1 d **2** b **3** f **4** a **5** g **6** c

5 Focus students' attention on the definitions and ask them to match these with words in the text. Point out that some of the words may be found in the missing sentences. Collect answers around the class.

1 complication
2 random
3 nerve-racking
4 relieved
5 mess up
6 expect
7 focus (on)
8 orphanage

Sum up

6 Ask students to order the events. Then ask them to work with a partner and retell the teenagers' experience in the order it happened. Circulate as students complete this activity, offering support when necessary.

1 e   2 c   3 a   4 d   5 b

Speak up

7 Read the rubric aloud to your students and ask them to discuss their ideas with a partner. Nominate students to report back on their partners' ideas.

Students' own answers.

To finish

Organise a light-hearted version of *The Speaker* competition in your class. Working as a class, generate a list of interesting topics and write them on the board. Ask students to pick one. Organise them into pairs and tell them they need to talk for one minute about their subject without hesitating or repeating themselves. Set a timer and monitor, choosing the three strongest speakers in the class to take part in the final. As a class, choose a topic for each of the final speakers. (You can choose challenging topics as this is the final.) The finalists must then speak on their allocated topic for one minute. The winner is the person who manages to speak for a minute without hesitation or interruption.

Homework

MyEnglishLab

VOCABULARY 1 (SB page 142)

Values

To start

Organise students into small groups. Tell them that they have a minute to write down and remember as many facts as they can about the final of *The Speaker*. After a minute, conduct class feedback. Award a point for each correctly remembered point and award double points for use of the new language learned in this lesson. The group with the most points at the end is the winner.

1 Focus students' attention on the words in the box and ask them to complete the sentences. Point out that three of the words are not needed. Check answers around the class and ask students if they can make sentences using the two words that they didn't need (*clear, clarity*).

2 conclude, conclusion

3 individual

4 view

5 admit

6 prepare, preparation

7 speech

8 argue

2 Read the words around the class, drilling pronunciation chorally and individually. Write the words on the board and elicit the stress patterns of each. Ask students to find and translate each word. Students should check their translations with a partner.

Students' own answers.

3 Tell students that they are going to listen to six people talking about values and ask them to match the speakers with the values in Exercise 2 which they describe. Point out that two of the values are not spoken about. Allow students to check their answers with a partner before conducting class feedback.

1

Presenter: So, guys, I want your opinions on what sort of values are most important to you.

Girl 1: I hate to see people arguing. I think any group of friends should stick together, you know? They should all feel part of the group, so they're almost like one person? That's what friends are for.

2

Boy 1: I think it's really important that everyone is equal. No one is more important than another person, whether it's a boy or girl, an old person or young person, or someone from another country. We're all the same.

3

Girl 2: I agree with Charlie. We're all equal, but the way you treat people is more important, especially teachers and students! You should think about the other person's feelings and listen to their point of view, even if you don't agree or don't understand them.

4

Boy 2: I think there are even bigger things to think about. All children should be given food and water. They need somewhere to live, they need to be healthy and they should have an education. There are laws about this and charities like UNICEF make sure children get these things.

5

Girl 3: Well, I just look at things on a more personal level, really. If you're open with your friends and family and you tell people the truth, I think that's the only value you need. It's that simple. If everyone was truthful, the world would be fine.

6

Boy 3: I think Flora's right about keeping things more personal. The way I look at it, everyone's got their strong points. We all have weaknesses, too, but you just need to look for the best in everyone, that's all. If you do that, you can really make a difference.

---

1 h **2** a **3** d **4** f **5** c **6** g

4 Tell students which value you think is the most important and give a reason for your choice. Say something like:
I think that equality is the most important, because we will never have unity or freedom in this world if some people have all the power and riches of the world.

Organise students into small groups and ask them to discuss this question, giving real examples to illustrate their choices wherever possible. Circulate, offering support wherever necessary and noting down any interesting choices and use of language to be discussed later.

Students' own answers.

Word XP

Point out the importance of noticing words which go together and focus on the example *be in love*. Stress the importance of learning the whole phrase and not just the verb *love*. Ask students to note down and learn the new collocations they will come across in Exercise 4.

5 Ask students to match the sentence halves. Check answers around the class and ask students to make a note of the new collocations.

1 c **2** d **3** b **4** a

6 Focus students' attention on the words in the box and ask them to complete the web page. Allow them to check their answers with a partner before reading the text around the class. Ask students if they think that Mill House sounds like a pleasant school to go to, and ask them if their school has similar values.

1 show **2** focus **3** speak **4** have **5** stand **6** take **7** take **8** believe **9** stand **10** stick

Game on

Explain that students are going to make a mini crossword for their partner. Choose a word from the page and write an example clue on the board, e.g. *when people are the same*. Elicit the answer (equality). Circulate as students prepare their crosswords, offering support where necessary. Students should then exchange and complete each other's crosswords.

To finish

Conduct a brief class discussion about the values of your students' school. Generate as many ideas as possible and write language on the board. Elicit what the logo of Mill House School is (a house). Organise students into groups and ask them to design a logo which reflects the values of their school. Conduct a class vote to see which logo is the most popular.

Homework
Workbook page 70
MyEnglishLab

GRAMMAR 1 (SB page 143)
Modal verbs (2)

To start

Practise the collocations your students learned in the previous lesson. Organise students into two teams. Tell students that you are going to say a word. The first student to put up their hand and tell you a word it collocates with wins a point for their team. The team with the most points at the end of the game is the winner.

Ideas:

the truth (tell)

a real difference (make)

advice (give or follow)

skill (learn)

respect (show)

focus (on)

stand up (for yourself/themselves)

stick (together)

Grammar XP

Read the information and examples in the Grammar XP box with students. Nominate a confident student to come to the front of the class. Tell them that she or he is going to mime a situation and that the rest of the class are going to guess what is happening using the target language.

Whisper to your student to mime *being at a disco* and ask your students to make guesses, e.g. *I'm not sure. She could be at a party. She's dancing. She must be at a disco!*

Repeat this a few times, nominating a few students to come forward and mime activities and writing students' suggestions and guesses on the board.

Suggested situations:

getting your exam results

waiting in the doctor's surgery

visiting the opticians

robbing a bank

dancing in a ballet

arguing with your boy/girlfriend

1 Focus students' attention on the task and ask them to decide if each pair of sentences have the same or a different meaning. Allow students to check their answers with a partner before conducting class feedback.

1 S (*may* has the same meaning as *perhaps*, i.e. 'not very sure')

2 D (*should* does not have the same meaning as *will*, i.e. 'not very sure' vs. 'sure')

3 S (*Could* has the same meaning as *Do you think?*)

4 D (*might not* does not have the same meaning as *won't*, i.e. 'not very sure' vs. 'sure'.)

5 S (*I don't think* does has the same meaning as *it can't*, i.e. 'sure')

2 Ask students to rewrite the sentences using the verbs in the box. Check answers around the class.

1 She must be feeling really nervous.

2 They should arrive at about six.

3 He may not get through to the next round.

4 They could be discussing the results.

5 You can't have forgotten your notes!

6 They could be members of the audience.

3 Students complete the text by choosing the correct answers and then compare their answers with a partner. Check answers by reading the text around the class. Elicit whether they have a debating society at school. If not, would they like to have one? Why/Why not?

1 A 2 C 3 A 4 C 5 B 6 A

Speak up

4 Read the question aloud to your students and ask them to discuss it in pairs, using the language from the Grammar XP box. Circulate as they complete the activity, focusing on accurate use of the target language. Nominate a few students to report back on their discussion.

Students' own answers.

To finish

Write questions on the board and ask students to discuss them with a partner, using the target language, e.g.

What might life be like in this school ten years from now? How do you think people will travel? What will people eat? How will people dress?

Homework

Workbook page 72

MyEnglishLab

VOCABULARY 2 (SB page 144)

Issues: fair or unfair?

To start

Find some newspapers or magazines with interesting pictures. Organise students into groups and ask each group to speculate on what is happening in the picture, using modal verbs, e.g.

There must have been a car accident.

She's surrounded by fans. She must be famous.

It's a European city. It could be Paris.

When students have had a chance to make some guesses, swap the pictures around. Continue until students have seen all the pictures. Conduct class feedback.

1 Ask students to choose the correct words to complete the sentences. Allow them to check answers with a partner before conducting class feedback. Explain that they will hear the correct answers in the next task.

1 mature   2 informal   3 responsible   4 illegal   5 unlucky

2 Play the recording so that students can check their answers. Encourage discussion about any of the statements which students find interesting and ask students whether they were surprised by any of the answers.

> **Track 12.2**

1

A: In Scotland you can vote at the age of sixteen because the government have decided that young people this age are mature.

2

A: In most countries everyone dresses up to attend a wedding; it's unacceptable to wear informal clothes.

3

A: Wearing a helmet when you ride a bike is responsible and saves lives.

4

A: Riding a motorbike without a helmet is illegal in most countries, but not everyone follows the law.

5

A: In China and Japan, the number four is believed to be unlucky, so many people don't want four in their phone numbers or car number plates.

Word XP

Refer students to the information in the Word XP box. Read the examples around the class and ask students to think of more examples to add to the list.

3 Focus students' attention on the words in the box and explain that they are going to have to make these adjectives negative by using the prefixes from the Word XP box. Students complete the sentences. Give them a minute to check their answers with a partner before reading the sentences around the class.

1 irregular   2 incorrect   3 unreliable   4 untidy   5 dissatisfied
6 impolite   7 illogical   8 dishonest

4 Ask students to complete the sentences. When the sentences are complete, students should compare their ideas with their partners. Nominate a few students to tell the class about their partners' ideas.

Students' own answers.

5 Focus students' attention on the title of the problem page and ask them to tell you their opinion. Students should then complete the letter. Read the letter around the class and ask questions to check understanding such as: *Why did Leo cheat in his exam?* (Because he had missed some work when he was ill and couldn't catch up.); *Why is Leo's friend upset?* (Because she got zero for the test.); *What does Leo's friend want him to do?* (explain the situation to the teacher).

1 impossible   2 informal   3 unlucky   4 unacceptable   5 dishonest
6 illegal   7 unfair   8 argument

Speak up

6 Ask students to work in small groups and discuss what advice they would give to Leo. Circulate as students complete this task, offering support if necessary. Conduct class feedback and generate a discussion about what things in life are unfair.

Students' own answers.

To finish

Tell students about a situation you think is unfair, e.g.

I parked my car to go and help an old woman who had fallen on the street. In the end I had to go to hospital with her and was there for hours. When I got back to my car, I had been given a parking ticket. Do you think this is fair?

Ask students to think of an unfair situation they have experienced and tell their partner about it. Nominate a few students to report back, and as a class decide how fair or unfair the situations were.

Homework

Workbook page 71

MyEnglishLab

GRAMMAR 2 (SB page 145)

Reply questions and question tags

To start

Organise students into two teams. Tell students that you are going to read out a list of adjectives. The first student to put up their hand and tell you the opposite form of the adjective wins a point for their team. The team with the most points at the end of the game wins.

Ideas:

satisfied

tidy

honest

correct

regular

logical

rational

possible

necessary

Grammar XP

Read the information and examples in the Grammar XP box aloud to your students. Generate some examples with your students and focus on how intonation changes meaning.

1 Ask students to match each reply question with the correct statement. Check answers around the class.

1 Hasn't he?

2 Won't she?

3 Were they?

4 Can't you?

5 Did you?

6 Must we?

2 Tell students that they are going to listen to two sentences and decide which one is asking for information and which one is expecting agreement. Play the recording, twice if necessary and check answers orally. Ask students to read the sentences following the intonation arrows.

➤ **Track 12.3**

1 Our speech should be two minutes long, shouldn't it?

2 There are three judges, aren't there?

1 asking for information

2 expecting agreement

3 Tell students that they are going to listen to more sentences and decide if the speakers are asking for information or expecting agreement.

➤ **Tracks 12.4 and 12.5**

1 We can't use notes for the real speech, can we?

2 We have to do a lot of research, don't we?

3 The advisors won't watch us, will they?

4 You don't know how big the audience is, do you?

1 I   2 A   3 A   4 I

4 Play the recording again and allow students to check their answers. Pause the recording after each sentence and ask students to repeat what they have heard. Focus on the correct intonation. Drill chorally and individually.

Students' own answers.

5 Ask students to complete the sentences with question tags. Check answers around the class.

1 don't they

2 will you

3 haven't we

4 isn't he

5 hasn't she

6 should you

7 aren't they

8 won't you

6 Organise students into pairs. Ask them to take it in turns to ask and answer the questions in Exercise 5. Monitor, offering support and modelling correct intonation where necessary.

Students' own answers.

7 Focus students' attention on the conversation. Ask them to complete it with one word in each space. Allow them to check their answers with a partner before conducting class feedback.

1 we   2 shall   3 might/may   4 am   5 is   6 will   7 must   8 did

Speak up

8 Refer students to the example and demonstrate the activity with a confident student. Organise students into pairs and ask them to take it in turns to make up statements and reply with a reply question, adding an extra comment. Monitor, focusing on correct intonation and accurate use of reply questions. Note down any problems to address in the class feedback session.

Students' own answers.

To finish

Organise students into pairs and ask them to talk about their plans for the weekend. Ask them to make a note each time they use a reply question. Conduct feedback and find out who has used the most reply questions in their conversation. Ask this pair to perform their conversation to the rest of the class.

Homework

Workbook page 73

MyEnglishLab

LISTENING (SB page 146)

To start

Tell students a short story about yourself to illustrate a proverb. Say something like:

I used to live in a really small house without a garden and I was always a little jealous of my neighbour who lived in a house with a nice big garden. Well, finally I moved into a house with an enormous garden and I'm just exhausted because it's such hard work. I'm so envious of my friend who lives in a flat. You know what they say – the grass is always greener on the other side.

Elicit that this is a proverb (*the grass is always greener on the other side*) and ask students to discuss what they think it means (it means that people always want what they don't have). Tell students they are going to learn about proverbs in this lesson.

Power up

1 Ask students to match the proverbs with their meanings. Ask students to check their answers in pairs and choose the advice they think is the best. Conduct class feedback. Find out which proverb students chose and ask them to give reasons for their choice.

1 e 2 f 3 d 4 a 5 b 6 c

2 Give students a minute to work with a partner, think of a proverb and try to translate it into English. Collect students' ideas around the class.

Students' own answers.

Listen up

3 Tell the class that they are going to listen to five students talking about their opinions on different subjects. Give students a minute to read the statements before playing the recording, twice if necessary. Check answers around the class.

1

Woman: Hi, I'm Alesha. I'm calling with some advice that more people should follow. My advice is: always, always tell the truth. Being honest is really hard to do, so it shows you have a good character, doesn't it? For example, if my boyfriend is wearing something I don't like, I tell him, 'It's rubbish,' or 'It doesn't suit you.' No messing about. He might not be too happy about it, but I can't stand being untruthful. My motto is 'Tell it like it is.' That way, there's no room for misunderstanding.

2

Man: I'd like to talk about our school anti-bullying campaign and how each person can make a difference. It's all about your actions. When I'm not sure what to do, I try to think of my gran's advice. She used to say, 'Your beliefs don't make you a better person; your behaviour does.' I think she meant that if you believe in something, like 'Stand up to bullies' you have to do something about it, too. So if you see someone being bullied or treated unfairly, you should step in and say something, shouldn't you?

3

Woman: I'm phoning to ask for volunteers or donations for *Neighbour Support*. When my parents came to this country, they didn't have much money, but they shared the things they had with their neighbours, like the iron or a hairdryer. Even food was shared – we often ate with the family next door. Now they're successful, but they always remember how difficult things were at first. They've set up a local centre to help people in the same situation. If you can spare an hour of your time or a packet of food, please call us: 546230073.

4

Man: I'm phoning in today with an appeal for more young people to join our charity run to raise money for UNICEF. The run is in the town centre next month and the closing date for entries is tomorrow. We'd love to hear from groups of friends who would do the run together. I know there are a lot of young people out there who are always ready to get their sports kit on to support this charity. The run is always fun and we usually raise a huge amount of money to help an orphanage in Africa. So, join us if you can!

5

Man: My best piece of advice to anyone would be 'Don't take everything so seriously, man!' I mean, so many people go around with a really long face, like this. What I say is why worry about things? Life's too short, isn't it? You should just go out there and have as much fun as you can. Hang out with friends, have a laugh, just chill. Oh, and one more thing: smile! 'Smile and the world smiles with you.' That's what my mum always tells me!

1 d 2 h 3 a 4 c 5 f

4 Ask students to tell you which speaker they think is in the photo. Encourage them to give reasons for their choice.

Speaker 3 (She talks about helping your neighbours and sharing food and the picture shows a large group of people sharing food.)

Speak up

5 Focus students' attention on the words and phrases in the box and drill pronunciation chorally and individually, focusing on any potentially tricky words, e.g. *behaviour* /bɪˈheɪvjə/. Ask students to discuss the statements from Exercise 4 and choose the ones they agree with most, giving reasons for their answers. Monitor as students complete this task, offering support where necessary.

Students' own answers.

6 Ask students to give their opinions and reasons for their answers. Encourage them to use the words in the box in Exercise 5 in their answers.

Students' own answers.

To finish

Organise students into small groups. Ask them to choose a short proverb and think of a story which illustrates it. Monitor as students prepare their story. Nominate students to tell their story to the rest of the class.

Homework
MyEnglishLab

SPEAKING (SB page 147)

To start

Write the beginning of a proverb from the Listening lesson on the board, e.g.
The early bird ...
Ask students to complete the proverb (*catches the worm*). Students should then write down the first part of three proverbs they learned in the previous lesson and read them to their partner who has to listen and complete the proverb.

Power up

1 Read the questions aloud to your students. Organise students into groups and ask them to discuss their ideas. After a few minutes, open this up into a class discussion. Generate as many ideas as possible and write students' suggestions on the board.

Students' own answers.

2 Focus students' attention on the photos and ask them to describe what they see. Ask them to compare the photos with their partners and discuss the advantages and disadvantages of each. Monitor, encouraging students to use phrases from the Language XP box.

Students' own answers.

Language XP

Refer students to the phrases in the Language XP box. Stress that this is very useful language to use when you are talking about a photo and you are not exactly certain of what you see.

Speak up

3 Focus students' attention on the rubric and the list of advice. Organise students into pairs and tell them they have a minute to add as many ideas to the list as they can think of, e.g. *make eye contact, speak in a loud voice*. Conduct class feedback and write ideas on the board.

Students' own answers.

4 Refer students to the list and ask them to choose a topic that they could speak about or to think of their own topic. Ask students to think of two arguments for and against each question. Monitor as students note down their ideas, offering support where necessary.

Students' own answers.

5 Tell students that they are going to listen to a teenager's one minute speech and answer questions about it. Play the recording, twice if necessary. Allow students to check their answers with a partner before conducting class feedback.

➤ Track 12.7

I'm here today to speak to you about respect. It's a subject that's very important to me because it's something my parents have always taught me. I think if you only have one value, this is the one you should have.

So what is respect? Respect means being polite, listening to other people's opinions and behaving to other people the way you would like them to behave towards you.

Adults often expect teenagers to show respect. They complain that too many young people behave badly and I don't think that's fair. In my opinion, the world would be a better place if more adults listened to young people; we have a lot of good ideas about how to change and improve things. You just need to listen.

So to conclude, respect is not a one-way street. It's not just about our behaviour towards adults. Respect is a two-way street. Thank you for listening.

1 2
2 C and B
3 C, B, A

6 Tell students that they are going to plan and write a brief speech, using the notes they made in Exercise 4 to help them. Organise them into pairs and ask them to practise their speech. Refer them to the Exam advice before they begin.

Students' own answers.

7 Elicit ways in which students can give each other constructive criticism, e.g. *I really liked what you said, but maybe you should say it a bit more loudly and clearly next time to make sure everyone hears.*

Students' own answers.

8 Nominate a confident student to deliver their speech to the class. Elicit positive feedback from the class and offer some constructive feedback of your own. Refer students to the list of things to think about and ask them to suggest one thing which could be improved for next time. Listen to a few more speeches and repeat this process.

Students' own answers.

9 Organise students into pairs. Ask them to turn to pages 158–159. Focus students' attention on the photos and the written prompts. Give them a couple of minutes to jot down ideas. When the time is up, ask them to start talking about their photos. Remind them to use the new language they have learned this lesson for making a sensible guess. They should then swap, so that their partner talks about his/her photos. Circulate, listening and noting down any good examples of language and any problems.

Students' own answers.

To finish

Students revisit the tips they wrote in Exercise 3. Ask students: *What other tips would you add now you have given a speech?* Ask students to make posters illustrating their top tips. Display the posters on the wall for future reference.

Homework
MyEnglishLab

WRITING (SB pages 148–149)

To start

Write the following sentence beginnings on the board:

Families are important because …

Friends are important because …

Ask students to complete the sentences with their own ideas. Allow students to compare their answers with a partner before reading sentences around the class. Encourage discussion about the subject of family, as this will help students when they come to do their writing task this lesson. Ask questions such as:

Are families less important now than they used to be?

Which plays a more important role in your life: your family or friends?

Who has the greater influence on you: your parents or your friends?

Generate as much discussion as possible and write new language on the board.

Power up

1 Focus students' attention on the photos and ask them to describe what they see. Read the question aloud to your students and ask them to discuss the examples and add some ideas of their own.

Students' own answers.

2 Elicit the meaning of the word *role model* (someone who sets a good example for you to follow). Ask students to discuss this question in groups and talk about their family and friends, giving reasons for their answers. Conduct class feedback.

Students' own answers.

Plan on

3 Read the rubric and the essay prompt aloud to your students. Allow them to discuss their idea for a third point with a partner. Elicit ideas, e.g. *money worries, parents' career opportunities, tension in the family, nobody for teens to talk to, doing things together as a family.*

Students' own answers.

4 Read the question aloud to your students and ask them to read the essay in silence. Ask them whether they agree with the student's point. Encourage them to give reasons for their answers.

Students' own answers.

Language XP

Draw students' attention to the phrases in the Language XP box. Explain that these are very important for writing an essay and that they should try to memorise one or two such phrases for use in their writing.

5 Challenge students to see who can be the first to find all the linking words in the essay. Conduct class feedback and point out the position of the linking words within the sentences.

so, while … others … , on the one hand, especially, like, on the other hand, too, although, because, in addition, in conclusion, in my opinion, but

6 Ask students to complete the sentences with their own ideas. Give students a chance to share their sentences with a partner before conducting class feedback.

Students' own answers.

Write on

7 Organise students into pairs. Ask them to read the essay prompt and discuss their opinions. Monitor as students complete this task, offering support where necessary.

Students' own answers.

8 Ask students to make a list of things they could write for the third point. Open this up into a class discussion and ask students to share and compare their ideas.

Students' own answers.

9 Ask students to make notes and organise their argument. Suggest that they refer to the model essay in Exercise 4 to help them structure their ideas. Monitor as students write their essay plan, offering guidance where necessary.

Students' own answers.

10 Read the Exam advice aloud to your students. Ask students to write their essay. When students have finished, write this checklist on the board and ask them to check their work:

– *introduction?*

– *conclusion?*

– *linking words and phrases?*

– *both sides of the argument?*

– *grammar and spelling?*

Nominate a few students to read their essay aloud to the rest of the class.

Students' own answers.

Model answer

In many families, parents and teenagers argue about housework. Often, parents think that teenagers should help at home, but teenagers sometimes disagree with this idea.

On the one hand, I agree with teenagers who think that life is too short to worry about housework. Teenagers are very busy with school work and so they don't want to come home to do boring tasks like tidying their rooms. On the other hand, it seems unfair for parents to do all the work, especially if they work full-time.

Although I am very busy at school, I take pride in the fact that my room is always tidy and I help with chores such as doing the shopping and washing-up. It's not always the most enjoyable work, but I think that it's important to help at home. What's more, knowing how to do housework will help me when I am an adult.

In conclusion, although I feel that my free time is precious, I think that teenagers should help at home. In my opinion, it is unfair and unreasonable of teenagers to think they can get away with doing nothing to help their parents.

To finish

Give students a nice souvenir they can take away from the last lesson of the course: *a friendship spider*. Distribute blank pieces of A4 paper. Take a sheet of paper, write your name in the middle, and draw a circle around it. Pass your piece of paper to the person on your right, and ask your class to do the same. Draw a 'leg' from the name in the middle of your piece of paper and tell learners that this is a spider's leg. At the end of the leg they are going to write something <u>nice</u> about the person whose name is in the middle of the piece of paper (Encourage them to make their language as interesting as possible!) This can be a compliment about the person's appearance, character, mention of a special talent this person has, an interesting fact you remember about this person or a positive prediction about their future.

Students keep passing their bits of paper round and adding comments until the paper has come full circle. Students can then read and enjoy the comments on their friendship spider.

Homework

MyEnglishLab

SWITCH ON (SB page 150)

Brittany speaks out

1 Focus students' attention on the question. Give them a minute to read the sentences and make their predictions. Play the video and ask students to check their answers against what they saw in the feedback. Conduct class feedback. Ask: *How many questions did you guess right?*

1 Rio de Janeiro
2 Date with History
3 Earth Summit
4 world and business leaders

2 Play the video again and ask students to answer the questions. Check answers orally.

1 New Zealand
2 young people (from around the world)
3 Yes, he was.
4 Yes, she did.
5 No, she didn't (she said it was busy).
6 She seemed confident. She said, 'It's going to be awesome. I can't wait – bring on tomorrow'.
7 the future
8 She thought it was excellent. She said, 'It's been amazing. It's changed my life'.

3 Ask students to discuss the question with a partner. Conduct class feedback, encouraging students to give reasons for their answers, e.g. *I think that Brittany delivered her speech really well because she made eye contact with her audience and didn't speak too fast or look too nervous.*

Students' own answers.

Project

4 Remind students of the speeches they made earlier on in the unit. Ask them to remember what they had needed to improve upon for next time. Organise students into pairs and ask them to discuss the points mentioned. Monitor, offering your input and suggestions where necessary. Students work in small groups and film their presentations. Play the film to the class and ask students watching to provide constructive feedback.

Students' own answers.

REVISION (SB page 151)

1

1 responsibility

2 confidence

3 argument

4 truth

5 pride

6 difference

7 conclusion

2

1 she may be at

2 must be asking everyone

3 it should be

4 Could that woman be

5 can't be right

6 might not come

3

1 A   **2** C

3 C   **4** A

5 B   **6** A

4

1 Was I?

2 Can't you?

3 Has he?

4 Must we?

5 Did you?

6 Aren't they?

7 Won't she?

8 Didn't they?

5

1 been

2 could

3 in

4 in

5 on

6 model

7 advice

8 difference

Homework

Workbook page 74–75

MyEnglishLab

Teaching notes for photocopiable activities

Starter

You will need: one set of cards per pair of students.

- Before the class, cut up one set of cards for each pair of students.
- Organise students into pairs and give each pair a set of cards. Tell them to lay the cards face down on the table.
- The students take it in turns to turn over a card and ask their partner the question on the card.
- Afterwards, ask students to report what they have learned about their partner to the rest of the class.
- As an additional or alternative activity students can write a paragraph about their partner based on what they learned in this activity.

Unit 1: Inside or outside?

You will need: one set of cards per pair of students.

- Before the class, cut up one set of cards for each pair of students.
- Organise students into pairs and give each pair a set of cards. Tell them to lay the cards face down on the table.
- Students take it in turns to lift **two** cards at a time. If they lift up an adjective **and** its definition they keep the pair. If they lift two cards which do not match, they must put them back on the table as they found them.
- The winner is the person who collects the most word pairs.

Unit 2: Making it happen

You will need: one worksheet per student.

- Before beginning the activity, ask students to close their books. Elicit as many technology words as they can remember and write them on the board.
- Give each student a worksheet. Tell students they must find thirteen words related to technology in the word search.
- Students work individually to complete the word search and find the thirteen technology words.
- Ask fast finishers to choose five of the words and write sentences.

A	B	O	G	T	U	G	M	Y	S
Q	B	A	T	T	E	R	Y	O	I
K	Z	D	H	W	V	J	S	W	G
C	O	D	E	E	Y	N	O	E	N
L	J	M	K	E	R	J	F	B	A
I	S	R	D	T	F	U	T	S	L
C	U	V	I	R	U	S	W	I	V
K	O	I	S	X	H	X	A	T	O
Y	N	N	O	Q	Y	U	R	E	M
R	L	R	N	G	Z	P	E	H	Z
X	I	J	I	E	B	D	L	V	P
J	N	K	Q	I	C	A	S	T	J
J	E	Y	U	B	Q	T	R	M	D
G	F	N	L	T	S	E	I	X	L
T	O	U	C	H	D	P	N	O	O
S	W	T	K	S	C	R	E	E	N
V	I	R	T	U	A	L	G	B	M

Unit 3: True story?

You will need: one set of cards per pair of students.

- Before the class, cut up one set of cards for each pair of students.
- Keep each of the three columns separate, so that you have three piles of cards in every set.
- Organise students into pairs and give each pair a set of cards, sorted into three piles. Tell them to lay the cards face down on the table in three separate areas.
- Students take it in turns to lift **three** cards at a time (one card from each area). If they can make a reasonable sentence out of the three cards, they keep those cards, e.g. buy – a birthday card – for us; *She bought a birthday card for us.* If they cannot make a sentence, they must put all the cards back on the table as they found them.
- The winner is the person who collects the most word sets.

Unit 4: Things they don't teach you

You will need: one set of cards per pair of students.

- Before the class, cut up one set of cards for each pair of students.
- Organise students into pairs and give each pair a set of cards. Tell them to lay the cards face down on the table.
- Students take it in turns to lift **two** cards at a time. If they lift up a noun **and** its definition they keep the pair. If they lift two cards which do not match, they must put them back on the table as they found them.
- The winner is the person who collects the most word pairs.

Unit 5: Green world

You will need: one board and one set of dice per pair of students.

- Organise students into pairs. Give each pair a copy of the game and a set of dice. Students use coins or rubbers as counters.
- Students take it in turns to throw the dice. When they land on a square, they have to answer the question or complete the sentence.
- If they can't answer the question or complete the sentence, their partner gets an extra turn. The first person to finish is the winner.

1 Students' own answers
2 Students' own answers
4 do my **bit**
6 Students' own answers
7 Students' own answers
8 plastic, paper, glass, aluminium
10 water shortage
11 growing things on unwanted land
12 drought
13 **makes** sense
14 Students' own answers
16 Students' own answers
17 somebody who thinks about the consequences of what they're buying, on people and the environment
19 **future** generations
20 alternative **energy**
21 somebody who buys things
22 a product you sell abroad
23 toxic **waste**
25 Students' own answers
26 a well

Unit 6: Before time

You will need: one set of cards per pair of students.

- Before the class, cut up one set of cards for each pair of students.
- Organise students into pairs and give each pair a set of cards. Tell them to lay the cards face down on the table.
- The students take it in turns to turn over a card and decide whether the statement is true or false by circling the correct letter.
- When all the pairs have finished, read out the correct answers. The pair with the most correct answers wins the game.

....

1 False (Both men and women did.)

2 True

3 False (They loved animals and thought they were incarnations of the gods.)

4 True

5 True

6 False (They believed it floated on an ocean of fresh water.)

7 True

8 False (It ended because of disease.)

9 True

10 False (They used mouse brains.)

Unit 7: The feel-good factor

You will need: one worksheet per student.

- Give each student a worksheet.
- Allow students time to read and complete the quiz.
- Organise students into pairs. Ask students to read the quiz again and predict their partners' answers.
- Students work in pairs to check their predictions. Students win a point for each correct prediction.
- Conduct class feedback and find out which student won the most points for their predictions.
- Now read the scoring system aloud to your students (below). Conduct class feedback. Who is the most positive person (or people) in the class?

....

What your scores say about you.

Mostly As: You are quite positive, but you need to be more self-sufficient. If you want things to turn out well, you need to take action yourself.

Mostly Bs: You aren't positive at all. Why not try looking on the bright side for a change? Life could be so much better.

Mostly Cs: You are very positive. Well done! You really know how to make the best of things.

Unit 8: Magic numbers

You will need: one set of cards per pair of students.

- Before the class, cut up one set of cards for each pair of students.
- Organise students into pairs and give each pair a set of cards. Tell them to lay the cards face down on the table.
- The students take it in turns to turn over a card and decide whether the statement is true or false by circling the correct letter.
- When all the pairs have finished, read out the correct answers. The pair with the most correct answers wins the game.

....

1 True

2 True

3 False (It's 70 percent.)

4 False (It's a word for a very large number.)

5 True

6 True

7 False (It's 417.7 metres below sea level.)

8 True

9 False (The temperature and the year are right but not the location: this happened in Vostok, Antarctica, July 21, 1983)

10 True

Unit 9: All change

You will need: one set of cards per pair of students.

- Before the class, cut up one set of cards for each pair of students.
- Organise students into pairs and give each pair a set of cards. Tell them to lay the cards face down on the table.
- Students take it in turns to lift **two** cards at a time. If they can make a reasonable sentence out of the two cards, they keep the pair. If they cannot make a sentence, they must put the two cards back on the table as they found them.
- The winner is the person who collects the most word pairs.
- Conduct class feedback and ask students what they would do in these situations.

Unit 10: Inspiration

You will need: one worksheet per student.

- Give each student a worksheet.
- Ask them to read the definitions and complete the puzzle with words related to science.
- Let them check their answers with a partner before conducting class feedback.
- Ask them to tell you what the secret word is.
- Fast finishers can choose five of the words and write sentences.

1 magnet
2 invisible
3 species
4 durable
5 odour
6 cells
7 topic
8 sound
9 waterproof
10 vision
11 delicate
Secret word: microscopic

Unit 11: The art of make-believe

You will need: one set of cards per pair of students.

- Before the class, cut up one set of cards for each pair of students.
- Organise students into pairs and give each pair a set of cards. Tell them to lay the cards face down on the table.
- The students take it in turns to turn over a card and make a sentence using that word. Each correct sentence wins a point. The student with the most points at the end of the game is the winner.

Unit 12: Find your voice

You will need: one set of cards per pair of students.

- Before the class, cut up one set of cards for each pair of students.
- Organise students into pairs and give each pair a set of cards. Tell them to lay the cards face down on the table.
- Students take it in turns to lift **two** cards at a time. If they lift up a sentence **and** the correct reply question, they keep the pair. If they lift two cards which do not match, they must put them back on the table as they found them.
- The winner is the person who collects the most pairs.

STARTER: All about me

Do you like football? Why/Why not?	Tell me about your perfect day.	Think of a sport. Name three pieces of equipment you need to play it.
Describe someone in your family.	What are your plans for the weekend?	Have you got a hidden talent? What is it?
Which three guests would you invite to your dream party?	How would your best friend describe you?	What makes you angry?
What job would you like to have in the future?	What's your favourite subject at school? Why do you like it?	Do you want to continue studying after school? If so, what will you study?
What is your favourite possession?	Do you prefer the city or the countryside?	Where do you like to hang out?
What's your least favourite subject at school? Why don't you like it?	What is your ideal holiday destination?	Where did you go on your last holiday?

GOLD EXPERIENCE

UNIT 01 Words describing work and skills

full-time	when you work around 40 hours per week
flexible	when you are happy to change your plans for other people
punctual	when you always arrive on time
sensible	when you think carefully about things
organised	when you keep everything in the right place
stressful	when something makes you feel anxious and worried
rewarding	when something you do makes you feel good
seasonal	work which you do at certain times of year

UNIT 02 Find the technology words

BATTERY CLICK CODE CONNECTION ONLINE SCREEN SIGNAL
SOFTWARE TOUCH TWEET VIRTUAL VIRUS WEBSITE

A	B	O	G	T	U	G	M	Y	S
Q	B	A	T	T	E	R	Y	O	I
K	Z	D	H	W	V	J	S	W	G
C	O	D	E	E	Y	N	O	E	N
L	J	M	K	E	R	J	F	B	A
I	S	R	D	T	F	U	T	S	L
C	U	V	I	R	U	S	W	I	V
K	O	I	S	X	H	X	A	T	O
Y	N	N	O	Q	Y	U	R	E	M
R	L	R	N	G	Z	P	E	H	Z
X	I	J	I	E	B	D	L	V	P
J	N	K	Q	I	C	A	S	T	J
J	E	Y	U	B	Q	T	R	M	D
G	F	N	L	T	S	E	I	X	L
T	O	U	C	H	D	P	N	O	O
S	W	T	K	S	C	R	E	E	N
V	I	R	T	U	A	L	G	B	M

UNIT 03 Sentence maker

bring	for me	a comic
buy	you	some apples
find	to her husband	a new outfit
give	for us	a job
make	them	a birthday card
offer	for Helen	an email
pay	to them	Spanish
promise	him	the tickets
read	us	a slice of pizza
send	to her	how to dance
show	it	a story
teach	to me	some money
tell	her	a present
write	for him	a letter

UNIT 04 Words related to money

bargain	very good value for money
voucher	a piece of paper with a special offer
bill	a written request for money which needs to be paid
cash	another word for money; coins and notes
discount	a reduction in the usual price of something
customer	a person who buys things in a shop
trolley	a thing with wheels which you use to put your shopping in at the supermarket
queue	a line of people waiting for something

UNIT 05 Go green!

START →	**1** Say three things you can do to help the environment.	**2** Name an endangered species.	**3** GO FORWARD 3 SPACES ↓
7 What can people do to reduce pollution?	**6** Name three environmental problems facing the planet.	**5** MISS A TURN →	**4** I want to do my ... for the planet.
8 Name three things which can be recycled.	**9** GO BACK 2 SPACES	**10** What do we call it when there is not enough water temporarily?	**11** What is guerrilla gardening?
15 HAVE ANOTHER TURN ↓	**14** Why is it a good idea to eat locally produced food?	**13** Recycling ... sense.	**12** What do we call a long period of time without any rain?
16 Name three green ways to travel.	**17** What is a responsible shopper?	**18** MISS A TURN ←	**19** I want to save the planet; not for me but for ... generations.
23 Factories shouldn't dump their toxic ... into rivers.	**22** What is an export?	**21** What is a consumer?	**20** Solar power is a source of alternative ... .
24 GO BACK 3 SPACES ←	**25** Which eco-friendly activity would you like to try? Why?	**26** Where can we get drinking water out of the ground?	**FINISH**

UNIT 06 How much do you know about ancient civilisations?

1 Egyptian men wore make up: not Egyptian women. T / F	**2** The Vikings believed that their purpose in life was to fight to the death. T / F
3 Egyptians never kept pets – they thought they brought bad luck. T / F	**4** Slaves were very important for the Romans. If you didn't have slaves, people thought you were poor. T / F
5 The Aztecs were really interested in pottery and sculpture. T / F	**6** The Mesopotamians believed that the Earth floated on a fluffy white cloud. T / F
7 In ancient China bones were often used to discover what the gods or nature wanted. T / F	**8** The Aztec civilisation ended because of war. T / F
9 The first Olympic Games were held in 776 BC at the Greek city of Olympia. The Olympics were actually a religious festival dedicated to the great god Zeus. T / F	**10** Romans used dogs' brains as toothpaste. T / F

UNIT 07 How positive are you?

1 You find out you've done really badly in a class test. What do you do?

   A Feel a bit down but try to forget about it. After all, everyone make mistakes sometimes.

   B Give up trying. What's the point?

   C Speak to your teacher and find out what you can do to help yourself.

2 You keep arguing with your sister and it's really getting you down. What do you do?

   A Try to stay out of her way until things improve and have a good moan to your friend.

   B Look forward to leaving home. Then you won't have to see her anymore.

   C Talk to her. Try to understand things from her point of view and explain how you feel, too.

3 You're feeling really tired and don't have your usual energy. What do you do?

   A Take a couple of painkillers and have an early night.

   B Worry that there's something really wrong with you.

   C Decide to start eating more healthily and think about changes you can make to your lifestyle.

4 You don't have enough money to buy the new pair of trainers you really want. What do you do?

   A Hope that you'll get them for your next birthday.

   B Try to forget them. You never get what you want anyway.

   C See if you can earn some money by doing chores at home. That way you can start to save for them.

5 Your best friend tells you she's moving to a different country. How do you feel?

   A Really sad, but hopeful you'll still see her during the holidays.

   B Totally miserable. You know you'll never see her again.

   C Sad, but also excited. You can't wait to go and visit her in her new home!

UNIT 08 Nature and numbers

1

The numbers we use today such as 1, 2 and 3 are based on the Hindu-Arabic numeral system which was developed over 1,000 years ago.

T / F

2

Different names for the number 0 include zero, nought, naught, nil, zilch and zip.

T / F

3

50 percent of the earth's surface is water.

T / F

4

The name of the popular search engine 'Google' came from a misspelling of the word 'googol', which is another word for a gigantic elephant.

T / F

5

A quadrillion, quintillion, sextillion, septillion, octillion and nonillion are all names for very large numbers.

T / F

6

A 'googolplex' is a number which is so big that it can't be written.

T / F

7

The Dead Sea is 800 metres below sea level.

T / F

8

The highest temperature ever recorded was 56.7 C in Greenland Ranch in California, July 10, 1913.

T / F

9

The lowest temperature ever recorded was –89.2 C in Scotland, 1983.

T / F

10

The Earth is between 4.5 and 4.6 billion years old.

T / F

If I could live anywhere I wanted,	I'd live in Monaco.
If I'd paid more attention in the last lesson,	I wouldn't have failed the test.
If I see him tomorrow,	I'll invite him to the party.
If I had saved some money,	I'd have been able to buy you a present.
If you burn toast,	it makes a terrible smell.
If you live in a flat,	you don't usually have a garden.
If I won a lot of money,	I'd travel the world.
If it rains tomorrow,	we'll cancel the picnic.

UNIT 10 Words related to science

Clues

1 a thing which attracts steel

2 used to describe something you cannot see

3 a kind of plant or animal

4 which is hard and lasts for a long time

5 another word for 'smell'

6 the tiny parts which make up our body

7 another word for 'subject' or 'theme'

8 what you can hear

9 used to describe something which water cannot pass through

10 the ability to see

11 very fragile and light

drawing	mess around	open-air
audience	paint	sketch
take somebody's place	brilliant	have a go
come true	bring something to life	go for something
rehearsal	expertise	be blown away
sound-proofing	nervous	comedy

UNIT 12 Did you really?

You're looking great today!	Am I?
Robert isn't coming.	Isn't he?
My mum made these cakes.	Did she?
It's cold today.	Is it?
They didn't enjoy their holiday.	Didn't they?
We must go home now.	Must we?
I come from Spain.	Do you?
I hadn't ever played football before.	Hadn't you?

Notes

Pearson Education Limited
Edinburgh Gate
Harlow
Essex CM20 2JE
England
and Associated Companies throughout the world.

www.pearsonelt.com

First published 2015

ISBN: 978-1-4479-7372-0

Set in Gill Sans MT 10/12

ARP Impression 98
Printed in Great Britain by Clays Ltd, St Ives plc